CULTURES, CONTEXTS, AND WORLD ENGLISHES

Yamuna Kachru
and
Larry E. Smith

Routledge
Taylor & Francis Group

NEW YORK AND LONDON

First published 2008
by Routledge
270 Madison Ave, New York, NY 10016

Simultaneously published in the UK
by Routledge
2 Park Square, Milton Park, Abingdon, Oxon OX14 4RN

Routledge is an imprint of the Taylor & Francis Group, an informa business

© 2008 Taylor & Francis

Typeset in New Baskerville by
Swales & Willis Ltd, Exeter, Devon
Printed and bound in the United States of America on acid-free paper by
Edwards Brothers, Inc., Lillington, NC

Library of Congress Cataloging in Publication Data
Kachru, Yamuna.
Cultures, contexts, and world Englishes/Yamuna Kachru, Larry E. Smith.
p. cm.—(ESL & applied linguistics professional series)
Includes bibliographical references and index.
1. English language—Variation. 2. English language—Dialects.
3. English language—Foreign countries. 4. English language—Social aspects.
5. Communication, International. 6. Sociolinguistics. I. Smith, Larry E.
II. Title.
PE1700.K28 2008
427.009—dc22   2007045123

ISBN10: 0–8058–4732–4 (hbk)
ISBN10: 0–8058–4733–2 (pbk)
ISBN10: 0–203–89134–1 (ebk)

ISBN13: 978–0–8058–4732–1 (hbk)
ISBN13: 978–0–8058–4733–8 (pbk)
ISBN13: 978–0–203–89134–6 (ebk)

CULTURES, CONTEXTS, AND WORLD ENGLISHES

This volume aims to familiarize readers with the varieties of world Englishes used across cultures and to create awareness of some of the linguistic and socially relevant contexts and functions that have given rise to them. It emphasizes that effective communication among users of different Englishes requires awareness of the varieties in use and their cultural, social, and ideational functions. *Cultures, Contexts, and World Englishes*

- demonstrates the rich results of integrating theory, methodology, and application;
- features critical and detailed discussion of the sociolinguistics of English in the globalized world;
- gives equal emphasis to grammar and pragmatics of variation and to uses of Englishes in spoken and written modes in major English-using regions of the world.

The Introduction outlines the underlying sociocultural reasons for language variation and discusses the status and functions of English in various parts of the world. Part I provides the background necessary to appreciate variation in English. Part II presents select features of grammatical and lexical variation to relate sociocultural contexts to the structural features of Englishes. Part III sets out the conventions of language use in the spoken and written modes across cultures. The Conclusion briefly discusses topics such as issues of standardization and codification, ideological stances with regard to linguistic imperialism and hegemony, violation of linguistic human rights attributed to the English language, and monolingual and "native-speaker bias" associated with practices in the English Language Teaching profession.

Each chapter includes suggestions for further reading and challenging discussion questions and appropriate research projects designed to enhance the usefulness of this volume in courses such as World Englishes, English in the Global Context, Sociolinguistics, Critical Applied Linguistics, Language Contact and Convergence, Ethnography of Communication, and Crosscultural Communication.

Yamuna Kachru is Professor Emerita of Linguistics at University of Illinois at Urbana-Champaign in the USA. She has taught in India, the UK, and the USA and has been invited as a speaker in Asia, Europe, and North America. Her research areas include structure of Hindi and other South Asian languages, and communication across languages and cultures using world Englishes. She was honored by the President of India for her contribution to Hindi linguistics with an award in 2006. Professor Kachru has authored and edited many scholarly papers and books on topics related to world Englishes.

Larry E. Smith is President of Christopher, Smith & Associates (CSA) LLC whose mission is to equip, empower, and inspire leaders for the twenty-first century. His experience includes over two decades as a researcher and administrator at Hawaii's East–West Center and a decade as Executive Director of the International Association for World Englishes (IAWE). He is co-founding editor (with Braj B. Kachru) of the professional journal *World Englishes: Journal of English as an International and Intra-national Language* and has authored, edited, and co-edited a number of volumes on the topic.

ESL & Applied Linguistics Professional Series
Eli Hinkel, Series Editor

Kachru/Smith • *Cultures, Contexts, and World Englishes*

McKay/Bokhosrt-Heng • *International English in its Sociolinguistic Contexts: Towards a Socially Sensitive EIL Pedagogy*

Christison/Murray, Eds. • *Leadership in English Language Education: Theoretical Foundations and Practical Skills for Changing Times*

McCafferty/Stam, Eds. • *Gesture: Second Language Acquisition and Classroom Research*

Liu • *Idioms: Description, Comprehension, Acquisition, and Pedagogy*

Chappelle/Enright/Jamison, Eds. • *Building a Validity Argument for the Text of English as a Foreign Language*(tm)

Kondo-Brown/Brown, Eds. • *Teaching Chinese, Japanese, and Korean Heritage Students: Curriculum Needs, Materials, and Assessments*

Youmans • *Chicano-Anglo Conversations: Truth, Honesty, and Politeness*

Birch • *English L2 Reading: Getting to the Bottom, Second Edition*

Luk/Lin • *Classroom Interactions as Cross-cultural Encounters: Native Speakers in EFL Lessons*

Levy/Stockwell • *CALL Dimensions: Issues and Options in Computer Assisted Language Learning*

Nero, Ed. • *Dialects, Englishes, Creoles, and Education*

Basturkmen • *Ideas and Options in English for Specific Purposes*

Kumaravadivelu • *Understanding Language Teaching: From Method to Postmethod*

McKay • *Researching Second Language Classrooms*

Egbert/Petrie, Eds. • *CALL Research Perspectives*

Canagarajah, Ed. • *Reclaiming the Local in Language Policy and Practice*

Adamson • *Language Minority Students in American Schools: An Education in English*

Fotos/Browne, Eds. • *New Perspectives on CALL for Second Language Classrooms*

Hinkel • *Teaching Academic ESL Writing: Practical Techniques in Vocabulary and Grammar*

Hinkel/Fotos, Eds. • *New Perspectives on Grammar Teaching in Second Language Classrooms*

Hinkel • *Second Language Writers' Text: Linguistic and Rhetorical Features*

Visit www.Routledge.com/Education for additional information on titles in the ESL & Applied Linguistics Professional Series

TO
SHARYN K. SMITH
AND
BRAJ B. KACHRU

Contents

Illustrations

FIGURES

TABLES

Preface

The genesis of this book goes back to 1983 to a colloquium held at the East–West Center in Honolulu, Hawaii. The focus of the colloquium was on discourse across cultures through the medium of world Englishes. It was then that a group of scholars from the Three Circles of Englishes discussed the desirability of a crosscultural study on this topic for a better understanding of complex issues related to intelligibility and global functions of Englishes. The idea was further strengthened subsequently when a number of investigators initiated research on topics such as conversation, speech acts, expository and argumentative writing, and literary creativity across cultures through the medium of English in Asia, Africa, and other parts of the world.[1] This book finally took shape when we were invited by Eli Hinkel to contribute a volume on this topic to her "ESL & Applied Linguistics Professional Series." Since the first conception of this volume, it has undergone several incarnations as the field has evolved, several approaches and methodologies have emerged and pedagogical studies have been conducted. The main goal of the volume, however, has remained constant.

The major objective of *Cultures, Contexts, and World Englishes* is to sensitize users of English to its varieties across cultures, and to emphasize that effective communication among users of different Englishes is possible by cultivating an awareness of the variation in Englishes and their cultural, social, and ideational functions. There continues to be a paucity of studies on how people from diverse regional, cultural, social, economic, and educational backgrounds use English in order to achieve their intended goals in the Three Circles of English. It is generally assumed that the privileged British, American—and now, in some Circles, Australian—varieties are communicating intentions and purposes across cultures in all contexts more or less clearly. It is not rare to be disappointed when one realizes that one has failed in successful and effective communication. It is our hope that *Cultures, Contexts, and World Englishes* will provide some insights in making users of English familiar with some of the linguistic and socioculturally relevant contexts that have motivated the development of varieties of English, not only in Anglophone Asia or Africa, but also in the Inner Circle of Englishes. We also hope that this book will further contribute toward awareness of and sensitivity to the formal and functional variation in Englishes.

The book is organized in three parts, preceded by an Introduction and followed by a Conclusion. The Introduction initiates the discussion on variation in English, points out the status and functions of English in various parts of the world, and describes what is covered in the individual chapters that follow. It emphasizes the impact of sociocultural background of Englishes and argues against attempts to characterize a mythical internationally accepted variety of English unmarked for users' sociocultural background for international communication.

Part I, "Verbal Interaction and Intelligibility," is devoted to the background that is necessary to appreciate variation in language so that it does not become an impediment in verbal interaction across cultures. It establishes the relevance of cultural context of language and its use and discusses the concepts necessary to view verbal interaction as a dynamic process where all parties engaged in the enterprise contribute to the outcome. Concepts from linguistic pragmatics, sociolinguistics, conversation analysis, psychology, and artificial intelligence are briefly presented to propose an integrated approach to analyze crosscultural exchanges among users of varieties of English. The notion of intelligibility is discussed in some detail and its components are identified to demonstrate what is involved in intelligibility across Englishes.

Part II presents select features of grammatical and lexical variation to relate sociocultural contexts to the structural features of Englishes. It is pointed out that the processes that operate in giving rise to observable differences in Indian or Nigerian or Singaporean English as compared to American or British English are the same that are responsible for variation among American, Australian, and British Englishes, and so-called dialects within each of these varieties. This phenomenon is not unique to English: histories of languages of the world provide considerable evidence that languages change when their geographical and sociocultural contexts change. That explains why there are different varieties of Arabic (Egyptian, Moroccan, Syrian, etc.) and Hindi-Urdu (in India where the two "high" styles share a colloquial variety called Hindustani; and Hindi has regional variation characterized as Eastern, Western and Southern), and why Spanish in Mexico is noticeably different from Spanish in Spain, or French in Quebec is not the same as French in France or Switzerland.

Part III deals with a crucial aspect of verbal interaction in world Englishes: it sets out the conventions of language use in the spoken and written modes across cultures. Similar to grammatical and lexical features, conventions of language use are responsive to sociocultural contexts. The relationship between culture and language is not deterministic, but the two are sensitive to each other and evolve together. This relationship is illustrated by looking at differing conventions in the organization of conversation, the performance of speech acts, and expressions of politeness in the spoken mode, and in writing letters, academic and argumentative texts, and creative literature in the written mode. An understanding of differing conventions is vital in interpreting intentions and purposes of users of Englishes from different backgrounds.

The Conclusion touches upon topics that are not dealt with in the preceding chapters, e.g. issues of standardization and codification, ideological stances with regard to linguistic imperialism and hegemony, violation of linguistic human rights attributed to the English language, and monolingual and "native-speaker bias" associated with practices in the English Language Teaching (ELT) profession.[2] All these issues merit full discussion, but they fall outside the scope of this volume.

Each chapter of the book is followed by suggestions for further reading, and also discussion questions or small research projects. Thus, the book is designed for a course on world Englishes with emphasis on crosscultural communication. We feel that such a course is eminently suitable in all ELT programs that are concerned with English language teacher education (MA in Teaching English as a Second/Foreign Language programs are a case in point). The book is relevant for courses on English in the world, sociolinguistics, crosscultural communication, and critical applied linguistics. Additionally, it can be used in training programs for professionals in various fields, e.g. in business and commerce, diplomacy, and media, as English is being used in all these domains increasingly across all languages and cultures.

We appreciate the suggestions and advice of Eli Hinkel, Editor of the series in which this volume appears. We are indeed grateful to her and to Naomi Silverman, Senior Editor, Lawrence Erlbaum Associates (now Routledge), for their understanding, patience, and faith in us; to Heeyoun Cho, who helped beyond the call of duty in overseeing the project, including the preparation of the final manuscript with dedication; to Prashast Gautam Kachru for the sketches of facial expressions and hand gestures in Chapter 3; and to the Research Board of the Graduate College of University of Illinois for their research support. Our deepest gratitude, as always, is to our families for their unfailing enthusiasm and cooperation in all our endeavors. We acknowledge our indebtedness to all those scholars whose works provided insights, ideas, and data that have been of immense value to us. This book would not have been possible without their inestimable research contributions.

Notes

1. See, e.g. studies by Nelson (1995), Smith (1992), Smith and Nelson (1985) on intelligibility; Bhatia (1993, 1996, 1997), Dissanayake (1985), Eisikovits (1989), B. Kachru (1981), Y. Kachru (1983), Liao (1997), Nelson (1985), Nishiyama (1995), Nwoye (1985, 1992), K. K. Sridhar (1991), S. N. Sridhar (1992), Tawake (1990), 1993, Thumboo (1985, 1992, 1994), and Valentine (1988, 1991, 1995, 2001) on conversation, speech acts, expository and argumentative writing and literary creativity.
2. See, e.g. works by Bamgboṣe (1992, 1998), B. Kachru (1983b, 1985a, 1985b, 1988a, 1991, 1996c), Pakir (1991, 1997), Quirk (1988, 1989), and Tickoo (1991) on standardization and codification; Pennycook (1994), Phillipson (1992), and Tsuda (1994, 2002) on the hegemony of English; Phillipson (1998), Skutnabb-Kangas (2000, 2001), and Phillipson and Skutnabb-Kangas (1997) on English and linguistic human rights; and Braine (1999), Canagarajah (2000), B. Kachru (1976, 1981, 1986f, 1987, 1988b, 1990a, 1995a, 1997c, 2001a, 2005a), Y. Kachru (1993a, 1994), Seidlhofer (1999), K. Sridhar and S. Sridhar (1992), and S. Sridhar (1994) on native-speaker bias in English language profession.

Yamuna Kachru and Larry E. Smith
August 15, 2007

Acknowledgments

The authors gratefully acknowledge the use of the following items from the sources identified in the chapters listed below:

- letters to the Editor from *The Straits Times*, April 6, 2000 and *The Indian Express*, April 6, 2000, in the Introduction;
- an excerpt from Dautermann (1995) in Chapter 1, suggested activities;
- an excerpt from a phone conversation out of A. Firth (1991) in Chapter 3, suggested activities;
- a letter to the Editor from *The Guardian*, Lagos, Nigeria, April 9, 2000 in Chapter 4, suggested questions for discussion;
- an excerpt from Mishra (1992) in Part II;
- two excerpts from Gumperz *et al.* (1979) in Chapter 5;
- a piece from *The African Reporter* cited in Vavrus (1991) in Chapter 9;
- a news item from *Daily Nation*, Nairobi, Kenya in Chapter 9, suggested activities; and
- one excerpt each from Marlene Nourbese Philip's poem entitled "Discourse on the logic of language" published in her collection *She Tries Her Tongue; Her Silence Softly Breaks*, NFS Canada Series (1989), and Sujata Bhatt's poem "Search for my tongue" published in her collection *Brunizem*, Carcanet, Manchester (1988).

Symbols

*	ungrammatical sentence
?	unacceptable sentence
ʔ or ´	glottal stop
ag.	ergative agent marker (in Hindi)
ç, C	a retroflex consonant in South Asian languages
ch or c^h	an aspirated consonant in South Asian languages
Δ	voiced interdental fricative
f	feminine gender
h.	honorific
T	voiceless interdental fricative, as in "think"
š	palatal sibilant
vv	a long vowel in South Asian languages
word^H or ^{H}word	word marked for honorific
x > y	x replaced by y

Abbreviations

APEC	Asia-Pacific Economic Cooperation
ASEAN	Association of South East Asian Nations
BBC	British Broadcasting Corporation
CAT	Communication Accomodation Theory
CE	Chinese English
CNN	Cable News Network (USA)
EFL	English as a Foreign Language
ELF	English as Lingua Franca
ELT	English Language Teaching
ESL	English as a Second Language
ESP	English for Specific Purposes
EU	European Union
FE	Filipino English
GE	German English
GhE	Ghanian English
IE	Indian English
IMF	International Monetary Fund
MATESL	Masters in Arts in Teaching English as a Second Language
NE	Nigerian English
NPR	National Public Radio
PE	Pakistani English
PIA	Pakistan International Airlines
PRI	Public Radio International (USA)
RELC	Regional Language Centre (since 1977)
RP	Received Pronunciation (British English)
SAARC	South Asian Association for Regional Cooperation

SAT   Speech Accommodation Theory
SgE   Singapore English
SME   Singapore–Malaysian English
TESOL   Teaching English to Speakers of Other Languages
UN   United Nations
VOA   Voice of America
WTO   World Trade Organization

Introduction: World Englishes and Cultural Contexts

ENGLISH IN THE WORLD

English is EVERYWHERE. At least it sometimes seems that way. In fact, that is not true. Most of the people on Earth do not use English. It is by no means a universal language. Perhaps 25 percent of the earth's population uses English for some purpose in their lives. If so, 75 percent do not. It is however interesting that often those who do use English are the best educated and the most influential members (the opinion makers) of their society. The spread, status, and functions of English around the world are impressive indeed. In recorded human history no other language has had such a position.

It is no longer the case that the English language is used by people from Korea, Thailand, or Switzerland just to speak with Americans, the British, or Australians. English is increasingly used by people from Asia to interact with those from Europe, and people from South America to interact with people from Africa. As was shown in the BBC documentary *The Story of English*, English is frequently used among interlocutors when no so-called 'native speaker' of English is present. The contexts for the use of English may be academic conferences, business, commerce, diplomacy, educational institutions, manufacturing, mining, print or audio-visual media, or tourism. One example of the pan-Asian use of English can be seen in the growing economic activity within the region. Tables 0.1 and 0.2 regarding Japan's profile of international trade and tourism make it clear that the language of international commerce and tourism is English, and such business and people-to-people contacts have been increasing dramatically (see also, B. Kachru, 2005a, pp. 91–93; Stanlaw, 2003).

TABLE 0.1 Japan's Trade with Asia			TABLE 0.2 Japanese Tourism in Asia	
Year	*%*		*Year*	*In millions*
1990	37.7		1989	4.62
1991	39.8		1991	5.08
1992	41.2		1992	5.35
1993	42.8		1993	5.42
1994	43.7		1994	6.20

Source: *Asiaweek* (April 28, 1995, p. 23).   Source: *Asiaweek* (April 28, 1995, p. 23).

As Table 0.1 shows, the total value of trade with Asia in 1994 was $252 billion. In 1995, analysts expected "Asian trade to surpass Europe and America combined" (*Asiaweek*, April 28, 1995, p 23). Within the last decade, the trend forecast in 1995 by *Asiaweek* has materialized decisively. According to the Japanese Ministry of Finance figures for 2002, Japan's trade with non-English-speaking regions of the world far exceeded trade with Inner Circle English-speaking areas of the world (see Table 0.3; the amounts are in billions of yen).

The English language includes at least three types of varieties: (1) those that are used as the primary language of the majority population of a country, such as American and British; (2) varieties that are used as an additional language for *intra*national as well as *inter*national communication in communities that are multilingual, such as Indian, Nigerian, and Singaporean; and (3) varieties that are used almost exclusively for international communication, such as Chinese and German. Most of these Englishes developed as a result of colonial imposition of the language in various parts of the world. Soon after the end of World War II, English achieved the status of an international language and left behind, in spread and frequency of use, other competing languages such as Spanish, French, Russian, and Japanese. Presently there are more users of the varieties of English of the second and third types than of the first type and it is primarily they who are instrumental in its further spread.

The term lingua franca has been used to characterize the global functions of the English language (e.g. James, 2000; McArthur, 2001; Seidlhofer, 2001) and there are attempts to define the core (e.g. Jenkins, 2000 is an attempt to do so in the area of the sound system) of this lingua franca English. This label, however, does not capture the phenomenon of world Englishes for several reasons, as has been explained in B. Kachru (1996b, 2005a; see also, Kahane and Kahane 1979, 1986).[1] Consider the case of English as used in the member states of the European Union (EU). Euro-English (Cenoz and Jessner, 2000, p. viii; Modiano, 1996) is not just a language used for utilitarian

TABLE 0.3
Trends in Exports and Imports by Country/Region

Exports from Japan

Year	Total	Asia	China	Korea	Taiwan	USA	EU	Middle East	Oceania
2000	51,654	21,254	3,724	3,309	3,874	15,356	8,432	1,047	1,110
2001	48,979	19,732	3,764	3,072	2,942	14,711	7,810	1,277	1,131
2002	52,109	22,439	4,980	3,572	3,281	14,873	7,663	1,423	1,278

Imports to Japan

Year	Total	Asia	China	Korea	Taiwan	USA	EU	Middle East	Oceania
2000	40,938	17,063	5,941	2,205	1,930	7,779	5,0435	5,310	1,929
2001	42,416	17,987	7,027	2,088	1,723	7,671	5,412	5,384	2,090
2002	42,228	18,358	7,728	1,937	1,699	7,237	5,482	5,095	2,074

Source: Ministry of Public Management, Home Affairs, Posts and Telecommunication, *Statistical Handbook of Japan.*

purposes of business, commerce, and tourism; it serves as a medium of academic, cultural, diplomatic, legal, political, scientific-technological discourses as well. In view of its mathetic function, Euro-English is no more a lingua franca in the term's original sense than South Asian or Singaporean or West African Englishes are. In fact, all these Englishes, including Euro-English exhibit internal variation as well, based on geographical and ethnic factors. Just because they have not been documented in grammars or dictionaries does not invalidate their existence; a large number of the world's languages have neither a writing system, nor have they been codified in grammars and dictionaries as yet.

Codification is not a prerequisite for legitimizing a language. For instance, Australians spoke Australian English for years before a dictionary of Australian English (*The Macquarie Dictionary*, 1981) was compiled and a grammatical description of Australian English (Collins and Blair, 1989) appeared.[2] Neither does codification prevent the natural processes of variation, as is clear from the histories of classical (e.g. Arabic, Greek, Latin, Sanskrit) and modern languages (e.g. English, French, Hindi, Spanish, Tamil).

We do not believe that there is a variety called world English, international English, or global English, although these terms, among others, have been given for the language that is being used in business, diplomacy, media, and other spheres (McArthur, 2001). These labels deny the pluricentricity of the medium and misdirect the research efforts at standardization of an abstraction at the cost of understanding the phenomenon of wide distribution and deep penetration of the medium across cultures. As McArthur (1998, p. xvi, see also Bolton, 2004) observes:

> The monolithic, linear model that takes us from Old English through Middle English to Modern English (culminating with Darwinian elegance in the standard international language of newspapers and airports) has, it seems to me, been asked to bear more weight than it can reasonably support. The emergence, therefore, of plural, non-linear models is a positive development, among whose advantages are a more accurate depiction of the diversity in which we are embedded and also a more democratic approach to the social realities of English at the end of the twentieth century.

It is also worth remembering that it is the range and depth of acculturation of English, and not the desire to homogenize the medium by standardizing an international variety, that has led to the spread of the language. We have to appreciate the variation and cultural pluralism denoted by the term *Englishes*, before any discussion of communication across cultures becomes meaningful. The efforts at collecting corpora in limited contexts (e.g. that of verbal interaction in Europe among users of English as an additional language) and describing the phonological system of Euro-English (Jenkins, 2000) have, of course, their uses. They, however, do not obviate the need for the world Englishes perspective in studying the phenomenon of the unprecedented spread of English around the world, which has resulted in a wide range of varieties (Mufwene, 1997).

According to B. Kachru (1985a), this diffusion of English is best captured in terms of three Concentric Circles: the Inner Circle, the Outer Circle, and the Expanding Circle. The Inner Circle represents the traditional historical and sociolinguistic bases of English in the regions where it is used as a primary language (including the UK, USA, Australia, Canada, and New Zealand). The Outer Circle represents the regions of the world formerly colonized by Britain and the USA. In these regions English has been adopted as an additional language for intranational purposes of administration, education, law, etc. (e.g. India, Nigeria, the Philippines, Singapore). The Expanding Circle includes the areas in which English is primarily used as a medium of international communication (e.g. China, Europe, Japan, Korea, the Middle East). This is an approximate characterization of the three Circles and there are many factors that influence how varieties of English are used in any particular context.[3]

The difference in the use of English in the three Circles is related to the diffusion of English around the world in what B. Kachru has termed the two diasporas of English (B. Kachru, 1992). In the first diaspora of the Inner Circle, a monolingual English-speaking population movement was responsible for bringing the language to new locations from the mother country, e.g. to Australia, New Zealand, and North America. In the second diaspora of the other two Circles, the language was transplanted to new locations. Of course, a handful of English-speaking people initially brought the language to the new locations primarily through education, trading, and missionary work. The main push for the adoption and diffusion of English, however, came from the local multilingual populations. And once the language was established, it was adapted to new uses and consequently went through processes of nativization in the new contexts (B. Kachru, 1983a; Pandharipande, 1987).

Actually, one can easily make a case for four diasporas of English. The first was to Ireland, Scotland and Wales, where local languages were supplanted by English; the second was to regions of North America, Australia, and New Zealand; the third to places such as India, Nigeria, Singapore, and the Philippines; and the fourth to countries such as China, Japan, Korea, Brazil, Germany, and Saudi Arabia, to name only a few in this category.

NUMERICAL STRENGTH AND STATUS

Currently the Outer and Expanding Circles are estimated to have approximately 800 million people using English along with one or more other languages (Todd and Hancock, 1986) as compared to just over 300 million people who use English as their primary language in the Inner Circle. All the countries in the Outer Circle are multilingual and multicultural. English has official status in their language policies. For example, the Indian Constitution recognizes English as an "associate" official language; in Nigeria and Zambia English is one of the state languages; in Singapore English is recognized as an official language; and in all of these countries as well as the Philippines, English continues to be the language of education, the legal system, and administration. In all of these places, English plays an important role in social interaction, and in literary creativity as well. Increasingly, it is also making its presence felt in popular culture (see Lee and Kachru, 2006). In the Expanding Circle English has no official status, but it is the preferred medium of international trade, and commerce, as well as the language of scientific, technological, and academic discourse.

Although the above represents a brief summary of the status of English in the Outer and Expanding Circles, the details are varied and complex (see McArthur, 1998, pp. 38–42). For instance:

1. Although there is no constitutional provision for an official language either in the American or the British system of government, English is in reality the official language. Standard American or British English,

of course, co-exists with other varieties (e.g. Scottish in Britain and African-American in America), as well as indigenous and immigrant languages/dialects/creoles in America and in Britain.

2. In the Anglophone Caribbean, English is the official language and is used in addition to the English-based creole and immigrant languages.

3. In Canada, English is the co-official language along with French, and co-exists with indigenous (Native American) languages and settler/ immigrant languages (e.g. Scottish, Gaelic, Ukrainian, Punjabi, and Cantonese).

4. In Kenya, English is the second national language with a status lower than Swahili, which is the official language.

5. In the Scandinavian countries English is a second language that practically everyone learns.

6. In the EU, English and French are the two working languages, though there are nine other languages also in the list of official languages.

7. In India, as mentioned earlier, English is an associate official language with Hindi, which is the official language. It co-exists with national languages (e.g. Hindi, Marathi, Tamil) of the vast territory and has the status of a national language, e.g. for the purposes of literary awards by the national academy of letters. In addition it is the official language of eight Union Territories directly controlled from New Delhi.

FUNCTIONS OF ENGLISH

As the above suggests, nations around the world use English for various purposes and in various contexts. The systems of government, the educational policies, the sociocultural contexts of literacy and language use, the legislative, administrative, and legal traditions all differ widely from context to context. It is, therefore, expected that functions of English—acculturated or not—will vary as well. In the Outer/Expanding Circle, there are countries where English is increasingly used in all domains of life (e.g. the upper echelons of Singaporean and Indian societies), or only in professional domains (e.g. most of South Asia, and Anglophone Africa), or only in restricted domains such as higher education, research publications in science and technology, international business, tourism, and commerce (e.g. East and Southeast Asia, most of Europe, and much of South America).

Table 0.4 from B. Kachru (2001b, p. 46) summarizes the functions of English in the three Circles. This shows a remarkable profile of the functional range of any human language. As the range is so wide and the users come from so many different backgrounds, the use of English offers a challenge to students of English studies. The issues we face are how best to characterize

TABLE 0.4
Functions of English in the Three Circles

Function	Inner Circle	Outer Circle	Expanding Circle
Access code	+	+	+
Advertising	+	+/−	+/−
Corporate trade	+	+	+
Development	+	+/−	+/−
Government	+	+/−	−
Linguistic impact	+	+	+
Literary creativity	+	+	+/−
Literary renaissance	+	+	+
News broadcasting	+	+	+/−
Newspapers	+	+	+/−
Scientific higher education	+	+	+/−
Scientific research	+	+	+/−
Social interaction	+	+/−	+/−

+ signals use in the domain; − indicates no use in the domain; +/− points to the use of English along with other languages in the domain.

what is going on, and at the same time spread awareness of the relevant factors in successful communication in Englishes across cultures. That is the purpose of this book.

THE ORGANIZATION OF THE BOOK

In this book, we attempt to look at the research findings in both usage (linguistic structure) and *use* (sociocultural conventions of speaking/writing) and discuss what insights are to be gained from them in the area of crosscultural communication through English.

The relationship between language and culture has been a matter of debate among linguists as well as anthropologists for a long time. Within linguistics there are two clear divisions: (1) those who believe linguistics to be an autonomous discipline and language to be a homogeneous system independent of culture and society; and (2) those who believe that the notion of language as an autonomous, homogeneous system is untenable; linguistic systems co-evolve with sociocultural conventions of language use and thus the context of use is as relevant as rules of usage. The former is based on a somewhat reified notion of language. We believe that in reality language is subject to great change and variation; it is not static and monolithic. Any discipline that aims at studying the phenomenon of language has to take into account cultural and social factors that are involved in human linguistic behavior.

As the focus of this book is on varieties of English around the world and especially on aspects of verbal interaction between and among users of these varieties, we rely on approaches and methodologies of research based on the latter view of language, an approach to linguistic study that is socially realistic (B. Kachru 1986b).

The first three chapters explore issues arising out of the interplay between linguistic and sociocultural norms of language behavior in social contexts. We are primarily concerned with linguistic interaction as a dynamic process rather than a static object. The use of language in performing acts, the cooperative nature of verbal communication, whether in the spoken or written mode, and the nature of sociocultural competence displayed in producing and interpreting linguistic performance are discussed in these chapters. The emphasis is on what it means to be polite in verbal interaction. We also bring in those aspects of non-verbal communication that have been identified as being responsible for successful communication or for failures in communication that lead to misunderstandings between users of different varieties.

The first chapter presents an integrated theoretical approach needed to discuss verbal interaction in world Englishes. The approach integrates the notions of speech acts, cooperative principle, and politeness from linguistic pragmatics, structure of conversation from conversation analysis, and sociocultural contexts and conventions of verbal interaction from sociolinguistics.

The second chapter provides a more detailed account of the cultural underpinnings of language use by utilizing the notions of context of situation from sociolinguistics, and structure of background knowledge from psychology and artificial intelligence. Interdisciplinary research aimed at studying conventions of speaking and writing in various societies has yielded useful insights, which are also briefly summarized in this chapter.

The third chapter examines conventions of politeness in some detail as different cultures have different notions of what polite behavior is. In one culture it may be inappropriate to ask questions about where an interlocutor is going, whereas in another culture it may be the formulaic greeting as in the state of Nagaland in India (Krishan, 1990). Additionally, different linguistic communities use different strategies—usually manifest in language use—to indicate politeness in interaction. For instance, in Inner Circle Englishes, it is more polite to use an interrogative form to make a request, e.g. *could you mail the letter on your way to the store?* However, in South Asian English, a direct imperative form may be considered equally polite if there are other indicators of politeness such as a term of address, e.g. *brother/ sister/uncle, bring me a copy of this book from the library!* (Y. Kachru, 1998a; K. Sridhar, 1991). This strategy is based on the substratum languages of India where direct imperative form has several realizations on the politeness scale

(Y. Kachru, 2006 for examples from Hindi). Ting-Toomey and Cocroft (1994, p. 313), discussing the Wolof speakers in the West African country of Senegal, state that a direct request or demand is actually perceived as more face-polite than the use of hedges and indirect request. Thus, the phrase "give me a drink" is perceived to be a much more polite expression than "I wish to have a drink."

The fourth chapter discusses issues of intelligibility in light of the factors identified in the previous three chapters. As different variety users have different cultural concepts, social conventions, and linguistic strategies, verbal interaction between them is not always smooth and successful. Although intelligibility is a familiar term and is used very frequently in the contexts of conversation and written texts, it is a complex notion when applied to situations involving interaction among language and culture-different interactants. This chapter explains the nature of intelligibility, analyses sources of difficulties, and suggests strategies to overcome them for successful communication across world Englishes (Nelson, 1982, 1985; Smith, 1992; Smith and Bisazza, 1982; Smith and Nelson, 1985; Smith and Rafiqzad, 1979).

Since certain conventions of the use of linguistic devices (e.g. stress and intonation patterns, certain kinds of words and sentence patterns) contribute to intelligibility, resulting in successful or unsuccessful communication, these are discussed in varying detail in appropriate contexts. Obviously, our judgments on these points are based upon existing and available research. Chapters 5, 6, and 7 summarize information we have on the sounds, grammatical patterns, and vocabulary of varieties of English. Features of Outer and Expanding Circle Englishes are discussed in greater detail, since their descriptions are scattered in journal articles, unpublished Masters theses and PhD dissertations. Because descriptions of Inner Circle varieties are more readily available, they are not under focus here.

Interactional features, more than grammatical differences, create the most serious problems of perception of one's partner in interaction. We therefore concentrate on these. Topics such as conventions of conversational exchange, patterns of agreement/disagreement, strategies of speech acts, etc. are dealt with in Chapter 8, and literacy practices of writing (e.g. writing of letters, argumentative, expository and narrative prose, academic writing, etc.) are dealt with in Chapter 9.

Most Outer Circle varieties already have, and some Expanding Circle varieties are beginning to acquire, a tradition of literary creativity in English. Chapter 10 explores the possibility of using the literatures in world Englishes from Africa, Asia, and the Caribbean as a valuable resource for creating awareness of conventions of language use across varieties.

Finally, the Conclusion discusses the need for creating more awareness of the consequences of globalization on the English language. One way of introducing professionals to the changing forms and functions of English is to initiate curricular changes in the program for training teachers who are involved in Teaching English to Speakers of Other Languages (TESOL) and other professional programs. This concluding chapter points out the wider implications of the preceding discussion to the English Language Teaching (ELT) profession. In addition it discusses the relevance of research in world Englishes to research in sociolinguistics, second language acquisition, bilingualism, and other areas where language, culture, and society intersect.

Each chapter is followed by suggestions for further reading, points for further discussion and, where appropriate, small-scale research projects to be carried out by the readers of this book. The book thus aims at stimulating more questions, consideration of alternative ways of thinking about issues, and actively engaging in English studies from various perspectives—those of learners and teachers of English, users of English active in academia, and various professions including business, commerce, diplomacy, law, media, and medicine.

THE SOURCES

In addition to the general theoretical literature from the various relevant disciplines (e.g. linguistics, philosophy, psychology, cultural anthropology, ethnography of communication, sociolinguistics, and artificial intelligence), a great deal of material is available on very specific types of verbal interaction such as those between doctors and patients (e.g. Candlin *et al.*, 1976), teachers and pupils in a classroom (e.g. Sinclair *et al.*, 1972), dentists and patients (e.g. Candlin *et al.*, 1983), and lawyers and witnesses (e.g. Labov, 1988). Most of these, however, are based on interaction among Inner Circle English speakers only. A few studies have focused on Inner Circle/Outer Circle interaction in various settings (e.g. Gumperz, 1982a, 1982b). Insights from such studies are incorporated in the discussion of the topics dealt with.

Notes

1. The term lingua franca has been used in the following four senses (B. Kachru, 1996b, pp. 906–907): (1) an intermediary or contact language ... used primarily by Arabs, and later, also by Turks, with travelers from Western Europe, by prisoners of war, and by crusaders; (2) language of commerce, e.g. Italian; it was said to be the lingua franca of the commerce in the Adriatic sea. The term lingua franca, from Arabic *lisan-al farang*, originally meant the Italian language; (3) a medium of communication stabilized without much individual variation; and (4) the exemplars of lingua franca are Swahili in East Africa, Hindustani in South Asia, Pidgin in West Pacific, and Sabir in the Mediterranean port. In view of the current profile of the language in the world, English cannot be assigned

to any of the above categories. For more discussion on this topic, see B. Kachru (2005a, pp. 222–24).

2. This, however, does not mean that codification is not important from the point of view of language learning and teaching, and several other practical considerations. As Bamgboṣe (1998, p. 4) observes: "The importance of codification is too obvious to be belabored . . . one of the major factors militating against the emergence of endonormative standards in non-native Englishes is precisely the dearth of codification. Obviously, once a usage or innovation enters the dictionary as correct and acceptable usage, its status as a regular form is assured."

3. Many of the world Englishes used in various parts of the world have been described, some in more detail than others. Examples are: Abdulaziz (1991) for Kenya; Baumgardner (1993) and Rahman (1990) for Pakistan; Bamgboṣe *et al.* (1995) and Bokamba (1991, 1992) for West Africa; Bautista (1996, 1997) for The Philippines; Bell and Holmes (1991), Bell and Kuiper (1999), and Hundt (1998) for New Zealand; Bloom (1986), Brown (1992), Crewe (1977), Foley (1988), Gupta (1993), Low and Brown (2003), Platt and Weber (1980), and Tay (1986, 1993) for Singapore; Bolton (2003) and Zhao and Campbell (1995) for China; Bolton (2002) and Tay (1991) for Hong Kong; Romaine (1991) for the Pacific; Cenoz and Jessner (2000), Deneire and Goethals (1997) and Hilgendorf (1996) for Europe; Chambers (1991) for Canada; Chishimba (1991) and Magura (1985) for Southern Africa; Collins and Blair (1989), and Guy (1991) for Australian English; de Clerk (1996), de Kadt (1993), and Mesthrie (1992) for South Africa; Foley (1995) for Mauritius; B. Kachru (1965, 1983a, 1985b, 1986a, 1986c, 1986d, 1996a, 1998a, 1998b, 2001a, 2001b, 2002, 2005a) and S. Sridhar (1996) for India; Kandiah (1981, 1991) for Sri Lanka; Newbrook (1999) for Thailand; Lowenberg (1986a) and Said and Ng (2000) for Malaysia; Proshina (2005) for Russia; and Stanlaw (2003) for Japan. For more bibliographical references of research publications on various aspects of Englishes, including dictionaries and literary works, see Bailey and Görlach (1982), Cheshire (1991), Glauser *et al.* (1993), Görlach (1991), B. Kachru (1997b, 2005b), Y. Kachru and Nelson (2006), and Schneider (1997); for brief sketches of Englishes—both standard and non-standard—see McArthur (1992).

Further Reading

Bolton, K. (2004) World Englishes. In A. Davies and C. Elder (eds), *The Handbook of Applied Linguistics* (pp. 367–396). Oxford: Blackwell Publishing.

Kachru, B. B. (1997) World Englishes and English-using communities. *Annual Review of Applied Linguistics*, 17, 66–87.

Kachru, B. B. and Nelson, C. L. (1996) World Englishes. In S. L. McKay and N. H. Hornberger (eds), *Sociolinguistics and Language Teaching* (pp. 71–102). Cambridge: Cambridge University Press.

Suggested Activities

1. Listen to/view news broadcasts on Cable News Network (CNN), the British Broadcasting Corporation (BBC), or the Voice of America

(VOA) and note the way the local correspondents use English. Discuss what you notice about their accents, vocabulary, and language use.

2. Compare the two letters to the editor from newspapers of two Outer Circle countries—India and Singapore. Do the two letters have grammatical or lexical features (i.e. sentential or vocabulary-related characteristics) that identify them as belonging to a particular variety?

A. Is this not a monopoly?

Dear Sir,

I just want to know if consumer is a king in [country name] or is always at the receiving end. Through this letter I just want to know if there is any organization which will listen to me as a consumer as I got a bad treatment from a cable company. I live in town (near [city name]) and the cable company of my area was having signal booster at the roof of my house. The cable company technicians used to check signal very often and used to disturb us a lot. Moreover after checking booster at the roof they used to enter the house to check the signal on TV. As cable company technicians never carried ID cards with them, anybody could have come as a cable company technician. As this was not safe, I asked the cable company technicians to remove the booster from the roof of my house. They not only removed the booster from the roof but also removed the cable wire from the roof for which I had already paid to them. They did not even tell me that they were going to remove the cable wire itself. When I was not getting my signal, I called them and they asked me to get the connection I would have to pay for the 20 meter wire. When I told them that I had already paid when I took my connection, I was told to pay again to get the connection. I think they did this to me not only to harass me but also to make me pay for removing the signal booster. As there is no other cable company in this area, they are having monopoly in this area and showing the monopolistic behavior. Is there any organization which will look into this case? If this company is harassing me and asking for more money, there is possibility that they can harass others also to make more money as they have monopoly in the area.

I.S.

B. Pass laws to stop unwitting harboring of illegals.

I REFER to the article, "Ignorance no defence for harboring illegals" ([Name of Newspaper], April 2).

I feel that the law is not fair to landlords who are unaware that their tenants should not be in the country in the first place.

The root of the problem is not the landlords renting out their premises to these illegal immigrants.

All the landlords want is to earn some money.

They are, by and large, not interested in the affairs of their tenants.

To ensure that such people are not taken advantage of by immigration offenders, we should try to stop the migrants entering the country by adopting more stringent checks at immigration checkpoints.

We can also pass laws to ban foreign workers from renting premises unless they are sponsored by their employers.

This will protect landlords from committing such offences unwittingly.

Of course, if it can be proven that a landlord knew of the illegal-immigrant status of his tenant, he should be punished.

Housewives, grandmothers and professionals who may not have realized their tenants were illegals have been caught and jailed for renting out their premises.

Such instances suggest that the law is too harsh and non-discriminating.

Seow Boon Wah, the church deacon appealing against a jail term for harboring an illegal, stood to gain nothing because the premises did not belong to him.

Yet, he is being punished.

I believe that he had no intention of breaking the law, and that, therefore, it is extreme to say that he was actually harboring illegals.

Perhaps the authorities could take another look at the problem, and stop people like Seow from running foul of the law unwittingly.

L.C.H.

PART I

VERBAL INTERACTION AND INTELLIGIBILITY

INTRODUCTION

There is no agreement about the relationship between language, culture, and society. Whether language is an autonomous system irrespective of its role as a means of human communication or whether it is primarily a medium of communication and therefore has a crucial role in social organization has also been a matter of vigorous debate. Credible arguments have been advanced on both sides of the debate. There is a vast body of literature that claims, following Chomsky's theory, that language is innate, biologically determined, species-specific; it is a biological entity, a mental organ (see, Anderson and Lightfoot, 2002). There is an equally impressive corpus of research that contends that language shapes and is shaped by social interaction (see, Halliday, 1973, 1978; Hymes, 1964, 1974; Labov, 1972b).

In this book we are interested in the use of various Englishes around the world, especially on how Englishes function in various communities to further their communicative goals. We, therefore, draw upon methodologies of research based on the latter view of language.

The aim of the first three chapters in this part of the book is to focus on the interaction of cultural assumptions, social configurations, and linguistic resources that manifests themselves in linguistic interchanges between users of English. The following chapter, Chapter 4, deals with issues of intelligibility in view of the discussions in the first three.

THEORETICAL APPROACH TO VERBAL INTERACTION

The first chapter briefly discusses the theoretical concepts of linguistic pragmatics (speech acts, cooperative principle, and politeness), conversation analysis (structure of conversation in terms of turns, adjacency pairs, floor, backchannel cues, etc.), and sociolinguistics (e.g. context of situation, conventions of speaking, writing, the role of silence and non-verbal cues in interaction, etc.).

The second chapter focuses on the interrelationship of culture and language and discusses language use. The chapter demonstrates one way of constructing the sociocultural bases of verbal interaction by utilizing components of context of situation from sociolinguistics, and structure of background knowledge from psychology and artificial intelligence. It also presents briefly the findings of interdisciplinary research on conventions of speaking and writing in various societies.

The third chapter presents various views of what it means to be polite in a variety of sociocultural settings. In one culture, it may be considered a violation of privacy to ask questions about one's marital status or how many children one has in casual encounters. In another, it may be a marker of one's effort to be sociable and friendly even if the encounter is short-lived, as in a train journey. In South Asia, it is quite common for passengers in the same compartment to ask such questions of each other in addition to sharing food and drinks. Koreo (1988, p. 19) recounts an anecdote about his experience of showing a group of Western scientists around soon after the end of World War II. After a day of walking about, he asked the visitors, "Aren't you tired?" He was surprised when, contrary to his expectations, one of them answered in the affirmative. When the following suggestion, "You must be hungry" was again followed by "Yes, I am," Koreo admits he was "taken aback." The unpleasant surprise was due to violation of expectations regarding polite behavior. According to Japanese norms, it is inconsiderate "to admit fatigue to a person who has acted as their guide all day" and in answer to the question about being hungry, it is polite to say something such as "just a little" or "I always have a late supper" to avoid worrying the host.

The strategies of politeness in verbal interaction may also differ across communities and cultures. Scollon and Scollon (1994, pp. 144–145) quote the following recommendation from *Li Chi*, dating from before Confucius: "When the elder asks a question, to reply without acknowledging one's incompetency and (trying to) decline answering is contrary to propriety." In many cultures, refusing to answer may be considered quite impolite.

INTELLIGIBILITY

The fourth chapter, as mentioned before, examines what is meant by intelligibility in the context of the discussions in the previous three chapters. The concept as discussed here differs from the popular use of the familiar term. It is analyzed into its component parts and related to pronunciation, grammar, and sociocultural conventions of language use to see why verbal interaction between culturally different interlocutors is not always efficient and successful. That any interaction can lead to misunderstanding and frustration is true of both conversation and writing; it is more so when the interlocutors do not share a common sociocultural background and a set of conventions of verbal interaction. The chapter presents a characterization of the nature of intelligibility, analyzes sources of complexity and suggests strategies to resolve difficulties to achieve communicative success across world Englishes.

The suggestions for further reading, recommendations for continuing discussions and small-scale research projects are intended to stimulate debates and exchanges on issues that arise due to the worldwide spread and use of English. The field of English studies is fraught with controversies and all users of English, teachers and learners included, have a stake in how some of the questions are answered and the answers in turn are implemented. It is our hope that what is presented in these chapters will inspire active participation of those who use English all across the Three Circles, whether in the fields of administration, business, commerce, diplomacy, education, finance, law, or media.

Chapter 1

Interaction as Cooperation

INTRODUCTION

Communicating through language—whether spoken or written—is a remarkably skilled social behavior. There are two major modes of using language for communication, spoken and written. The written mode is not universal, there are many languages in various parts of the world that are spoken, but not written. Written language, where it exists, imposes a severe restriction on channels through which participants communicate with each other. The spoken mode, on the other hand, allows for a number of channels to be utilized. We speak with our vocal organs, but we converse and communicate with our entire bodies. Obviously, the written mode cannot utilize the channels of gesture, body posture, facial expression, etc. to the same extent, though there are some symbols devised for (informally) indicating smile, frown, etc.

These differences notwithstanding, a broad generalization in terms of spoken vs. written mode of linguistic interaction is possible, since the dichotomy spoken vs. written is not discrete, e.g. a phone conversation utilizes the spoken channel, but does not share all the features of face-to-face conversation. In a phone conversation the speaker and hearer are unable to see each other's body posture, facial expressions, gestures, and other non-verbal cues. The technology is not widely available as yet for the participants in a conversation to see each other as they speak, hence, facial expression, gesture, body posture, etc. are not transmitted in phone conversations. For our purposes, we will, for the most part, concentrate on features common to the spoken and the written modes. Most of what we have to say about verbal interaction in this chapter apply to both the modes.

INFORMATION EXCHANGE

In both the spoken and the written modes, participants exchange three types of information. The first may be termed **conceptual information**, i.e. the purely factual content of linguistic signals exchanged. "Factual" does not mean "true"; the sentence, "The Fairy Godmother transformed Cinderella into a princess by a wave of her magic wand," has a cognitive content, and therefore, conveys a certain "factual information," although it is not "true" in the real world.

The second type of information exchanged is what Abercrombie calls **indexical information** (Abercrombie, 1967, p. 6), i.e. information about the speaker/writer himself/herself. Listeners/readers use this information to draw inferences about the speaker/writer's identity, attributes, attitudes, and mood. For instance, the utterance, "It is clear that Jeremy is the culprit" makes it obvious that the speaker is making a firm assertion, whereas the utterance, "I think Herbert was fired" indicates that the speaker is not sure of his/her facts.

The third type of information exchanged is what has been called **interaction-management information** (Laver and Hutcheson, 1972, p. 12), i.e. information that enables participants to initiate or terminate an interaction, indicate transitions, control time-sharing, etc., in an acceptable way in the spoken mode, or signal **cohesion, coherence**, etc., in the written mode. For instance, the utterance, "That's all I have to say about it" signals explicitly to other participants in the conversation that the speaker has completed his/her turn and is ready to give a chance to someone else to claim a turn. Similarly, the utterance of "Did you hear what happened to Margie?" provides a clear signal to the participants in the conversation that the speaker wishes to narrate a significant event. Similarly, expressions such as "It is claimed in this study that . . ." and "I will argue in this paper that . . ." clearly signal academic argumentative writing. More about such devices in the spoken and written modes are pointed out in Chapters 8 and 9. Here, we will focus on some concepts that are crucial in analyzing verbal interaction.

RELEVANT CONCEPTS

In order to understand how successful communication through language is achieved by conveying the three types of information mentioned above, it is useful to look at several areas of study. The linguistic-philosophic-semantic discussions of **speech acts** (Austin, 1962; Searle, 1969) and **cooperative principle** (Grice, 1975) are useful in providing a great deal of insight into language use in general. The research on face-to-face interaction, including conversation, with a social science bias is extremely helpful in structuring conversation. The structure of conversation is looked at in terms of units such as **turn** (distribution of talk across participants; Sacks *et al.*, 1974), **exchange** (response by one participant to another), and **adjacency pair** (paired utterances by two different participants, e.g. question–answer, compliment–response, apology–minimization). Social scientists such as Goffman have also looked at face-to-face interaction as ritualistic behavior (Goffman, 1955, 1967) and discussed **face** as an important concept in characterizing the image that people attempt to project, negotiate, and maintain in such interaction. The concept *face* is inextricably linked with the concept of **politeness** as well as the concept of cooperation in Gricean terms. The contribution of sociolinguistics and ethnography of communication in structuring the social context of language use is as relevant as that of artificial intelligence and psychology: the former provides the concept of **context of situation** or *context*, the latter several constructs for structuring **background knowledge** or **sociocultural knowledge** essential for analyzing conversation or discourse structure. They are discussed in relation to crosscultural communication through English in the following pages.[1]

In this chapter, we will discuss some of the concepts mentioned above in some detail. We will look at two instances of a conversation and analyze them in terms of speech acts, Gricean cooperative principle, and conversation analysis, taking into account sociocultural context and background knowledge.

Consider the following verbal interaction between a Vietnamese (A), a recent immigrant to the USA, and an American college student (D) in the college lounge (*Take Two*, 1983, pp. 94–95). Both are women and have heard the teacher pronounce their names, which may not be enough in case of unfamiliar names.

1. D: Hi Ann, How ya doin'?
    A: Oh hi. Uhm, I'm reading.
    D: Mind if I sit down?
    A. Please.
    D: Thank you. You getting ready for class?
    A: Yes.
    D: I was wondering—you're from Vietnam, aren't you?
    A: Yes.

From the point of view of interaction management, this conversation does not seem to be going well. The addressee, addressed as Ann, is not very communicative. Out of the four *exchanges*, she replies in monosyllables in three. Now compare the above with the following interaction (*Take Two*, 1983, pp. 109–110):

2. D: Hi Ann. How ya doin'?
    A: Oh, hi. How are you?

> D: Fine, thanks. You mind if I sit down?
> A: Oh, have a seat.
> D: Thanks. Getting ready for class?
> A: Yes, I'm prepared. (A: slight laugh)
> D: Your name is "Ann", isn't it?
> A: Uh, no, it's "Anh", <u>A</u>—<u>N</u>—<u>H</u>. In Vietnamese, it's "Anh".

It is obvious that this interaction has a better chance of succeeding in establishing some social relationship between the participants. Anh is more forthcoming and does not confine herself to monosyllables. A more detailed look at (1) and (2) in terms of speech acts, Gricean cooperative principle, and conversational analysis is helpful in understanding the nature of interaction exemplified by these texts.

Speech Acts

The notion of speech acts is a simple one: uttering a string of meaningful sounds is not only performing the act of speaking, but also performing a variety of acts such as informing, questioning, ordering, etc. via the act of speaking. These latter are the subject matter of the field of research known as speech acts. Philosophers and linguists have been aware of the fact that in discussing meaning in natural languages, determining the truth or falsity of utterances is not enough, since some utterances such as questions or requests are neither true nor false; they are the means of performing acts that may be appropriate or inappropriate in a given context. For instance, if one utters the example in (3), depending upon a number of conditions, the request may be judged appropriate or inappropriate, but not true or false:

> 3.   Open the door!

The request is appropriate if it is uttered by a parent and directed to his/her child, for instance, but inappropriate if uttered by a hotel employee and directed toward a hotel guest. Similarly, there is no conceivable way of determining the truth value of utterances such as the example in (4) below:

> 4.   Why are you frowning?

Again, it may be appropriate or inappropriate to ask such a question under certain conditions; it makes no sense to ask whether it is true or false.

According to Austin (1962), every linguistic utterance represents an act. Some are **explicit**, as in case of a judge passing a sentence on an accused by saying *I hereby sentence you to. . . .* Others are **implicit**, as in case of a statement, which is not prefaced normally by *I hereby declare that.* . . . In fact, if such a preface were added to the ordinary statement *I don't feel well today,* the listener(s) would consider the utterance very odd. In addition to **direct speech acts**, which may be either *explicit* or *implicit*, there are **indirect speech acts** (Searle, 1975), such as interrogative structures signaling greetings or requests, as mentioned before and exemplified by (5):

5.   Would you mind closing that window?

Most readers would agree that the speaker who utters (5) is requesting the addressee to close the window, but that is not the literal meaning of the sentence in (5). When "one illocutionary act is performed indirectly by way of performing another" (Searle, 1975, p. 60), it results in an indirect speech act. The illocutionary act performed in (5) is a question, but the question is used to perform the act of request.

Why people resort to indirect speech acts is a separate question. It is not difficult to guess the reasons: indirect speech acts are generally more polite, they are more tactful ways of correcting, questioning, reminding, requesting (as in (5) above), etc. Part of being a competent speaker of a language involves judgments with regard to when to perform direct or indirect speech acts, and when to remain silent. It is obvious that performing and interpreting speech acts in a second or n-th language presents more problems than in a language one grows up with.

Speech acts in crosscultural and cross-linguistic situations present even more fascinating challenges, since it is normally the case that the interactants do not share the same sociocultural conventions and background knowledge in such situations.

Looking at the conversation in (1) above, it is clear that Anh misinterprets D(iane)'s *How ya doin'?*, she interprets it as a question and answers *I'm reading.* In a sense, what Anh does is not unreasonable: the locutionary act of uttering an interrogative structure signals an illocutionary act of question, as is clear from the following exchange:

6.   X: What time is it?
     Y: It's five past four.

In (6), Y is an appropriate response to X in case X intends to ask for information and Y provides the information being sought. In (1), however, Diane does not intend to seek information, as is clear from her phrasing, i.e. her use of *how* instead of *what.* However, Diane's intention is not obvious to Anh. Why Anh's interpretation of Diane's utterance results in an inappropriate response in the given context can better be understood in terms of Gricean cooperative principle.

Conversational Implicature and Gricean Maxims

Anh's failure to interpret Diane's apparent question as greeting leads us to the idea of conversation as a cooperative venture. Successful interaction depends on the addressee's ability to arrive at the **conversational implicature** of the speaker's utterance, i.e. the addressee's ability to understand the speaker's intention in uttering something. *Implicature* refers to what the speaker implies, suggests, or means, as distinct from what (s)he says literally. According to Grice (1975), *conversational implicatures* are derived from a general principle of conversation and a number of **maxims** that speakers normally obey. The general principle, called the *cooperative principle*, is as follows (Grice, 1975, p. 45):

> 7. A. Make your conversational contribution such as is required, at the stage
>   at which it occurs, by the accepted purpose or direction of the talk
>   exchange in which you are engaged.
>   The **maxims**, or conventions which support this principle are as follows:
>   B. *Quantity*: Make your contribution as informative as is required (for the
>   current purpose of the exchange). Do not make your contribution more
>   than is required.
>   *Quality*: Do not say what you believe to be false. Do not say that
>   for which you lack adequate evidence.
>   *Relation*: Be relevant.
>   *Manner*: Be perspicuous.
>   Avoid obscurity of expression.
>   Avoid ambiguity.
>   Be brief (avoid unnecessary prolixity).
>   Be orderly.

Grice does not claim this to be an exhaustive list, for instance, he notes that a maxim such as *Be polite* is normally observed. It has been suggested that the maxim of manner does not apply to "primarily interactional conversation" and that "*Be relevant* seems to cover all the other instructions" (Brown and Yule, 1983, p. 32). Note also that if the purpose of the interaction is served by violating any of the above instructions, participants do violate them, e.g. if the purpose is to mislead, the **maxim of quality** is violated, and so on. Whatever the controversies might be with regard to these maxims, they are useful as a point of departure for our discussion. One word of caution, however, is necessary. The maxims are not meant to be prescriptive; they represent the normal assumptions on which verbal interactions are based. Any violation of the maxims thus leads to inferences regarding the intent of the speaker utterance.

In conversation (1), the source of Anh's misinterpretation lies in her not recognizing the linguistic convention that operates in American English. Consequently, she interprets "How ya doin'?" as a genuine question, rather than a greeting. Equally important, Diane could have been more "cooperative" and used a more conventional opener, such as "*How are you?*," which Anh would perhaps have recognized more easily as a greeting. Thus, D's use of an indirect speech act, though conventionalized in American English, in this context of interaction with Anh represents a violation of the maxim of manner in that it appears opaque to her interlocutor.

Conversation Analysis

In both (1) and (2), the total number of turns is the same and both Anh and Diane take four turns each. However, this equal number of turn-taking is deceptive.

In (1), as the interaction progresses, it seems that "Diane leaves Anh very little time to respond to questions. The total exchange lasts for approximately one minute and ten seconds, with Diane's utterances taking approximately 66 percent of that time." The explanation for Diane dominating the conversation is suggested by the following observation: "it is not uncommon for a native speaker to react to discomfort in an exchange . . . by increasing verbal activity. Abhorrence of silence could almost be a cultural trait in dominant U. S. culture" (Grumperz *et al.*, 1979, p. 97).

In conversation (2), Anh recognizes Diane's apparent question as an opener (i.e. a greeting), responds to it, and in subsequent exchanges, is more willing to ask questions instead of answering Diane's question in mono-syllables. The turns are more even, and it seems likely that as the conversation progresses, both participants feel at ease and then part feeling comfortable about their relationship. The conversation in (2), thus, conforms more closely to the norms of such verbal interactions in the American English-speaking community, at least in the setting of academic institutions.

Linguistic and Sociocultural Conventions

The examples above establish it clearly that in order for an interaction to succeed, the participants have to be aware of the **linguistic conventions** of the language of interaction (e.g. the use of an interrogative structure in the function of "greeting" in American English). In addition, they have to be aware of the **sociocultural conventions** that the participants follow (e.g. the participant's observance of a certain duration of silence before contributing to the exchange). Cultures vary with regard to their tolerance of silence, and where silence is appropriate, in conversation.[2] These conventions are discussed in some detail in the following chapters in the context of varieties of English (see Chapters 8 and 9). Next we explore the relevance of the concept *face* to verbal interaction briefly.

The Concept *Face*

When an interaction is not going well, both participants engaged in it may feel uncomfortable. This is because in face-to-face interaction, participants are not only exchanging messages, they are also projecting their self-images. Failure in interaction poses a threat to this self-image, or *face*. According to Goffman (1967, p. 5), "*face* is an image of self delineated in terms of approved social attributes. . . ." Since "maintenance of *face* is a condition of interaction" (Goffman, 1967, p. 12), any threat to face leads to the threatened participant abandoning the interaction. In order to keep the interaction going, attempts are made to retain the ritual equilibrium (Goffman, 1955). Two good examples of such attempts in conversation (2) are the return greeting *How are you?*, and the explanation by Anh, *In Vietnamese, it's "Anh."* The first reciprocates Diane's attempts at getting a conversation going, the second is to make sure Diane is not embarrassed at being corrected in the pronunciation of Anh's name.

Let us look at another example. Consider the following conversation between two friends:

8. i.   A: We will be delighted if you could share a meal with us on Saturday evening.
   ii. B: Why go to so much trouble? After all, everyone is so busy during the week. The week end is the only time when one can relax. We will drop by and see you some time during the week end.
   iii. A: It will be no trouble at all. It will be a simple meal, nothing elaborate.
   iv. B: Shall we bring some thing?
   v.   A: Just yourselves, and a good appetite. See you at 7 PM.
   vi. B: We will meet then.

To give a brief account of what is going on in the above exchanges, it may be hypothesized that both participants are conscious of each other's face or the image of themselves that they want to project to the society as a whole. A's invitation is not accepted immediately because that would either imply that A is obliged to invite B for some reason, or that B has to accommodate A's wishes for some reason. The first alternative would be detrimental to A's image, the second to B's. Also, B has to be sure A is sincere in inviting him/her before accepting the invitation. Thus, the initial reluctance saves both participants' images. A's subsequent insistence in (iii) indicates the sincerity of the invitation, so B hints at his/her willingness to accept the invitation in (iv). The eventual acceptance of the invitation restores social harmony and enhances the image of each participant. The concept of face is discussed in greater detail in Chapter 3, since it plays a major role in politeness across cultures.

The Concept *Context*

Maintaining the ritual equilibrium is easier when the participants share a common sociocultural background. A simple illustration is what the participants know about each other as individuals and as members of a sociocultural group. Let us take a second look at the conversation in (8) from this perspective. Note that both participants take it for granted that according to the norms of their culture and society, a dinner invitation is a matter of negotiation and not of immediate acceptance or rejection. It is polite on part of the guests to offer contributing to the dinner by bringing in a dish to share; it is, however, not polite of the hosts to accept the offer, except in rare circumstances. It is not customary among friends to thank each other for such invitations. At a personal level, both participants seem to know that they are working couples, hence the mention of week end. The host is sure that the guest knows where the hosts live, hence the location of the dinner is not specified. The guest seems to know that the hosts know the dietary habits of the guests, hence no mention is made of any dietary restrictions, e.g. a vegetarian dinner.

Even this brief example makes it clear that specifying whatever is meant by "sociocultural background" is not easy. Sociolinguists, sociologists, ethnographers of communication, and psychologists have, however, attempted to provide some key concepts that are helpful.

CONCLUSION

The sociolinguistic concepts of *context* and *context of situation* are crucial in analyzing verbal interaction; they provide the essential categories required for structuring the sociocultural background of interaction. The context of culture is discussed in greater detail in the next chapter.

Notes

1. For those who wish to consult the original sources for these concepts, the following list may be helpful: for a general approach to analyses of language use, see Green (1989); for *speech acts*, see Austin (1962), Sadock (1974), Searle (1975); for a discussion of *cooperative principle* and *conversational implicature*, see Grice (1975); for conventional implicature, see Karttunen and Peters (1979). Goffman (1967), Laver and Hutcheson (1972), and Duncan and Fiske (1977) are good sources for becoming familiar with the social scientific approach to face-to-face interaction. The concept of *context of situation*, first discussed as relevant to linguistic analysis in Firth (1957a, 1957b), and Hymes (1964), is elaborated in Halliday (1973, 1978), and Saville-Troike (1982), respectively. How encyclopedic and sociocultural knowledge that participants bring to verbal

interaction is utilized in utterance text production and interpretation has been studied in many diverse fields. From the perspective of cognitive psychology and artificial intelligence, Bartlett (1932), Minsky (1975), Schank and Abelson (1977), and Sanford and Garrod (1981) provide the concepts of **schema**, **frame**, **script**, and **scenario** for structuring background knowledge essential for success-ful conversation or for structuring discourse. Some of these latter constructs have been shown to be relevant for the analysis of discourse in Chafe (1980), Freedle (1979), Tannen (1982a, 1982b), Brown and Yule (1983), and Y. Kachru (1983, 1987, 1988).

2. For a description of these conventions in some cultures, see Philips (1983), Scollon and Scollon (1981), Tannen (1984), and Tannen and Saville-Troike (1985).

Further Reading

Brown, G. and Yule, G. (1983) *Discourse Analysis.* Cambridge: Cambridge University Press. [Chapters 2 and 7.]
Green, G. M. (1989) *Pragmatics and Natural Language Understanding.* Hillsdale, NJ: Lawrence Erlbaum.
Schiffrin, D. (1994) *Approaches to Discourse.* Oxford: Blackwell. [Part II.]

Suggested Activities

Consider the following excerpt from a conversation in a professional setting (Dautermann, 1995, pp. 205–207) and discuss the following questions:

1. What is the purpose of this interaction? Do you have any background knowledge to answer this question fully? If not, what more information do you need?

2. Are the participants being cooperative? What devices are they using to signal their cooperative stance?

3. What face-saving strategies, if any, are they using?

4. What can you say about the geographical location, if anything, of this interaction? How do you deduce the location?

5. Does the interaction achieve its purpose? What suggests the interaction has succeeded or failed?

Excerpt from an interaction between nurses working in a hospital drafting a document:

de: Procedures.
jd: Alright. Procedures.

di: "Procedures is the process used to . . ." not to document technical intervention, but to . . .

jd: Standardize?

di: Okay, there's a good one, "standardize the technical steps, the technical—?"

jd: Intervention?

di: mm. hmm. Steps and intervention, the same thing. "Technical intervention."

jd: But nursing intervention? "Technical nursing intervention—?"

di: Nah. Too much.

jd: Okay.

di: "Technical intervention applied—"

jd: mm. hmm. To—"in response to patient care plan?"

di: Well is it in response to a patient condition? or is it in response to an expected condition? or\\

de: //Response to an order. That's what we are doing. A procedure we do because we have an order to do it.

di: "A process used to standardize the technical intervention applied— _"

jd: "In response to an order?"

di   "To physician order?" Is it a physician order?

jd: Hummm.

de: "A procedure is a tool that is used—"

di: Here finish this statement. [Hands draft to jk.]

jk: "Procedure"

jd: "to standardize the technical intervention in response to—"

di: What?

jd: To what? Patient care needs? People's orders?

jk: We have to say what they are in response to.

de: "A procedure is a tool that defines the technical steps\\

jk: //involved in nursing intervention."

de: No.

jd: Okay, hold it. "A procedure is a tool that is used to standardize technical intervention by nurses."

di: That's it.

jd: Okay.

de: I like that. Good. Excellent.

[Transcription conventions: —indicates a pause inviting comment from the others; . . . indicates text not read aloud; \\ indicates utterance is continued or interrupted by another speaker; // indicates an utterance that attaches to someone else's utterance.]

Chapter 2

Context of Culture

INTRODUCTION

It is not easy to define what is meant by terms such as **culture** and **context of culture**. Culture has been defined in various ways in different disciplines. For instance, one definition says that culture is "a historically transmitted pattern of meanings embodied in symbolic forms by means of which men communicate, perpetuate, and develop their knowledge about and attitudes toward life" (Geertz, 1973, p. 89). Another definition suggests that culture is what people "must know in order to *act* as they do, *make* the things they make, and *interpret* their experience in the distinctive way they do" (Quinn and Holland, 1987, p. 4, emphasis added). Thornton (1988) argues against a static, reified notion of culture and observes that there is not much point in discussing what "culture" is. Rather, what can be useful is to say what culture does. According to Bloch (1991), culture, which is an important area of anthropological research, can be defined as that which people must know in order to function reasonably effectively in their social environment. Social environment consists of social organizations and behaviors that are the instruments through which people relate to each other.

Although it is difficult to define precisely what is meant by the term "culture," what is clear from all the attempts at defining it is that culture is both historic and immediate; it shapes action—verbal as well as a variety of other actions—and in turn is shaped by them. It is a dynamic process rather than a static, monolithic entity with a stable existence.

It is equally difficult to define what is meant by the term **society**. For example, Ginsberg (1932, p. 40) defines a society as "a collection of individuals united by certain relations or modes of behavior which mark them off from others who do not enter into those relations or who differ from them in behavior." Linton (1936, p. 91) observes that a society is "any group of people who have lived and worked together long enough to get themselves organized or to think of themselves as a social unit with well-defined limits." The social scientists view society as a system, that is, a social system consisting of

> groups whose members together perform certain functions that they do not accomplish as separate groups. The groups are thus interdependent, and they are interdependent in a particular arrangement. That is to say, the participants in each group act in regular, anticipated ways toward members of other groups and toward the external environment. When some participants do not carry out the kind of interchange that others in the system anticipate, the others respond in regular ways of counterchange to restore some systemic regularity to their relations. (Mandelbaum, 1970, pp. 4–5)

Examples of such groups are parents and children, teachers and students, employers and employees, etc.

Human actions, including verbal interactions, take place in institutions defined by societies, such as the institutions of family, workplace, education, worship, and others. It is thus relevant to look at the sociocultural contexts in which language is used in order to gain insight into linguistic behavior. For this endeavor the concepts of *context* and *context of situation* as characterized by linguists such as Firth (1957a) and ethnographers such as Hymes (1964) are useful.

CONTEXT AND CONTEXT OF SITUATION

According to Firth (1957a, p. 182), "context of situation" is best used as a suitable schematic construct to apply to language events. He suggests the following categories to relate "context of situation" to "language events":

1. a. The relevant features of participants: persons, personalities.
        i.   The verbal action of the participants.
        ii. The non-verbal action of the participants.
     b. The relevant objects.
     c. The effect of the verbal action.

For instance, in a classroom situation, both teachers and pupils engage in speaking (e.g. both teachers and pupils ask questions and give answers). The verbal interaction involves objects, such as books, chalk, blackboard, etc., and actions such as raising hands, opening books, pointing at a pupil, writing on the blackboard, etc.

A similar approach is found in Hymes (1964, 1974) where further details of context are specified. For instance, the notions of **speech situation** (which may comprise both verbal and non-verbal events, e.g. a ceremony or a hunt) and **speech event** ("activities, or aspects of activities that are directly governed by rules or norms for the use of speech," e.g. a church service) are relevant for a sociolinguistic description. Components of speech include **message form** ("how things are said," e.g. the linguistic form of the utterance including silence), **message content** ("what is being talked about," e.g. topic), **setting** (place and time of the event and the non-verbal actions of the participants), **scene** (psychological setting, e.g. informal/formal, serious/festive), **participants**, including **speaker**, **addressor**, **addressee**, and **audience**, i.e. person(s) other than the addressee(s), **purposes**, including **outcomes** and **goals** (what the participants intended to achieve as a result of the communicative event), **key** (evaluation of message form, e.g. as mock/serious, perfunctory/painstaking), **channels** (e.g. speech, writing, smoke signals, drum beats), **forms of speech** (e.g. language, dialect, code, variety), **norms of interaction** (rules that govern speaking in a community), **norms of interpretation** (how certain behaviors, including verbal behaviors such as hesitation, are interpreted within or across communities), and **genre** (e.g. poem, myth, tale, riddle, curse, chanting).[1]

Drawing upon Hymes' categories, Saville-Troike (1982, pp. 139–140) discusses the following components of a communicative event: *genre* or type of event (e.g. joke, story, lecture, conversation, etc.); *topic, purpose,* or *function,* both of the event in general and in terms of the interactional goals of individual participants; *setting,* including location, time, season, and physical aspects of the situation; *participants,* including their age, sex, ethnicity, status, and relationship to one another; *message form,* including both vocal and non-vocal channels and the code used; *message content* (i.e. what is communicated); *act sequence* (i.e. ordering of speech acts, including turn-taking); *rules for interaction;* and *norms of interpretation.*

All these features are relevant in the interpretation of a communicative act in the same way as a feature of the sound is. That is to say, changing [p] to [b] in *pet* signals a different meaning, i.e. *bet,* and thereby establishes the fact that the feature "voicing" has a meaning. Similarly, each feature of context has a meaning, and changing any one of the features signals a different meaning. For instance, the following signal two different meanings:

2.   A: Is he at home?
       B: Is he at his residence?

Just the difference in the use of the lexical items *home* vs. *his residence* signals the difference between intimate vs. a more formal domain.

Another example may reveal the relevance of the components of context of situation more completely. Most fluent speakers of a language share experiences of participating in speech events that are similar in many respects. They are therefore able to understand texts by "supplying" the missing components in speech when faced with a piece of text such as the following exchange:

3.   A   Don't you have to go to school tomorrow morning?
      B: I just have one more math problem to solve.

One can infer several contextual features from this. One set of inferences may be that B is a student, and A is either a parent, or a caregiver. B is still young enough for the caregiver to suggest when (s)he should go to bed, but not young enough to be ordered to go to bed. The time is most likely to be late evening, and the location is likely to be A's and/or B's home. The domain of interaction is intimate, and the purpose of interaction is expression of solidarity. That is, A wants to convey to B his/her concern about B getting enough rest for the next day, and B's purpose is to reassure A that (s)he is mindful of the time as well as his/her duty to complete the school assignment for the next day and that (s)he is almost finished. Note that any change in any contextual feature of the interaction will lead to a change in the coding of the interaction. For example, a change in the participants' age and relationship will lead to a difference in message form, e.g. if both A and B were college roommates, the following rather than (3) may be a possible interaction:

4   A: What time do you have to go to the class tomorrow?
      B: I just have one more short chapter to read.

It is noteworthy that the exchange in (4) is much harder to interpret without more contextual clues. A's question may show concern for B; on the other hand, it may also be a hint that A wants to rest, and therefore B should turn off the light. It is clear that depending upon the relationship of the two participants (parent–child, roommates), and other contextual factors, such isolated exchanges may have several different interpretations. In case of actual conversational exchanges, however, the relevant factors constrain the choice of interpretations much more narrowly.

STRUCTURE OF BACKGROUND KNOWLEDGE

People organize the background knowledge essential for verbal interaction not only in terms of context of situation or features of context that are within the domain of immediate experience, but also in terms of conceptual organizations established on the basis of earlier experiences. These organizations have been discussed in a variety of disciplines using various terms such as *schemata, frames, scripts, scenarios*, etc. The terms differ because the perspectives of the relevant disciplines to speech situations differ. For instance, within psychology, the concept of *schema* arose in the context of research on memory and recall. Bartlett discussed *schemata* as structures in memory which remain "active" and "developing." According to Bartlett, "[t]he past operates as an organized mass rather than as a group of elements each of which retains its specific character" (1932, p. 197). The concept of *schema* is invoked in the concept of memory for discourse. For example, a text such as in (5a) may be remembered as in (5b):

5. a. Samantha and Kimberly were going shopping when they met with an accident.
    b. Two friends were going shopping when they were hit by a car.

The person who recalls (5a) as (5b) has actively reconstructed the text in (5a) using the schemata of friends going shopping together and a car accident.

As opposed to this concept of dynamic *schema* is the concept of static *frame*, which is conceived on a much broader scale in sociology. According to Goffman (1974), who makes use of the notion of *frame* proposed in Bateson (1972), most members of a society come to understand a situation in accordance with principles of organization that govern events in which they are subjectively involved. His aim is "to isolate some of the basic framework of understanding available in our society for making sense out of events" (Goffman, 1974, p. 10). Goffman discusses not only framing situations and events that facilitate our understanding of what is going on, but also misframings that lead to misunderstandings.

The notion of *frame* has been adapted to the needs of research in artificial intelligence, where it has been suggested that human knowledge is stored in memory in the form of data structures that represent stereotyped situations called *frames* (Minsky, 1975). *Frames* are "remembered framework[s] to be adapted to fit reality by changing details as necessary" (Minsky, 1975, p. 212). As applied to linguistic knowledge, we may say that our knowledge of a certain area of human activity is stored in a *frame* labeled SCHOOL. This *frame* has certain **slots** such as "class room," "teacher," "blackboard," "chalk," etc. The **slots** are filled by **fillers**, i.e. specific lexical materials that occur in a text.

Whereas a *frame* is static, a *script* is dynamic in that it incorporates "a standard sequence of events that describes a situation" (Riesbeck and Schank, 1978, p. 254). One way of clarifying what is meant by script is to show how people come to understand texts. For instance, it is not difficult for most readers to fill in the blank in (6) with an expression:

6. A: I am thirsty.
    B: _____

Any of the following and several others would be appropriate:

7. B: Would you like some water/juice/coffee/tea/soft drink?

The expectation that A's utterance demands the offer of some drink is satisfied by the utterances in (7). Given the context, however, that both A and B are shopping in a big department store that has a coffee shop on the fifth floor, the expected response is more likely to be something like:

8. B: Shall we go to the coffee shop on the fifth floor?

That is, A's utterance in (6) evokes a script that contains certain stereotypical "actions," e.g. offer of a drink, or offer of accompanying A to some location where drinks are available. Such expectations, based on conceptual knowledge as they are, play a significant role in constructing interpretations of texts.

One other concept invoked in accounting for discourse interpretation, based upon that of script, is that of *scenario*. According to Sanford and Garrod (1981) knowledge of settings and situations may be thought of as constituting the interpretive scenario behind a text. To the extent that a piece of text invokes an appropriate scenario for a reader/ listener, it is interpreted successfully. For example, a text that mentions going to a restaurant invokes a scenario in which waiters, menus, seating, etc. play a role.

Some examples may make the applicability of these concepts clearer. For instance, the following exchange between a foreign visitor and a native host in the USA may prove problematic for the foreigner unless (s)he has the relevant background knowledge, i.e. (s)he is aware of the holidays in the USA:

9) Visitor: I was thinking of cashing in some cheques on Thursday.
    Host: Thursday is Thanksgiving.

The host's utterance indicates that "Thanksgiving" is part of the background knowledge that a speaker of American English possesses. What the visitor is expected to infer is that the banks will be closed on Thursday, so his/her plans will have to be revised. If the visitor has never heard of Thanksgiving, obviously, the American host's utterance is a puzzle for him/her. Note that it is not the competence in the English language that is relevant here, it is the sharing of the sociocultural (background) knowledge that is crucial for successful communication to occur in this instance. This, of course, is a very simple example and depends on a piece of information that is easily obtainable. A more complex example is the following:

10. Before carrying the rice up into the barn, the time arrives for making merit at the threshing floor. They make a pavilion and set up a place for the Buddha image and seats for monks at the threshing ground. In the evening of the day appointed for making merit at the threshing floor, when the time arrives monks come and perform evening chants at the threshing ground. (Rajadhon, 1968, p. 368)

Although the above text is in English, it is difficult for all users of English to come up with an interpretation of this piece of text. What can be deduced is the following: the writer is the *addresser*, the reader is the *addressee*, the *topic* seems to be farming; the *code* is English; the *channel* is writing; the *genre* is expository prose; and the *purpose* seems to be "to inform" the reader about some *event* connected with farming. However, several components of the *context* are unclear. It is not clear what geographical region the text comes from. It is not clear what "making merit" refers to. For those familiar with rice farming, it is obvious that the general context relates to rice farming. The expressions "Buddha image" and "monks" indicates a Buddhist locale. The text is about threshing rice and subsequently storing it in the barn. For people who can interpret "making merit" in the intended way, a great deal is clear. For others, the *schema* (e.g. knowledge representations of rice farming, and Buddhist ceremonies), *frame* (e.g. knowledge of components of "making merit"), *script* (knowledge of event sequences in "making merit"), and *scenario* (e.g. "actions" associated with "making merit") are unclear because they have no experience of "making merit" and therefore don't have mental structures for it. They don't have the frame for it since they do not know what slots are available to be filled in with which components of "making merit."

Given the information that the event is located in rural Thailand, that "making merit" is a ceremony that people engage in after the threshing, and that the ceremony may last for more than one evening depending upon the abundance of the crop, a richer interpretation becomes possible. A full interpretation is possible only when several other questions are answered, such as, who does the pronoun "they" refer to—an individual farmer and his family, or the whole village? Does the "merit" accrue to someone, and if so, to whom—the host(s), the monks? What events and actions by whom occur in "making merit"? Obviously, a Thai Buddhist user of English can interpret the text much more easily and completely than users of any other variety, unless they possess the same *background knowledge* and can invoke the same *schema*, *frame*, *script*, and *scenario* and fill in all the items, events, and activities associated with "making merit" and the slots.

The concepts discussed above are invoked in subsequent chapters in discussing texts from other varieties. Therefore, there is no need to provide further illustrations at this point. It is, however, worth keeping in mind that all these are relevant for demonstrating the role sociocultural knowledge plays in constructing and understanding texts.

CULTURE, CONTEXT OF SITUATION, AND LANGUAGE USE

The concepts discussed above are all invoked in discussing language use and usually, one comes across generalizations that apply to oppositions such as

American vs. Japanese culture or Western vs. non-Western cultures, or Western European vs. Asian cultures. Labels such as American or British or Indian or Thai culture are referred to as if they are monolithic entities with no internal variation. That, however, is not true. Each one of these cultures represents variations based on factors such as region, ethnicity, age, gender, class, social status, education, and profession.

Consider the differences within the American culture and those of Australia, New Zealand, and the UK. There is a divide between norms of interaction referred to as the Southern style and other geographical regions of the USA. The distinct ethnic style of New York Jewish conversation is documented in Tannen (1984). Age, gender, and ethnicity-related differences are documented with reference to Australian and New Zealand cultural contexts in Eisikovits (1989) and Stubbe and Holmes (1999). The differences between women who come from diverse ethnic communities in Britain are recorded in Coates and Cameron (1988). How gender identities are constructed and maintained in the Indian English speech community is described in Valentine (1995, 2001).

CONCLUSION

A great deal of caution needs to be exercised when we make generalizations about cultures with reference to nations or regions. It is as important to be aware of the differences between smaller groups—based on age, gender, ethnicity, profession, etc.—when we discuss verbal interaction within or across such groups as it is when we generalize across national or regional cultural contexts. It is common to speak of "American Culture" or "European culture" or "Japanese culture" as though every individual from these regions instantiates all the conventions of behavior associated with these labels. The associations between cultures and behavior are usually formed by what one learns from scholarly sources, e.g. anthropological or sociological descriptions, or popular sources, such as travelogues or folklore. No matter whether the descriptions are based on careful observations or casual impressions, broad generalizations are just that. Meticulous ethnographic studies detail how groups, subgroups, professional networks, and other units of human society—too many to list exhaustively—have their characteristic behavior patterns, including linguistic behavior (e.g. Eisikovits, 1989; Morgan, 1996; Stubbe and Holmes, 1999; Tannen, 1981). Although we ourselves use broad terms such as Indian, or Native American, or Polish cultures, where relevant, we have to be aware that specific instances of behavior may not be attributable to these categories. We have to remember, all tools are useful, but they may not be used indiscriminately without danger of doing harm.

Note

1. For a detailed description of these categories, see Hymes (1974, pp. 51–62).

Further Reading

Saville-Troike, M. (1996) The ethnography of communication. In S. L. McKay and N. H. Hornberger (eds), *Sociolinguistics and Language Teaching* (pp. 351–382). Cambridge: Cambridge University Press.

Suggested Questions for Discussion

1. How would you define culture?
2. To what extent is it true that "language is culture?"
3. If English is the common linguistic code, i.e. the language is used by speakers of diverse languages all over the world, what else is needed for successful communication in the areas of, say, academia, business negotiations, diplomacy, media, and social interaction?
4. Have you noticed any difference between how you use language in interacting with (a) your parents; (b) your friends; and (c) your colleagues (fellow students, co-workers, etc.)? Catalogue a select list of features of sounds, words, and expressions that you may use with one but not the other category of participants in conversation.

Chapter 3

Parameters of Politeness

INTRODUCTION

Two types of concepts have been discussed previously: those that relate to the context of interaction in a crucial way, such as politeness, and those that are important from the point of view of structuring the context, such as schema, frame, etc. The concept of politeness is crucial in any communication, but it is more so in crosscultural communication. Hence, a detailed discussion of politeness phenomena is taken up next.

Politeness Formulae

All human speech communities have "politeness formulas" (Jespersen, 1933, p. 266) such as "good morning," "thank you," "God bless you," "bye-bye." Ferguson (1976, p. 138) hypothesizes that humans have "innate predispositions to the use of interjections and ritualized exchanges in which a given formula triggers an automatic response." Such politeness formulae, however, are not the only way in which human beings interact politely. There are several other devices or strategies that are used, and these vary from one speech community to another. Sociocultural conventions play a very important role in deciding the strategies used in any speech community:

> [A]ll languages have devices to indicate politeness and formality. But, for some languages, politeness must be encoded into every sentence: there are obligatory markers of status, deference and humility. Other languages express politeness less overtly, or differently: perhaps by smiling or in the stance, or distance kept between participants in an encounter. A speaker from one

culture translated to another will not, perhaps, know how to match his feelings
to the signals he is supposed to give. (Lakoff, 1974, pp. 13–14)

There are similarities across cultures in the kinds of strategies used to express
politeness, but there are also clear differences of form. These differences are
what create problems for the users of a second or additional language: the
politeness strategies employed by his/her mother tongue or first language
may be very different from those of the second or additional language used
as a primary language.

The following is an attempt to set out the parameters along which
politeness functions and the instruments or verbal strategies used to display
politeness. No society makes use of all these parameters or instruments, and
in order to function efficiently in a given society, one must determine what
that society's choices are. Politeness is closely tied to cultural values and one
must know the latter if one is to use the former correctly. For example, one
of the questions to be asked is: Does the culture defer to the addressee's desires
and opinions in a direct manner? In America, the answer is "yes." If a guest
refuses the offer of more food, for instance, his/her refusal is accepted at face
value and the offer is not repeated. In Poland and India, however, the guest
would be encouraged to eat some more and the host will practically insist that
(s)he do so. It does not mean that the Polish and Indian cultures do not defer
to the wishes of the guests, it simply means that a refusal of offer for food or
drink is not to be accepted readily. Such acceptance suggests the host was not
sincere in his/her offer. Only repeated refusals can be accepted with regret.[1]
Similarly, the conditions under which compliments are to be paid and how
they are to be accepted or rejected differ from culture to culture.

Parameters of Politeness

The following twelve parameters are important for a study of what being
polite means in different cultures:

Values: The cultural values of a society must be taken into consideration.
In Australian society, for instance, social distance (see pp. 45–46) has a
positive value because it is interpreted as showing respect for individuality.
In Polish society, however, social distance has a negative value because it is
taken as showing hostility and alienation or lack of intimacy. In some Native
American cultures there is a positive value placed on silence in situations
where in other cultures people would speak out (Basso, 1970; Plank, 1994).
According to Albert (1972, p. 75), in the African nation of Burundi,

> practical and esthetic values take precedence over logical criteria in all but a
> few classes of communication situation. A well-brought up Murundi [a citizen
> of Burundi] would suffer agonies of shame in the presence of the naked truth

and would hasten to provide the esthetic covering called for by the cultural value system.

Cultural values play a role in determining what participants do in verbal interaction, what and how face is projected and maintained, what avoidance strategies are utilized when face is threatened, how "ritual equilibrium" is maintained and restored, etc. (Ting-Toomey, 1994). Hall (1960) mentions the values attached to time, space, material possessions, friendship, and legally documented vs. orally accepted or given agreements in the context of international business and describes how various societies differ in each of these areas.

Face. Following Goffman (1967), Brown and Levinson (1987, p. 61) see the desire to maintain "face" as playing an important role in social interaction. "Face" is defined as the "public self-image that every member wants to claim for himself," consisting of two related aspects:

1. a. *Negative face:* the basic claim to territories, personal preserves, rights to non-distinction, i.e. to freedom of action and freedom from imposition.
   b. *Positive face:* the positive consistent self-image or "personality" (crucially including the desire that the self-image be appreciated and approved of) claimed by interactants.

In the Western cultural contexts, especially those of English-speaking ones, many speech acts are considered face-threatening acts (Brown and Levinson, 1987, pp. 65–68). They are face-threatening because they restrict the addressee's freedom of action and freedom from imposition. The following are examples of utterances that illustrate the concepts of negative and positive face-threatening speech acts:

2. a. Negative face-threatening speech acts:
      i.   Could you lend me a hundred dollars for a couple of days?
      ii. If I were you, I would consult a doctor as soon as possible. That cough sounds dangerous to me.
      iii. You are so lucky to have such good friends all over the world!
   b. Positive face-threatening speech acts:
      iv. Weren't you supposed to complete the report by now?
      v.   I am not sure I agree with your interpretation of the by-laws.
      vi. (One girl friend to another) Mabel thinks you have put on some weight.

The utterance in (i) is said to threaten the negative face of the addressee by imposing a request for a loan on him/her. Suggestions as in (ii) and compliments as in (iii) do the same (Brown and Levinson, 1987, p. 66): advice and suggestions attempt to put a limit on addressees' choice of action and compliments may signal that the speaker is envious of the addressee and is desirous of acquiring what the addressee has.

Even mild criticisms, such as in (iv) above threaten the positive self-image of the addressee; they seem to attribute to the addressee the undesirable qualities of not being reliable, or being inefficient. Disagreements, as in (v) above, suggest that the speaker thinks the addressee is mistaken, and any bad news (weight gain, in this case) about the addressee, as in (vi) above, signals that the speaker is not averse to causing distress to the addressee.

It has been suggested that the applicability of the notions of positive and negative face to speech acts is not universal. For example, in Eastern cultures, not all speech acts are considered face threatening in the sense of Brown and Levinson (1987). Not even all requests are considered threatening to the negative face of the interlocutor(s). Depending upon the context, they may be considered affirming the positive face of the interlocutor(s) instead (see Chapter 8).

Status: According to Linton (1936, p. 113), "status . . . is simply a collection of rights and duties." It is suggested that when the social analyst refers to the term "status" [e.g. mother/child], (s)he is referring to an institutionalized, systematic relationship. (S)he is more likely to use the term "role" when referring to a social relation that is less institutionalized (e.g. host/guest). According to E. Goody (1978: 11), status is "hierarchy and position in a system of roles." It is obvious that "status relationships are based upon norms (external to immediate interaction) that have a broad consensus by third parties in ego and alters social networks or some larger community" (Cicourel, 1967, p. 13). In most societies, the rule seems to be, the higher the status, the more politeness expected from the lower status participants in an interaction.

Some languages have conventionalized the assignment of politeness in the use of language for social interaction. According to Makino (1970), Japanese has the following conventions or Politeness Assignment Rule: if the speaker is lower in social status than the hearer, then the utterance has to be polite. If the speaker is higher in social status than the hearer but is lower than the subject of the sentence he is uttering, then the utterance has to be polite. Otherwise, the utterance can be without the markers of politeness.

Some of the circumlocutions in the other varieties of English that the Inner Circle speakers of English find hard to interpret are motivated by concerns of politeness in the speech of the users of these varieties.

Rank: Rank is hierarchically organized with reference to a social institution, e.g. the principal of a school, the commander of an army, etc. In an environment where rank takes precedence over all other considerations in determining speech levels, as in military organizations, there will usually be no ambiguity. One's rank title will often serve as the term of address and will cue the required level of politeness (Corbett, 1976).

Cultures vary as to which relationships are treated as rank relationships and which ones are treated as status relationships. For instance, in some cultures, a teacher not only commands respect by virtue of his/her rank, (s)he also has a high status. This explains why for many users of Englishes, it is unthinkable to address one's teacher by his/her first name. This is true of most Asian and African cultures.

Role. Role refers to the less institutionalized position one assumes in some interaction. Examples are host/guest, captain of the team/players in sport, etc. Note that even a lower status person in the role of guest deserves polite treatment in many cultures. Similarly, the status of older vs. younger brother may not override the role of player vs. captain of the team in a sports event.

Power. Brown and Levinson (1987) describe this as the "ability to impose one's will on others." Power can also be seen as related to status. The higher one's status, the more power is ascribed to one and the more politeness is directed toward one. This seems to be the rule of interaction in general. It is true that in some cases, high status and power do not necessarily coincide. This is true of the system of constitutional monarchy in several countries. In spite of the circumscribed power of monarchy, however, as far as language use is concerned, the royals are still treated as though their status confers power. In British English, or in Japanese, or in Thai, terms of address and other markers of polite language use still signal the monarch's high status and power.

Age. The relative ages of the speaker and the hearer determine how politeness is to be expressed. In many speech communities, for example, a younger person may not address an older person by his/her name, even if the younger person is of higher status. In India, those domestic servants who have served the family for decades are addressed by a kinship term suffixed to the given name by the children in the family. Martin (1964, p. 41) notes that in nineteenth-century Okinawa a difference in age of only one day was sufficient to require the use of a different level of speech. In Burundi (Albert, 1972, p. 81), "[t]he order in which individuals speak in a group is strictly determined by seniority." Seniority in status, however, takes precedence over seniority in age in Burundi.

Sex. In English, women's speech is supposed to be more polite, and in the presence of women, males are supposed to eschew "the coarseness of ruffianly men's language: no slang, no swear words, no off-color remarks" (Lakoff, 1975, p. 52). In Hindi, although men may express intimacy and solidarity by using swear words and terms of abuse in face-to-face interaction with their intimate friends, women are not supposed to behave in a similar fashion. Note that sex-difference takes precedence over intimacy in male–female interaction. In many parts of the world, women are not supposed to speak at all in a group meeting. In others, women assume an equal role in debates on social, political, economic, religious and philosophical issues.

Social distance. Brown and Levinson (1987) characterize this as a factor affecting politeness. Social distance is inextricably linked to intimacy: the more intimate the participants are, the less social distance there is between them. Also, the more intimate the participants are, the less polite they are to each other. In fact, in many cultures, use of a markedly coarse style, full of curse and swear words, is a strong indicator of a high degree of intimacy among men (Y. Kachru, 1983).

Intimacy: This may be seen as intimacy of participants or of the setting or both. That is, participants may be in a relationship that is intimate, e.g. husband/wife, brother/sister, friends, and that allows for relaxations of rules of politeness. Or, participants may be in a relationship that is not intimate, such as an employer and an employee, and still may be able to relax the rules of politeness in an informal setting such as a dinner at a mutual friend's home, or a party.

Kinship: The relationship between the participants decides the kind of instruments (i.e. linguistic exponents) used. For instance, in India, one invariably uses the honorific/plural forms of pronouns and agreement patterns in addressing or referring to one's parents-in-law. In Burundi, (Albert, 1972, p. 79), mother-in-law and son-in-law must address each other as *mufasoni*, "noble," irrespective of their actual caste position.

Group membership: In certain societies, group membership is important in deciding the politeness strategies used. In Japan, for example, certain honorifics are used with out-group members only. With in-group members, a different set of honorifics is used (Goody, 1978, p. 186), or honorifics may be dispensed with altogether. African Americans in the USA use certain verbal strategies, such as signifying and marking (Mitchell-Kernan, 1972), only with in-group members.

It is worth noting that the parameters listed above are not all equally discrete. Whereas status, role, and rank are clearly distinguishable, kinship, group membership, social distance, and intimacy are partially overlapping. Kins belong to the same group, but groups may include non-kin members, such as professional colleagues and friends, too. Social distance and intimacy seem to be the two opposing ends of the same cline: intimacy involves minimum social distance. However, intimacy of setting is not included in this cline of social distance. For example, even in the boss's home, employees are expected to use more politeness markers toward the boss than with their co-workers.

All these parameters of politeness interact with each other in complex ways. The following observations may be helpful in grasping the complexities resulting from such interactions. First of all, cultural values determine which parameters interact with each other, and which ones are weighted more heavily in comparison with the others. In Western culture, generally speaking, individual face wants are attended to more systematically than the demands of status or age or rank in interactions. In Eastern cultures, status, rank, and age interact with kinship, group membership, social distance, and intimacy in complex ways and take precedence over individual face wants (see Chapter

8 for further discussion). This is a very broad generalization that needs finer analysis. The generalization may apply to certain domains of interaction and not to others. Any generalization in terms of whole cultures is suspect. Domain-specific analyses, and especially changing norms of rapidly modernizing societies need a great deal of attention.

Interaction of parameters of politeness: The following three dimensions are useful in analyzing linguistic politeness: social distance vs. intimacy, power vs. lack of it, and formality vs. informality. It is safe to say that those who share their group membership and interact with greater frequency feel closer, e.g. friends, colleagues, family members. Nevertheless, power relations may interfere with intimacy: normally, a worker does not feel close to a boss though they are members of the same group (i.e. they work for the same company or firm). Also, linguistic display of intimacy is much less in formal contexts than in informal contexts, e.g. two Indian lawyers, even though close friends, must refer to each other as 'my learned friend' in a court setting.

Tact: A discussion of Leech's concept of linguistic *tact* is relevant here. Tact refers to linguistic politeness behavior (Leech, 1983). The factors that are relevant are the same: social distance, power, and formality. For instance, in the context of a departmental office at an American university, a head of the department may say to his secretary: "Get me the file on our budget for the forthcoming conference." He may not, however, in the same context say: "Get me a cup of coffee." What is considered polite, tactful request depends upon the role relationship: in a boss–secretary relationship, request for a file is appropriate, request for personal service such as a cup of coffee may have to be phrased much more tactfully. If, however, the boss and secretary happen to be good friends in their social context, a more casual verbal interaction is possible.

Instruments of Politeness

Several linguistic devices are used as instruments (i.e. exponents, or linguistic markers) of politeness in different languages (see, D'souza, 1988 for a description of such devices in South Asian languages). It does not follow that what is polite in one language is necessarily polite in other languages, too. For instance, establishing a relationship on first-name basis as quickly as possible is considered polite in social relationships in the USA. This was not true of Britain until recently, and even now it is not favored in all situations; it is even less true in India. The following twelve devices—some linguistic and others extra-linguistic—have definite functions in expressing politeness:

Pronouns of address: **Status** (or relatively greater social distance) and **solidarity** (or intimacy or group membership) are two dimensions of social relations relevant to the choice in the forms of address in any language. Many languages (e.g. French, German, Hindi, Spanish) have a form of second person pronoun that is grammatically singular and used for addressing a person younger in age, lower in status, or intimate in relationship, and another which is grammatically a plural or honorific or both and is used for a person older in age, higher in status, or distant in relationship. Following the French second person pronominal forms, these are known as the T and the V forms. According to Slobin (1963, p. 193):

> Brown, et al., have found what may be a "linguistic universal" in all of the languages they have investigated: the form used vertically to address status inferiors (the T-pronoun) is also used horizontally to address intimates, and vice-versa.

In many languages of the Indian sub-continent, status and solidarity are still independent variables and interact in complex ways, whereas in many languages of Europe, the equilibrium has been destroyed as the solidarity criterion is applied vertically as well as horizontally (Slobin, 1963, p. 194). That is, status differences are minimized on the vertical level as are age, role, and sex differences on the horizontal level within the same status.

Brown has noticed a tendency in European languages in recent times to avoid non-reciprocal use of second person pronouns by using only the solidarity dimension as relevant to the choice of a pronoun (Brown and Gilman, 1960). Thus, in this evolving unidimensional system, there is increasing tendency to address all intimates, regardless of status, with the T-pronoun, and all strangers with the V-pronoun. A similar process has been taking place in Russian since the 1917 revolution and the resultant change in the reflection of social class in language (Corbett, 1976).

Slobin (1963) investigated "the semantics of social relations underlying the usage of the second person pronouns in Yiddish, as it were spoken in Eastern Europe before World War II" (p. 194) and found that "ascribed status, and, if exceptional, achieved status prevail over solidarity in the semantics of pronouns of address" (p. 201). However, he noted that "the exception is the strong solidarity of kinship, which is also based on ascribed, rather than achieved values" (p. 201). He concludes that "the general picture resembles that drawn by Brown and Gilman [1960] for nineteenth century Europe, retaining situations of non-reciprocal address. The 'linguistic universals' linking intimacy and condescension, distance and deference, were again found to hold true" (p. 201).

In Thai, there is an elaborate system of pronoun usage with sets of pronouns to be utilized for referring to the speaker, the addressee, and participants other than the addressee(s). The use of pronouns is determined by status, rank, age, sex, social distance/intimacy, and kinship/group membership.

Honorifics: The use of honorifics is a very common way of showing politeness. One society that makes maximum use of this device is the Japanese. The following will give us some idea of the complexity of the Japanese system of using honorifics to convey politeness.

According to Yamanashi (1974), the Japanese language has three basic types of honorifics:

3. H-I: Speaker honors individuals whose social status is higher than his by marking them, their states of affairs, and/or actions with honorifics.

    H-II: Speaker indirectly honors individuals of higher status by marking in a humilitary way the individuals in the speaker's group, their states of affairs, and/or actions.

    H-III: Speaker honors his interlocutor, whose status is respected, in the performative act by marking the end of the whole surface sentence.

For instance, if the speaker is of higher social status than the referent Yamada, and his son, the speaker may say:

4   a.   Yamada ga musuko to syokuzi o tanosinda.
        Yamada enjoyed dinner with (his) son.

If, however, the speaker is not of higher status, he will use:

    b.   Yamada-*san* ga musuko-*san* to *o*-syokuzi o tanosim-*are*-ta.
       Yamada^h enjoyed$^{h\ h}$dinner with (his) son^h.
    [The superscript ^{h} indicates honorific marking, the Japanese honorific elements are in italics. Note that the item *are* is a marker of passive. The passive morphology is used in referring to the actions of people of higher status.]

If the son being mentioned is the speaker's son and the speaker is of lower status than Yamada, the following is appropriate:

    c.   Yamada-*san* ga musuko to *o*-syokuzi o tanosim-*are*-ta.
       Yamada^h enjoyed$^{h\ h}$dinner with (speaker's) son.

Similarly, different forms will be used if the son belongs to someone whose social status is higher than speaker and in addition, the speaker is higher than Yamada.

Since English does not make available devices such as special honorific pronouns or honorific markers dispersed throughout the sentence, users of other varieties use certain English items, such as *honorable* or *respected* or *sir*, in the same way as their native language expressions. In India, it is not uncommon for visiting British or American professors to find themselves being addressed as "Respected Sir Professor X."

Kinship terms: Kinship terms are sometimes used for people unrelated to the speaker. Thus, in order to soften a request or a refusal, in many of the Indian and other Asian languages, the speaker will address the listener as *mother, brother, sister,* or with some other kin term. Even complete strangers may be thus addressed, e.g. in a shop, if the shopkeeper cannot agree to the price the customer suggests as a fair price for the merchandise. In many of the world's languages, including the Indian languages, *Uncle* and *Aunt* are appropriate terms of address for strangers older than oneself in ordinary circumstances. Among the Nuer people of the Sudan, older men will address younger men as *gatada,* "my son." In return the younger will address the older as *gwa,* "father" (Evans-Pritchard, 1948).

Set formulas: Ferguson (1976) notes that "in general the structure of politeness formulas varies in constituency and intensity in correlation with a number of social dimensions." He lists these "social dimensions" as:

5. a. length of time elapsed since previous encounter,
    b. distance between communicators,
    c. number of individuals in the relevant groups, and
    d. relative social status of the communicators.

In a study of Syrian Arabic politeness formulas, Ferguson (1976, p. 137) notes that "the Syrian Arabic speech community uses hundreds of politeness formulas, many of them occurring in stereotyped initiator-and-response sequences." A specific initiator formula is automatically followed by the appropriate response, e.g.

6. a. *alla maʔak*   "God be with you" is invariably replied to with:
    b. *alla yihfazak*   "God preserve you."

In the Hindi speech community in India, the greeting addressed to an elder, *praṇaam,* is always replied to with *xuš raho* 'May you be happy' or, *jiite raho* (masculine) or *jiitii raho* (feminine) "May you live long." Some such pairs may seem deliberately non-communicative as in the Korean formulaic "Where are you going?" (said upon meeting an acquaintance in the street) and the response "Just over there."

Plurals: In many languages, the plural may be used to indicate politeness when addressing a single person, e.g. in certain dialects of Polish, which makes a gender distinction, polite forms are plural and masculine regardless of the sex of the addressee. In Standard Russian, Czech, and Serbo-Croatian, the pronoun, the verbs, particles, and adjectives that are in agreement with the pronoun are all plural, only the predicate noun remains in singular if the addressee is a single person, e.g. *Vi ste* (pl.) *bili* (pl.) "You were good," as opposed to *Vi ste* (pl.) *bili* (pl.) *studentkinja* (sg.) "You were a good student" (Comrie, 1975, p. 408).

Questions: In some societies, questions are used to express politeness, e.g. in English, "Could you tell me the time?" is more polite than "Tell me the time!" (Note that not all questions are polite, e.g. "What time is it?" is not very polite in English. Usually, the questions need to take account of the addressee's ability or convenience.) In other societies, e.g. the Gonja in Ghana (Goody, 1978, p. 32), questions are highly institutionalized and cannot be used in this fashion.

In Gonja society, the significance of asking questions depends on the relative status of the questioner and the respondent. Goody notes four main functions of questioning in Gonja society:

7. a. information seeking;
   b. control (when questions are asked of inferiors by superiors);
   c. rhetorical (used in joking challenges, greeting exchanges, court cases, etc.);
   d. deference (sanctions questions from juniors to seniors because this strategy "by at least *seeming* to ask for information, implies ignorance by the questioner of the answer." (Goody 1978: 32)

Among the aborigines of South-East Queensland, direct questions are seldom used (Eades, 1982). The questioner must make assumptions, and then ask questions on the basis of these assumptions. In Japan it is considered more polite to ask negative questions such as "You're not going?" (Martin, 1964), which may sound to a non-Japanese to be presupposing a negative response.

Indirect speech acts: It has already been pointed out in the discussion on Gricean *maxims* (Grice, 1975) that people do not always say what they mean. The same ends may be accomplished by various means, some of them indirect. The discussion on indirect speech acts (Searle, 1975) makes this clear. For example, in English, one may say "It's cold in here" when what one really means is "Close the window." In Bengali, requests are sometimes made through plain statements, e.g. in a clothing shop, a person may say:

8. *aamaar šarṭ dorkaar*
   to me shirt need
   I need a shirt.

This is interpreted as a request and is a more polite way of asking for the shirt than saying "I want to see some shirts."

In many cultures, talk about some unrelated topic is first indulged in before the real subject is mentioned. Thus, in refusing a request for a ride to the airport by a friend leaving town, the speaker may first make oblique references to him/her already being delayed for an appointment, etc.

Topicalization and focus: In English, topicalization and focus can effect the degree of politeness. Given the following sentences:

9. a. If you don't mind my asking, where did you get that dress?
    b. Where did you get that dress, if you don't mind my asking?
Sentence (9a) is seen as more polite than sentence (9b) (Goody, 1978, p. 98),
if we assume that (9a, b) will be pronounced as follows:
9a If you DON'T MIND my asking, . . .
9b. WHERE did you get that dress, . . .

That is, the emphasis is on the part of the utterance that signals to the hearer
that this is a request in (9a) whereas the emphasis is on the question in (9b),
which sounds as though the speaker is making a demand.

Effort: Brown and Levinson (1987, pp. 93–94) note that the greater the
effort expended in face-maintaining linguistic behavior, the greater the
politeness, e.g. "I wouldn't dream of it since I know you are very busy, but I
am simply unable to do it myself, so . . ." They claim that this phenomenon
is universal.

Use of "a little": Many languages use the phrase "a little" to convey the
meaning carried by English "please" in imperatives, e.g. Tamil *koncam* "a
little" (Brown and Levinson, 1978, p. 144), Tzeltal *ala* "a little" (Brown and
Levinson, 1987, p. 182), Bengali *ektu* "a little", Hindi *zaraa* "a little", etc. The
following sentences illustrate this use:

10. a. Tamil: *oru paise koncham kutunka caami.*
                   one cent a little give   sir
                   "Could you please give me a cent?"

     b. Tzeltal: *ya hk'an ?ala pesuk.*
                   "I want a little peso's worth as it were."

     c. Bengali: *jaamaata debe   ektu?*
                   shirt cl. give will a little
                   "Will you give me the shirt, please?"

     d. Hindi: *zaraa id^har aanaa.*
                   a little here come inf.
                   "Come here, please."

In Japanese "chotto" (a little) can be used by itself to express a number of
meanings such as "Excuse me," "Please pay attention," or "Come here."

Hedges: Hedges are often used for politeness, e.g. "John is sorta short"
instead of "John is short." Lakoff (1974) suggests that hedges are used in
societies in order to reduce friction in that they leave the way open for the
respondent to disagree with the speaker and the speaker to retreat.
Hesitations serve much the same purpose. According to Goody (1978, p. 6),
"one might say that strategic elements like hesitation and high pitch appear
to have similar meanings across cultures because there is something about
social interaction which gives them a sort of 'basic meaning'." Hedges are
encoded in particles, adverbials, parenthetical clauses, and gestures and body
postures (Brown and Levinson, 1987, p. 145ff.).

Gaze, gesture, and body posture. In many societies, certain types of gaze, gestures, and body posture convey politeness and others convey the opposite meaning. For instance, in the Inner Circle, it is not considered polite to get closer than 20 inches to the person one is conversing with. In certain Arab societies, however, to maintain such a physical distance is considered rude.

Hall (1966) and Watson (1970) divide cultures into two types: contact and non-contact. Those from contact cultures tend to stand closer, speak louder, and touch more while those from non-contact groups do not touch much in similar situations of interaction. In some cultures, touching certain parts of the body (e.g. head in Thai culture) is forbidden. In many Asian societies, couples do not touch each other in public.

The non-contact groups do not face each other as much or look at each other as much in an interaction as do the contact groups. According to Argyle and Cook (1976), once gaze patterns have been learnt in childhood, they remain unaffected by later experience. Navaho Indians are taught not to gaze directly at another person during a conversation (Hall, 1966). The Japanese are taught to look at the neck, not at the eye. Indians are taught to look down, toward the interlocutor's feet, when talking to elders. Too much direct gaze is regarded as superior, disrespectful, threatening, or insulting by Africans, Indians, and Asians in general.

Arabs, Latin Americans, and Southern Europeans belong to the contact group whereas Asians (including South Asians), Northern Europeans, and in general Americans are in the non-contact group. Nevertheless, there is a difference in mutual gaze between Asians, Africans, and Native Americans on the one hand, and Europeans on the other. In the USA, the English-speaking community certainly considers an unwillingness to look directly in the eye as signaling insincerity or lack of respect.

Bowing is another way of showing politeness. It is very common in East Asian societies such as the Japanese and, to a lesser extent, the Korean. The depth and duration of the bow varies according to status, age, etc. In India, in general, to sit with one's head bowed is seen as a mark of respect for the elders present in the room.

In the USA and several parts of the world, nodding one's head up and down signals "yes" or agreement, and shaking one's head side to side signals "no" or disagreement. In Southern India, however, bending one's head from side to side, with the head inclined toward the shoulder, signals "yes" and nodding one's head side to side, with the head held straight, signals "no."

Particular gestures have particular meanings in different cultures. For example, in the USA, raising a hand and making a circle with the thumb and the forefinger is a signal that something is fine, or perfect. But in Japan, it is a gesture for money; in France, for zero, and hence worthless; and in Greece, an obscene comment or insult to a male or a female (Morris, 1977, p. 39).

CONCLUSION

This discussion has serious implications for the training of individuals interested in crosscultural communication, whether in the field of language teaching, training of language teachers, translators and interpreters, business people involved in international trade, or whatever. It is clear from the above discussion that it is not enough for participants to master the vocabulary and grammar (s)he needs to function in English or another target language. As Wolff (1964, p. 441) notes, "in some areas there is a very low correlation between similarity in vocabulary and grammar on the one hand and intelligibility, claimed or proven, on the other." One must also have a sense of the values of the target culture, the nuances of the posture, intonation, deference strategies, etc. that are so crucial to successful communication. A common language alone is no guarantee of success, one must also be aware of the different ways in which language functions in different societies.

Conventions for expressing politeness in linguistic interaction have been developed in speech communities to reduce conflict and maintain ritual equilibrium. As has already been said, English speakers all over the world do not represent a single speech fellowship (B. Kachru, 1997a). Conventions for being polite vary among the member fellowships of this speech community (Y. Kachru, 2003). An awareness of different possibilities, discussed above, goes a long way in reducing misapprehensions.

In spite of variation among communities, attempts have been made to suggest a universal set of rules of politeness on the basis of observed regularities. For instance, R. Lakoff (1975) sets up the following rules of politeness:

11. a. Formality: keep aloof (use formal pronouns, titles, etc.).
    b. Deference: give options (use question intonation, tag questions, euphemisms, etc.).
    c. Camaraderie: (show sympathy, use colloquial language, nicknames, etc.).

The order in which these rules apply is not the same in all cultures. According to Lakoff (1975, pp. 69–70), at a first meeting, a German will emphasize rule (a), a Japanese rule (b), and an American rule (c). More empirical research is needed to confirm such claims.

Note

1. Throughout this and subsequent chapters, broad generalizations are cited about local (Kashmiri), national (American), and regional (Western) cultures. Most of these have been taken from published sources (e.g. works such as Brown and Levinson, 1987; Hill *et al.*, 1986). It is worth remembering that not all of these represent results of careful ethnographic investigations and need to

be established as such by further research. Meanwhile, they are convenient abstractions that researchers use to arrive at insights that are useful in discussing conventions of language use.

Further Reading

Kachru, Y. (2003) Conventions of politeness in plural societies. In R. Ahrens, D. Parker, K. Stierstorfer, and K. Tam (eds), *Anglophone Cultures in Southeast Asia* (pp. 39–53). Heidelberg: Univesitätsverlag Winter.

Silva, R. S. (2000) Pragmatics, bilingualism, and the native speaker. *Language & Communication*, 20, 161–178.

Sridhar, K. (1991) Speech acts in an indigenized variety: sociocultural values and language variation. In J. Cheshire (ed.), *English around the World: Sociolinguistic Perspectives* (pp. 308–318). Cambridge: Cambridge University Press.

Suggested Activities

1. The following excerpt is from a short story by R. K. Narayan (1990, p. 107). The Talkative Man is arranging for Nagaraj to have some Sanskrit lessons from a pundit (Sanskrit scholar). Read the dialogue cited below and discuss answers to following questions:

   > The Talkative Man finalized the arrangement. Turning to Nagaraj he asked, "Do you start tomorrow?"
   >
   > Before he could answer, the pundit interposed to say, "Let me look into the almanac and find an auspicious day and hour for starting the lessons."
   >
   > "When will you see the almanac?" asked the Talkative Man.
   >
   > "Tomorrow morning after my puja. I won't touch it now."

   a. What does the word *puja* mean?

   b. Why does the pundit want to look into an almanac and find an auspicious day?

   c. Why can't he look into the almanac at the time the interaction was taking place?

   d. What information do you need to interpret what is going on here?

   e. Do you have the concept 'auspicious day' in your culture?

2. The following is a phone conversation between a Danish Export Manager of a Dairy Company (H) and an Indian Commodity Buyer for a Saudi Arabian Company (G). A and B are members of staff of the Saudi Arabian company. Note that in the transcription, underlining shows emphasis, (:) shows length of the segment, (numeral) shows the duration of silence in seconds, (.) shows micro-pauses of less than 0.2 seconds, and (( )) contain relevant contextual information, (::) preceding and following h indicate audible inhalations and exhalations,

and AA shows emphatic, loud enunciation. Four participants can role play and act out the conversational exchanges and then discuss the following aspects of the segment given in (a)–(c) below.

1. A: ello?
2. H: yes hello er saudi royal import export company:?
3. A. ye:s?
4. H. it's er michael hansen er melko dairies speaking. (0.8) could
5.   I speak to mister guptah please?
6. A: moment
7.   (17.0)
8. B: allo:?
9. H: yes hello er michael hansen melko dairies speaking
10. B: one minute
11.   (4.0)
12. G: hello?
13. H: hello mister guptah (.) how are you?
14. G: fine. (.) how're you?
15. H: fine than' you (0.6) you know now the summer time has
          come to denmark as well
16. G: ((laughing)) huh hhe:h heh heh heh : : hh
17. H: so for: : the: – us here in denmark it's hot (.) it's er twenty
18.   five degree, but for you it will be- it would be cold (.) I think
19. G: no, here in this er: forty – forty two
20. H: yes?
21.   (1.0)
22. G: yes
23. H: well I prefer tweny five. (.) it's better to me
24.   (0.9)
25. G: yeah
26.   (1.1)
27. H: GOOD er- I got a telex for er- from you
28.   (1.3)
29. G: yeah
30. H: you don' er: (.) accept our prices.
31.   (1.2)
32. G: for this er cheddar

                                        (Firth, 1991, pp. 52–53)

a. What impression do the opening sequences in lines 12–26 create about the participants?
b. What does the laughter in line 16 indicate?
c. Could this conversational exchange take place in your culture?

3. Watch a video of three to five minutes of an interview program or a soap opera. What instruments of politeness were used (e.g. linguistic devices, gestures, body postures)? What politeness parameters do they reflect (e.g. intimacy vs. distance, power relationship, cultural value, age, sex)?

4. Look at the following pictures of facial expressions and hand gestures (Figure 3.1–3.5). What do they mean in your own culture?

Figures 3.1–3.5 Pictures of facial expressions and hand gestures

5. Go to a library, a fast food place, or any other site where service encounters take place. Observe how people make requests and respond to requests, and what the accompanying gestures and body postures are. Discuss them with your fellow participants in the discussion group.

Chapter 4

Intelligibility and Interlocutors

Soon after arriving to live in Australia, David Cervi was invited to an informal party and was to bring a plate.

"Of course," he replied. "Is there anything else you're short of—glasses, knives and forks, for example?"

"No," replied his host, "I've got plenty of dishes. Just bring some food for everyone to share."

David immediately realized that, although as a native speaker he had understood the words, he had misunderstood their meaning.

(Cervi and Wajnryb, 1992, p. 18)

INTRODUCTION

Questions of intelligibility arise whenever there is variation in language use. World Englishes, by definition, exhibit variation; therefore it is natural that intelligibility becomes an issue for those using world Englishes across cultures. The concern most often expressed is that with the great diversity in varieties of English, it may soon occur that people speaking fluent English may not be intelligible to other fluent users of English. The fact is that for at least the last 200 years there have been native English-speaking people in parts of the world who have not been intelligible to other native English-speaking people in other parts of the world. Today with millions (Crystal, 1998) of people using many different varieties of native and non-native English, it is inevitable that this will continue but not necessarily lead to a modern day Tower of Babel (Genesis, 11: 1–9). Prior research (Smith, 1987; Smith and Bisazza, 1982; Smith and Rafiqzad, 1979) indicates that (1) native English speakers are often not intelligible to fluent non-native English users;

(2) native English speakers are not better than non-native users in understanding varieties of English different from their own; and (3) even if users of English as a second or additional language can understand one Inner Circle variety of English, they may not be able to understand other varieties of any Circle unless they have had experience interacting with those who use such varieties.

IS INTELLIGIBILITY ALWAYS NECESSARY?

It should not be seen as necessary for every user of English to be intelligible, at all times, to every other user of English. One's English needs to be intelligible only to those with whom (s)he is attempting to communicate. The *intra*national use of English by locals of a region may not be intelligible to English-using outsiders and the locals may prefer it to be that way. For example, the English used by an Indian family among themselves may not be understood by an American because the Indians may want to keep some of their family conversation private. Of course the Indians can use English *inter*nationally to communicate with outsiders, including the American, and when they do, they want and expect to be understood.

Many people have had the experience of being part of an educated English conversation with an international colleague in his/her office in his/her country when the phone rings and (s)he speaks in a localized variety of English with vocabulary, pronunciation, and intonation that makes it difficult or impossible to understand the telephone conversation. (S)he then hangs up and automatically continues his/her conversation in an English that is so easy to follow that it isn't given a second thought. This kind of experience is not unusual and will become more common as fluent users of English are able to move with ease from one variety to another. Localized varieties that are frequently used in local situations with different objectives are often not understood by outsiders, i.e. non-locals. One need not find this surprising or disturbing and should not expect to understand every lectal variation of English used all over the world. In fact, not all educated speakers of American or British English understand all lectal varieties in the US or Britain.

However, one can expect to understand an educated variety of English whenever and wherever it is used for *inter*national communication (the educated variety has also been referred to as "acrolect" in literature, e.g. in discussing the Singaporean variety of English in works such as Tay, 1986). It may take a few minutes to adjust to a pronunciation and intonation that is not familiar, but the more practice one has in hearing them, the easier it becomes. As one learns to expect differences, one then develops an attitude for understanding varieties different from one's own. People should not be shocked when others misunderstand their intentions even when using varieties of educated English. One must remember that misunderstanding of meaning (illocutionary act of the speaker, see Chapter 1) is not uncommon among those using the same educated variety (even in the same biological family) so it will certainly be no less so when multiple varieties are in use. These misunderstandings can be repaired without great difficulty and need not be feared.

INTELLIGIBILITY DEFINED

Understanding and intelligibility are often used interchangeably in conversation. It is not uncommon for "intelligibility" to be the cover term in language and linguistic discussions for all aspects of understanding. We believe it is wise to disentangle these and make intelligibility only one of the three dimensions of understanding. The other two are **comprehensibility** and **interpretability**. Let's examine each one separately.

Intelligibility is the recognition of a word or another sentence-level element of an utterance. For example, if one were to hear "anyone lived in a pretty how town," one would probably recognize this as an utterance made up of six English words. When told that this is the first line of an e. e. cummings' poem, one could accept that but still have no idea of what the utterance may mean. To check intelligibility of the utterance, one could be asked to repeat the utterance or to write it as dictation. The results would be an intelligibility rating, or the level of understanding of the speaker's locutionary act. Volume, clarity, and speed of the recitation, as well as presence/absence of outside noise, would affect the results. If, for example, for whatever reason, one found the second and fifth words to be unintelligible one could ask specifically for them to be repeated (i.e. "I'm sorry I didn't hear the second and fifth words. Would you repeat them please."). If, when the words are repeated, one recognizes the seven words, and demonstrates the recognition by repeating them or writing them as dictation, one's intelligibility of the statement is high even if one cannot attach any meaning to the utterance. An example from a real conversation indicating a lack of intelligibility for part of the conversation is the following:

A: Her family name is Vogeler. (There was some outside noise when the last word was spoken.)
B: Is that spelled V-O-G-E-L?
A: No. Vogeler. V-O-G-E-L-E-R.
B: Oh, Vogeler.

B knew that the word (s)he didn't understand was the last word and that it was a family name, but perhaps because of the noise, B wasn't sure what the name was. (S)he believed it sounded like "Vogel," a family name familiar to B so (s)he asked for clarification by spelling what (s)he thought (s)he heard. As the word was repeated and spelled out (s)he discovered that indeed (s)he had not heard the word correctly. The misunderstanding had nothing to do with the meaning of the word. B probably knew the word "Vogeler" as well as the word "Vogel" as a family name but had heard only two syllables spoken rather than three and decided that the word was "Vogel" or something similar. The misunderstanding had more to do with something interfering with the recognition of a word. It was an intelligibility error.

COMPREHENSIBILITY

Comprehensibility refers to the recognition of a meaning attached to a word or utterance, i.e. the contextual meaning of the word in a sociocultural setting as well as the illocutionary force of an utterance. Note that comprehensibility includes the hearer's crucial role in recognizing the speaker's intent unlike the notion of illocutionary act that is only concerned with the speaker's utterance. For example, when we hear the word "please" we ordinarily understand it to be related to a request or directive, usually polite. In such a case the comprehensibility of the word, or the recognition of the illocutionary act of the speaker, is high. When we say or write "Please be prepared to leave the area by 3:00 p.m.," we can check the comprehensibility in at least two ways. One way would be to ask for the utterance to be paraphrased by the listener/reader. If the response to that is something like, "Kindly be ready to depart this place by 1500 hours," we can be fairly certain that there has been high comprehensibility of the utterance. Another way to check comprehensibility would be to ask a question about the statement such as "What time are we expected to leave the area?" and if the answer is "3:00 p.m." we also can be confident that the comprehensibility of the utterance has been high.

INTELLIGIBILITY VS. COMPREHENSIBILITY

Intelligibility and comprehensibility are certainly interrelated but are not the same. Intelligibility usually, but not always (see Frenck and Min, 2001) refers to perceptions of speech whereas comprehensibility commonly refers to what is conveyed by what is spoken or printed. It is possible to have intelligibility without comprehensibility and it is possible to measure the differences between them. As an example, suppose one was given the text below with every third word (italicized) deleted and represented by a blank space. If someone read the passage at a regular rate of speech and if one wrote in the missing words as it was being read, this performance would demonstrate how intelligible one found the speaker.

> In South *and* Southeast Asia, *given* the general *identification* of internationalisms *with* Euro-American colonialism, *purification* shows tendencies *of* combating 'cultural *colonialism*' much more *than* neighbouring vernaculars, *all* the more *so*, since the *latter* have little *if* any national *significance*. (Foreword by J. Fishman, in Rubin and Jernudd, 1971, p. 15)

The greater the number of correct words the higher one's intelligibility score. If one were asked to paraphrase the sentence or answer questions about it, the ability to do so would be a measure of one's comprehensibility of the text. It might be relatively easy to fill in the blanks in the passage yet very difficult, if not impossible, to write a paraphrase or answer specific questions about it. If that were the case, by our definition of the terms, the intelligibility of the passage would be considered high but the comprehensibility of it low. As a second example, if someone were to read aloud the following portion of page 41 of B. Mukherjee's 1972 novel, *The Tiger's Daughter*, one would hear:

> On her third day in Calcutta, Tara's mother took her to visit the relatives. . . .
> "Take us to Southern Avenue first," the mother said to the chauffeur . . .
> "Yes, memsahib."

If one were able to repeat the words as spoken or write them correctly as dictation, this would demonstrate the high intelligibility of the speaker. The one word that might not be recognized is *memsahib*, but if one could say it or write it the way it sounds and if one's efforts were acceptable to the person who had read the passage, then that would show high intelligibility. If one could paraphrase the sentences or answer questions based on the text, that would be evidence of comprehensibility. Once again the word *memsahib* could present a problem to the listener/reader, but it might be clear that it is a respectful form of address. If so, that would indicate a level of understanding of the contextual meaning of the word in the sociocultural context of modern India by the reader/listener and thus some comprehensibility of it.

In the quote from Cervi and Wajnryb at the beginning of this chapter, there was perfect intelligibility, but David did not comprehend the contextual meaning of the item *plate* as used in Australian English, so he followed up with the question about knives and forks. Once the question was answered, the utterance of the host became perfectly comprehensible.

INTERPRETABILITY

Interpretability refers to the recognition by the hearer/reader of the intent or purpose of an utterance, i.e. the perlocutionary effect the speaker/writer is aiming at. Again, note that interpretability is not the same as a perlocutionary act, since it involves the hearer/reader crucially into the recovery of speaker/writer's intent. It is a more complex feature of understanding than either intelligibility or comprehensibility because one must know something about the cultural context of the statement in order to have medium to high interpretability. John Hersey recognizes this in *A Single Pebble* where he has his protagonist say,

> I had approached the river as a dry scientific problem; I found it instead an avenue along which human beings moved whom I had not the insight, even though I had the vocabulary, to understand. (1989, p. 18)

One may have the vocabulary and be able to attach some meaning to what has been heard or read and still not be sure of the intention of the speaker/writer. For example, if the phone rings and a friend asks "Is Sean there?" The person answering the call may say several possible things. If Sean is not present, (s)he may say, "No, he isn't." That would indicate clear comprehension of the question and would be evidence of high intelligibility and comprehensibility. If Sean is present, (s)he may say, "Yes, he is." That too would be evidence of high intelligibility and comprehensibility but low interpretability. To demonstrate high interpretability (s)he would need to recognize that the caller is really requesting to speak with Sean and (s)he would reply with something like, "One moment please."

INTELLIGIBILITY, COMPREHENSIBILITY, AND INTERPRETABILITY

To illustrate the differences among intelligibility, comprehensibility, and interpretability read or listen to someone read the following passage at a normal reading pace:

> With hocked gems financing him, our hero bravely defied all scornful laughter that tried to prevent his scheme. "Your eyes deceive you," he had said, "an egg not a table correctly typifies this unexplored planet." Now three sturdy sisters sought proof, forging along—sometimes through calm vastness, yet more often over turbulent peaks and valleys. Days became weeks as many doubters spread fearful rumors about the edge. At last, from nowhere, welcomed winged creatures appeared, signifying momentous success. (Dooling and Lachman, 1971, p. 216)

If someone read the passage aloud, the listener will probably recognize all of the words and could easily repeat each phrase as it was said or write each one as dictation to demonstrate a high degree of intelligibility. It is also very likely that one would be able to recognize a possible meaning for each sentence and could even paraphrase each one. If so, one's comprehensibility of the text would also be considered high. We doubt however that anyone will have much confidence in explaining the story after hearing it only once. Upon first reading, it is difficult to know the author's intentions. One might guess that it is a science fiction tale or the plot for a children's television cartoon feature. If however one is given the author's title of "Christopher Columbus Discovers America," and is allowed to hear the passage once more, this time one will probably have quite a different response. The first time one heard the text, one may have been confused because one lacked the cultural context of situation. Providing the title will be enough to give that context to some people and will increase the likelihood of their high interpretability along with high comprehensibility and intelligibility.

Sometimes difficulties in comprehension and interpretability are related to the way a particular culture uses a word or utterance. For example, reading the following from the Thai novel *Little Things* by Prajuab Thirabutana (1973, p. 15) may present some interpretability problems:

> "So you've come? Is this your daughter that you've told me about?" a woman who was sitting on a low raised place in the shop greeted us.
> "Yes. Ee-nang, salute Koon Maa."

If the passage were read aloud, the listener would probably have little difficulty with intelligibility since all of the words, except "Ee-nang" and "Koon Maa" are common and easy to recognize. The first sentence may seem a little strange as a greeting, but since the author tells us that it is used as a greeting, one can comprehend it accordingly. Even the words "Ee-nang" and "Koon Maa" are intelligible (i.e. recognizable as words) and will perhaps be comprehended as names or forms of address. However the passage is not easy to interpret. One must have certain information about Thailand in general and the Northeast of Thailand in particular to do so with confidence. One must know that in Northeast Thailand "Ee-nang" is a term used by parents to address their youngest daughter and that "Koon Maa" is a typical Thai term for respectfully addressing an older woman as if she were a member of one's family. Unless one knows this about Thai culture, these terms cannot be interpreted appropriately. The word "salute" may also create some confusion and prevent high interpretability. In this context, it is usually correctly comprehended as "greet." However, unless one has some knowledge of the way young Thai girls respectfully greet older people, one cannot interpret the word properly or guess the kind of action the young girl is being directed to perform.

Bokamba (1992, p. 132) reports a conversational example from African English of the same phenomenon:

> "Hasn't the President left for Nairobi yet?"
> "Yes."

If the speaker speaks clearly and there is no outside noise to interfere, the intelligibility (recognition of words) and comprehensibility (understanding of a possible meaning) may be high, but the interpretability (knowing the intentionality) of the speaker will be low. It may not be clear to one unfamiliar with African English if the President has or has not left (in this case, he has not).

Intelligibility and comprehensibility (utterance recognition and utterance meaning) are relatively easy when compared to interpretability (knowing the meaning behind the words).

RELATION TO LANGUAGE FLUENCY AND CULTURAL COMPETENCY

English language fluency and grammatical competence facilitates successful intelligibility and comprehensibility but it is clearly not sufficient for successful interpretability. For that, one must have cultural competence as well. One must remember that when communicating with people who use a different variety of English than one's own, those people will likely use a different pronunciation, intonation, and vocabulary. More importantly they will also use their own cultural conventions of communication (e.g. politeness strategies, appropriate topics of conversation, sequence of information) as well as speech act functions (e.g. ways of greeting, showing agreement, using directives, making refusals, leave-taking, etc.).

EXAMPLES OF CULTURAL CONVENTIONS OF COMMUNICATION

When Japanese use English to communicate with non-Japanese, the non-Japanese are sometimes confused by Japanese conventions of communication. For example, consider the way Japanese use the word "Yes." While a non-Japanese is speaking, the Japanese listener may frequently say "Yes" accompanied by a nod of the head. The intelligibility and comprehensibility here are probably high. The non-Japanese person knows the word "Yes" and recognizes a nod of the head. If (s)he were to use these verbal and non-verbal behaviors in a similar situation, (s)he would most likely use them to convey that there was understanding and agreement between the speaker and listener. Unless (s)he knows something about Japanese culture, (s)he will probably believe the Japanese do the same. If so, the interpretability of the behavior will be low. (S)he will be surprised to learn that when Japanese say "Yes" and nod their heads they do so to encourage the speaker and to indicate that they are listening and trying to understand what is being said. These behaviors do not mean that the Japanese listener understands and agrees with the speaker. Even when they do understand what is being said, these behaviors do not mean that the Japanese agrees with it.

Another common statement with an extended meaning when used by Japanese is "I'm sorry." It is used frequently, not as an admission of guilt/fault (although it can be) but as a verbal lubricant to prevent open friction among the parties involved. It is a politeness strategy and a mark of civility. To the Japanese its use is evidence of "good breeding" and "superior training."

Just as what sounds like an apology (i.e. "I'm sorry") may not be one, what does *not* sound like a refusal may be intended as one. Ikoma and Shimura (1994) provide the following example:

> While living in the United States, a Japanese woman was invited by an American friend to a disco party. Since she didn't care for disco, she wanted to refuse the invitation and said, "Well, I don't like discos very much but I'll consider it." The "I'll consider it" was her way of making a polite refusal which she thought her American friend understood. She was surprised and displeased therefore when her friend called her on the day of the party to say, "Are you ready? I'm on my way to pick you up."

Although the intelligibility and comprehensibility were high between this Japanese woman and her American friend, the level of interpretability was low for each of them.

Koreo (1988, p. 21) observes that

> [t]he Japanese dislike specifying things down to the last detail. This has led some Westerners to conclude that Japanese speech is like Japanese ink painting. Ink painting creates an effect by the use of blank spaces, and unless one is able to read those empty spaces, one can not understand the work.

That seems to be true in a great deal of social interaction, as the example above shows. It, obviously, cannot be true in case of mathematical proof or scientific work.

Nishiyama (1995) writes about the importance of the sequence of information as a tool of interpretability when using world Englishes across cultures. He gives an example of an American businessman making a proposal to his Japanese counterpart. After the American finished, the Japanese spoke for several minutes. He began with several statements about how interesting the project sounded. Then he told the American about the studies his company had been conducting on similar topics. At this point the American assumed that the proposal was going to be accepted easily because that would be what he would mean if he were structuring the information in this way. The American was shocked when at that point the Japanese said, "however" and refused the offer. Nishiyama reminds us that, unlike Americans, when Japanese are speaking, the end of the statement is usually more important than the beginning. If a non-Japanese does not know this, (s)he is likely to have low interpretability and therefore to feel misled by such behavior.

Nishiyama offers another example of how the Japanese structure of information can create serious problems of interpretability for Americans. Some fluent English-speaking Japanese leaders and American leaders were holding a televised conference about trade and economic relations between the US and Japan. During the discussion, one American asked whether the change in exchange rates, bringing the dollar down to about half of what it had been against the yen, would seriously affect Japan's exports to the United States. This question was directed to a particular Japanese participant. The Japanese responded by first explaining Japan's policy to support and promote free trade. He then spoke about Japan's efforts to restructure their industries to cope with changes in exchange rates. He finally ended by saying that, therefore, Japan would continue to have a healthy trade relation with the United States. A portion of the TV screen showed the face of the American as the Japanese responded. Obviously, according to Nishiyama, the American was puzzled trying to understand why the speaker was speaking in such a "round about" way. He probably expected a more direct answer like, "Exports will be seriously affected" or "Exports will not be seriously affected" after which an explanation would be given. The American did not realize that when a Japanese person answers a question (s)he will likely begin with an explanation of the answer before the answer is given. S/he may move from the periphery to the center of the topic, and what is not said is almost always more important than what is spoken. The American should have known that the US way of structuring information was not the Japanese way and that speaking English fluently did not change that. Each of these people had high intelligibility and high comprehensibility but low interpretability of the other's statements/intentions. Neither of them was adequately prepared for the other.

CONCLUSION

With the global spread of English and the development of multiple varieties of English, issues of intelligibility will continue to be matters of concern. It may be helpful to distinguish dimensions of understanding into intelligibility, comprehensibility, and interpretability. It is important to remember that communication is usually between two parties and that intelligibility, comprehensibility, and interpretability are "interactional" activities. They are not speaker or listener centered. Inner Circle English speakers cannot claim to be better judges than Other Circle users of what is or is not intelligible, comprehensible, or interpretable to others. Neither can they claim that Inner Circle English speakers are more intelligible, comprehensible, or interpretable than Other Circle users. Although one's English proficiency is correlated with his/her ability to understand another person communicating in English, crosscultural competence is more important for understanding than grammatical competence. Inner Circle English speakers need as much cultural information and as much exposure to different varieties of English as do Other Circle speakers if they are to increase their levels of intelligibility, comprehensibility, and interpretability of world Englishes.

Further Reading

Baker, W. and Eggington, W. G. (1999) Bilingual creativity, multidimensional analysis, and world Englishes. *World Englishes*, 18(3), 343–357.

Frenck, S. and Min, S. (2001) Culture, reader and textual intelligibility. In E. Thumboo (ed.), *The Three Circles of English* (pp. 19–34). Singapore: UniPress.

Kachru, B. B. (1992) *The Other Tongue: English across Cultures* (2nd edn). Urbana, IL: University of Illinois Press.

Nelson, C. (1995) Intelligibility and world Englishes in the classroom. *World Englishes*, 14, 273–279.

Wolff, K. H. (1959) Intelligibility and inter-ethnic attitudes. *Anthropoligical Linguistics*, 1(3), 34–41.

Suggested Questions for Discussion

1. Is comprehensibility built upon intelligibility? Is intelligibility necessary before comprehensibility/interpretability is possible?

2. How does the question of standard English relate to issues of intelligibility?

3. Read pages 29–61 of Burkhardt (1990) and discuss how the notions of intelligibility, comprehensibility, and interpretability are related to Speech Act Theory. Do the notions of intelligibility, comprehensibility, and interpretability correspond one-to-one with the notions of locutionary, illocutionary, and perlocutionary acts? If not, what are the differences?

4. Listen to an interview on National Public Radio (NPR), the BBC or any other international network and see how much can be understood when the interlocutors are using world Englishes across cultures. Is it possible to determine when misunderstandings occur if it is because of low intelligibility, low comprehensibility, or low interpretability?

5. Read the following letter to the Editor published in *The Guardian*, Lagos, Nigeria, April 9, 2000. If you are not a user of Nigerian English, is the letter intelligible to you? Is it comprehensible? Is it interpretable? If not, identify the factors that play a role in the letter not being intelligible, comprehensible, or interpretable.

Killing the Joy of Democracy

To the Editor: On May 29, Nigerians collectively agreed by national consensus, that we were all going to embrace democracy and sustain it.

But eight months into our democracy, the indices that have impacted on the polity have rather been more negative than one would ordinarily have expected. The collective realization of these negative manifestations cuts across every facet of the three arms of government but as is natural, the executive comes in for a lot of flak in the calculation of these negative happen-stances.

And so where can one start, is it not from Odi where perhaps the darkest points of our democracy was recorded. Closely inter-woven with this is the Niger-Delta issue which has achieved albatross status and is currently dominating the political discourse.

Interestingly, the human rights activists have surprisingly remained silent over the manifestation of all these negative things particularly the obvious anomalies and violations that have characterized the trials of Mohammed Abacha, Hamza Al-Mustapha and company. Even the press has not helped matters by apparently misleading and fashioning public opinion with their sensational tales and reports concerning the trials of Abacha loyalists and the Abacha family.

To add to this, the avalanche of promises which ushered in this democracy, have largely been unfulfilled. Again, uncertain attempts at poverty alleviation, curbing corruption, the weak exchange rate of the naira, the rising violent crimes, have all contributed to give our nascent democracy a negative picture.

Rather, what the press has done is to kill the joy of our democracy by continuing to indulge in Abacha saga and sensationalizing the trials of Mohammed Abacha and company beyond permitable legal and moral limits.

One hopes this millennium, the press, the government and indeed all Nigerians will stop killing the joy of democracy.

KI, Ibadan

PART II

SOUND, SENTENCE, AND WORD

INTRODUCTION

By now, the readers are, we assume, familiar with the background information about the English language, consisting of the historical context of its spread around the world and the resultant variation in its use across languages and cultures. Additionally, they are also cognizant of the fact that societal language use takes place in a cultural context and concepts necessary to discuss such contexts and their impact on language are essential if one wants to study the current place of English in the world. These concepts are drawn from various disciplines, including sociolinguistics and linguistic pragmatics, ethnography of communication, cognitive psychology, and artificial intelligence with relevance to language. Part II continues the discussion and brings in the science of language, or linguistics, into this conversation.

In order to use language for communication, one needs to have two types of competence: linguistic and communicative. Linguistic competence is normally characterized as the knowledge of the rules of usage, i.e. the sound system, the grammatical structures, and the vocabulary. Communicative competence refers to the knowledge of rules of use, i.e. how the symbolic system is utilized to express the intended meaning in real-life situations. In Part II of the book, we will focus on the rules of usage that characterize world Englishes: Chapter 5 discusses the sound system; Chapter 6 the grammatical structure; and Chapter 7 the vocabulary.

LANGUAGE VARIATION

It is a well-recognized fact that different language-speaking communities have different ways of speaking. By different ways of speaking is meant use of a different set of rules regarding rhythmic patterns, word-order, and other devices to indicate meanings such as what is being talked about, emphasized, or related to preceding utterances. Recent research in language use in real-life social contexts such as job interviews, court cases, and doctor–patient interactions, in addition to normal conversational exchanges, has shown that different speech communities use language differently. In fact, different ethnic groups living in the same speech community use a shared language quite differently (Tannen, 1984). For instance, African Americans in the USA use English in different speech functions as compared to other Americans and use talk for different purposes (e.g. Goodwin, 1990; Labov, 1972a, Ch. 8; Mitchell-Kernan, 1972, 1973; Morgan, 1996; Schilling-Estes, 2000; Smitherman, 1995). Furthermore, speakers of different ethnic communities signal their intentions in inter-ethnic communication in a way which is sufficiently different to cause problems for listeners who do not share their ethnic background (e.g. Hansell and Ajirotutu, 1982; Hecht *et al.*, 1992; Mishra, 1982, among others). A much more serious problem is caused when participants in an interaction come from different speech communities and use a common language such as English in significantly different ways.

RHYTHMIC PATTERNS

There are patterns of stress, pitch, and loudness that convey specific meanings. Some are universals, e.g. a high level of pitch and increased loudness conveys excitement or signals new information (Chafe, 1972). Others are culture-specific. For example, loudness may convey emphasis in one culture, but aggression in another. A high pitch may be obligatory in speech for certain categories of speakers in one culture, but may be associated with "childish" behavior in another.

As has been mentioned earlier, speakers of Inner Circle varieties of English are normally tolerant of what they perceive as "errors" of pronunciation and grammar. For instance, they normally attempt to adjust to features such as the following in the other varieties: simplification of final consonant clusters (e.g. *lef* for *left*), wrong assignment of stress in a word (e.g. *'success* for *su'ccess*), missing articles (e.g. *he gave me tough time*), use of wrong preposition (e.g. *We are ready to eat, go sit on the table*), and failure to observe verb agreement patterns (e.g. *That time I see him, he tell me. . .*). Differences in the use of certain other devices, however, create severe problems. Rhythmic patterns of speech are especially problematic.

Stress and intonation in English and other languages are used to signal topic, focus, emphasis, etc., in characteristic ways. These are not subject to correction very easily as they signal speaker intentions. Therefore, certain features of the Outer and Expanding Circle varieties, such as their use of rhythmic patterns, are usually attributed to the personality of the speaker rather than to his or her competence in language. This reaction, of course, is not one-sided. Users of all varieties of English perceive one another as being rude, conceited, untruthful, hesitant, etc., if their utterances are interpretable as such following the conventions of the hearer's use of English.

A few examples of interaction where the characteristic features of the Outer and Expanding Circle varieties led to serious problems in interpretation by the speakers of an Inner Circle variety may clarify this point. A detailed example of a real-life incident, in which precisely this kind of misunderstanding occurred, is given in Mishra (1992, pp. 100–129). The interlocutors were M, a female British staff member in the National Institute of Industrial training, England, and K, an Indian male worker. K was desirous of taking a course and needed a set of forms to apply for admission to the course. In M's judgment, the course was meant for a specific professional group and K did not qualify for admission. She did not get the forms he wanted and could not send them to him when K requested them. Failing to get the forms by mail, K personally went to find out why the forms were not being sent, and had the interaction reported in Mishra (1992). The interaction ended in M feeling K was insulting her by calling her a liar, and K feeling he was discriminated against because of his national origin, and his competence in English.

According to Mishra (1992), the features that were responsible for this frustrating experience for both the interlocutors are the following. The first factor is a mismatch of background knowledge, i.e. what terms such as "suitable," "qualification," and "professional interest" mean. For M, the current job a person has defines suitability, qualification, and professional interest. For K, being already enrolled in the institution where the course is to be taught defines qualification and personal interest in a future profession defines suitability for the course. Since the course has been advertised in the papers, the fact that he did not get the application forms as requested means that he is being discriminated against. The second factor is K's use of *yes* and *no* to signal more than agreement and disagreement; he uses them to signal that he is listening to M. Every time he says *yes*, M thinks he is agreeing with her, but then she finds out that is not what he means. She, therefore, repeats what she has already said, and the process exhausts her. She is unable to figure out what his *yes* means. The same is true of K's *no*; he uses it as a turn opener. Both of these characteristics can be seen in the following excerpt (Mishra, 1992, pp. 121–122). The *yes* in turns 382, 389, and 398 do not signal agreement (the turns are numbered as in Mishra, 1992). Similarly, the *no* in turn 401 simply means K is ready to take his turn.

381.   M: Mr. K I know "more about this course /than you do/ I designed it
382.   K: [yes//
388.   M: I "don't have an equal say actually/ it's—
389.   K: yes//
390.   M: ++I am <telling you/++I-<know//
391.   K: (acc.) if if if you feel somebody/ who is not suitable
392.   ""you""can""say""no( )//
395.   M: (acc.) its got nothing to do with me//if "you have applied to
396.   E. technical College/that's as far as I'm concerned/that's
397.   <<that//it's up to_<<them.it's got nothing to do with me/at all/
398.   K: "yes/still uh you have say//you have opinion//
399.   M: Mr. K stop_<<telling me/what I'm doing/what I'm not doing//
400.   I_<<know what I am "doing//
401.   K: no/++I'm not telling you/what you do/or what you not to
402.   [do/but I I "know.the.fact/what you're/and what you what
403.   did your opinion will be//

[Note: In the transcription above, [indicates overlap, / signals minor tone group boundary, // indicates major tone group boundary, " signals high pitch level, "" marks sustained high pitch level, ++ indicates high pitch, _ indicates low level tone, (acc.) signals an accelerated rate, and << marks gradual falling tone.]

In addition to the background knowledge and the use of *yes* and *no*, the stress patterns mean different things to the two interlocutors. Stress and rhythm are discussed in some detail in Chapter 5.

GRAMMATICAL PATTERNS

Grammatical categories of number, tense, aspect, etc., carry specific meanings. Each language exploits a different patterning of these categories to signal meanings salient in the language. Outer and Expanding Circle varieties of English differ from established Inner Circle varieties in utilizing these categories, leading to misunderstandings in some cases, and judgments of speaker competence in other cases.

For instance, sentences such as the following from Jamaican English are not difficult to understand or process (Shields, 1989, pp. 50–51):

1. This shop is safe; it is here approximately for 35 years.
2. Political tribalism is going on now for over 20 years.

The context of the durational adverbs, *for X years*, makes it clear that the speaker or writer means that the shop *has been* there for X number of years and that tribalism *has been* rampant for over X number of years. Nevertheless, depending upon one's experience with varieties, it may take some adjustment to arrive at an interpretation of such sentences. Additionally, speakers of Inner Circle varieties may view a speaker of the Jamaican variety as a user of *non-standard* language and may not be willing to accept it in, say, the written mode.

Select grammatical patterns and how they differ in world Englishes are discussed in some detail in Chapter 6.

VOCABULARY AND IDIOMS

Place and time have immense impact on the vocabulary of any human language. Compare the dictionaries of the British, American, and Australian Englishes, and this becomes obvious. Also, comparing the first and the ninth editions of Webster's is enough to convince anyone of the difference a passage of years makes in the lexicon. Word such as *opossum, moose, hickory, squash, moccasin, caucus* came into the English language via the American variety (Mencken, 1936), and words such as *sputnik, byte,* or *software* are not listed in the dictionaries produced in the 1940s and 1950s. Idioms such as *to play possum, to have an ax to grind, to pull up the stakes* also represent American innovations (Mencken, 1936).

Outer and Expanding Circle varieties show the same sensitivity to the geographical locations and the sociocultural contexts of the users of the varieties by developing new lexical items and new idioms. For instance, items such as *gherao* (a sit-in by protesters that confines the authorities to their chambers), *lathi-charge* (charge by the police with batons), *satyagrah* (non-violent non-cooperation with authorities) are common in Indian English newspapers, and idioms such as *your tongue flies* (you cannot be trusted not to repeat what you hear) are common in Caribbean English. Philippine English newspapers may carry reports on the activities of a *carnapper* [*carjacker* in American English] or a *reelectionist* "one who stands for reelection" or *studentry* "student body."

The characteristics of vocabulary, including idiomatic expressions, in world Englishes are discussed in Chapter 7.

Chapter 5

Sounds and Rhythm

INTRODUCTION

The following is a description of how the messages that the speakers of Outer and Expanding Circle varieties wish to convey are coded in terms of the organization of sounds of English and how some of the devices that they use may sometimes result in miscommunication.

STRESS AND RHYTHM

Consider a constructed example of the rhythmic pattern resulting in miscommunication in the setting of a British bank. (Gumperz *et al.*, 1979, pp. 21–24):

1. Customer: Excuse me.
   Cashier: Yes, sir.
   Customer: I want to deposit some **money**.
   Cashier: Oh. I see. OK. You'll need a deposit form then.
   Customer: Yes. **No, No**. This is the **wrong** one.
   Cashier: Sorry?
   Customer: I got my account in **Wembley**.
   Cashier: Oh you need a Giro form then.
   Customer: Yes, Giro form.
   Cashier: Why didn't you say so the first time.
   Customer: Sorry, Didn't **know**.
   Cashier: All right?
   Customer: Thank you.

The items that the customer emphasizes are in bold letters. It is obvious that the customer is not a speaker of British English. According to Gumperz *et al.* (1979), the emphasis on *no* and *wrong* in the third exchange of the dialogue gives the wrong signal; it suggests to the cashier that the customer thinks it is his/her fault. The customer's repetition of *Giro form* in the fifth exchange is his/her way of expressing apology, which goes unnoticed and the cashier's irritation is expressed in the same exchange. The sixth exchange is an attempt to repair the damage, but again, the emphasis on *know* gives the wrong signal. The result is that neither participant is very happy.

Contrast the above with (2) below where both the customer and the cashier are speakers of British English:

2. Customer: Good Morning. I want to **deposit** some money, please.
   Cashier: Certainly sir, you'll need a deposit form.
   Customer: Thank you very much. Oh no. This is the wrong **one**. My account is in **Wembley**.
   Cashier: Oh I see. In that case you'll need a Giro form, sir. There you are.
   Customer: Thank you
   Cashier: You're welcome.

The British speaker of English emphasizes *one* rather than *wrong*, and does not have as much pitch variation on *Wembley* as the Indian English speaker (Gumperz et al., 1979, p. 24), therefore, the cashier does not feel s(he) is being blamed for suggesting the wrong form or not knowing where the customer's account is located.

The following information about stress assignment in the Outer and Expanding Circle varieties is useful. Stress assignment in words in these varieties does not follow the rules that operate in the Inner Circle varieties. For instance, word stress in the Outer and Expanding Circle varieties seems idiosyncratic from the perspective of a speaker of American or British variety; *'success* for *su'ccess* (Nigerian English; henceforth, NE), *recog'nize* for *'recognize* (Indian English; henceforth, IE), etc. Actually, as most such varieties have a syllable-timed rather than a stress-timed rhythm (Bamgboṣe, 1992; B. Kachru, 1983a), it is probably the case that the stress assignment follows the values attached to the **mores** (weight of syllables in terms of duration) in these varieties. This seems to be the case in IE. Since the vowels in the syllables *re-* and *-cog-* are short and not as weighty as the diphthong in *-nize*, the primary stress goes with the heavy syllable. Rhythm in these varieties is based on the mores of the syllables; the long syllables are twice as long as the short, but the quality of the vowel in long as well as short syllables remains the same. In case of a word with several long syllables, all the syllables are pronounced long irrespective of their stressed or unstressed character. In Inner Circle varieties of English, the stressed syllable has a longer duration as compared to the unstressed syllable; in fact, the characteristic rhythmic pattern of British

English is such that in a multisyllabic word, the duration of the several unstressed syllables is roughly equivalent to the one stressed syllable. Consequently, vowel quality has a strong correlation with stress. To the Inner Circle speakers of English, the Outer and Expanding Circle varieties sound as though they have a staccato rhythm.[1]

In most Outer and Expanding Circle varieties, there exists a phenomenon known as "spelling pronunciation." For instance, a word such as *lamb* or *comb* is pronounced with a final -*mb* cluster since the word is spelled as such. As English is learned in schools from teachers who themselves have spelling pronunciation for a large number of vocabulary items, the tradition of such pronunciation continues. It is, therefore, natural for speakers of these varieties to arrive at a value for syllables following the conventions of their first languages and assign stress accordingly. For instance, in words such as *biology*, IE speakers assign the value to syllables as follows: *ba-yo-lo-ji*. In most Indic languages, the vowels *a*, *o*, and *i* are long. In most major Indic languages, the first long syllable, or the penultimate syllable, if long, receives the primary stress. Thus, one hears both '*bi-o-lo-gy* and *bi-o-'lo-gy* in IE.

In addition, these varieties do not utilize stress in the same way as do the Inner Circle varieties. For instance, they do not utilize stress to make a distinction between nouns and verbs in pairs such as '*import* and *im'port*. They do not utilize contrastive stress for focusing, either (Bamgboṣe, 1992; Gumperz, 1982a, 1982b). Instead of *JOHN did it*, the Nigerians say *It was John who did it* (Bamgboṣe, 1992), the Zambians say *Me I am going to sleep* (Tripathi, 1990), and the Indians say *John only did it* (Gumperz, 1982b). Emphasis and focus as well as the distinction between *given* and *new* information are signaled by utilizing pitch and intonation in a way which is very different from those utilized by the Inner Circle varieties as discussed in Gumperz (1982a, 1982b). This is discussed further in relation to the signaling of focus and theme in the Outer and Expanding Circle varieties (see Chapter 6).

The pronunciation of segmental sounds in the Outer and Expanding Circle varieties hardly ever leads to a communication breakdown or a serious misunderstanding. This is because as interlocutors get familiar with each other's system of phonological organization, they accommodate their habitual patterns to those of the other speaker(s). According to the Speech Accommodation Theory (SAT, first proposed in Giles, 1973), speakers slowly converge toward the speech patterns of the interlocutor they are interacting with. Later, the theory was made broader and renamed Communication Accommodation Theory (CAT, Giles *et al.*, 1987) so that an interdisciplinary rather than a purely linguistic account of social interaction could be given. The more comprehensive description then would involve verbal means of communication, i.e. the linguistic variables, and also the non-verbal (gesture, body posture, etc.) and discursive dimensions of interaction. Although the theory initially dealt with speakers accommodating to their addressees, by now it is used to account for both speakers and hearers, as in an interaction both sets of participants change roles as speakers and hearers. It is worth remembering that

> accommodation is to be seen as a multiply-organized and contextually complex set of alternatives, regularly available to communicators in face-to-face talk. It can function to index and achieve solidarity with or dissociation from a conversational partner, reciprocally and dynamically. (Giles and Coupland, 1991, pp. 60–61)

We *accommodate* or adapt to others by adjusting our verbal behavior to the role we have in a given interactional context.

In research on intelligibility also, it has been found that the more experience interlocutors have with varieties of English, the less difficulty they have in processing what they hear (see Chapter 4). In view of these findings, the differences in sounds have not been dealt with in detail here. However, the following information about the characteristic use of sounds in these varieties may be helpful to users of all varieties.

SOUNDS

In pronunciation, most Outer and Expanding Circle varieties are different from the Inner Circle varieties. They share this characteristic with the regional dialects within the Inner Circle varieties of English. Some of these differences lead to grammatical consequences which affect comprehension. One such feature is the simplification of final consonant clusters, e.g. *lef* for *left*. By itself, in most contexts, presumably there will be no serious difficulty. It is noteworthy, however, that this feature leads to a loss of past tense endings on verbs, e.g. *pick* for *picked*, and a loss of plural markers on nouns, *des* for *desks*. There is potential for misunderstanding in such cases. It is worth keeping in mind that this is true not only of the Outer and Expanding Circle varieties, but also of certain varieties of American English, e.g. African-American Vernacular English (see Labov, 1972a).

The English sounds that are pronounced differently in the Outer and Expanding Circle varieties are as follows. Consonants and vowels are different as compared to the Inner Circle varieties in the following ways:[2]

1. Voiceless plosives, *p, t, k*, lose their initial aspiration so that the speakers of Inner Circle varieties perceive them often as *b, d, g*. In colloquial varieties, e.g. Malaysian English (Schneider, 2003, pp. 56–57), the final stop is often replaced by a glottal stop, e.g. *ba'* "back"; *be'* "bet" or "bed."
2. Fricatives *f v θ ð s z ʒ* are often replaced by other sounds: *f* by *ph* (IE), *v* by *bh* or *w* (IE), *θ* by *t* (Chinese English or CE, Ghanian English or

GhE, Singapore–Malaysian English or SME) *th* (IE), by *d* (GhE, CE, IE, SME), or *z* (German English or GE), *z* and *ʒ* by *j* in most varieties. In many varieties (e.g. SME), initial *p*, *t*, *k* are pronounced without aspiration and *b*, *d*, *g* are devoiced. As a result, *pig: big, town: down, could: good* may be pronounced identically (Brown, 1986, p. 4).

3. The clear and dark *l* are not distinguished in most varieties.

4. Some speakers of African Englishes (e.g. Zambian) and Expanding Circle varieties (e.g. Japanese) do not distinguish between *r* and *l*; these may be substituted for each other freely.

5. Final consonant clusters are simplified in most East and Southeast Asian varieties. In some varieties, such as IE, initial consonant clusters with initial *s* are either simplified by inserting a neutral vowel between the two consonants or pronounced with an initial vowel so that the cluster is no longer initial, e.g. *saport* "sport," *islow* "slow" (IE). It is true that in Sanskrit borrowings in educated or High Hindi, such clusters are present, for example, in *skand^h* "shoulder," *spard^{h}aa* "competition," and *st^{h}aapit* "established." However, in colloquial (less well-educated) Hindi, they are pronounced as *askand^h*, *aspard^{h}aa*, and *ast^{h}aapit*.

The conflation of sounds described above make words such as the following homophonous in some varieties, e.g. SME (Brown, 1986, p. 4): *theme* and *team*; *then* and *den*; *thin* and *tin*, etc. Some varieties (e.g. IE, Pakistani English; henceforth, PE), however, maintain the contrast by pairs such as *t^{h}iim* "theme" and *ṭiim* "team" and *den* "then" and *ḍen* "den," where the *t^h* and *d* are dental and the *ṭ* and *ḍ* are retroflex plosives. In most cases, context of occurrence helps disambiguate what is being said, though there are occasions when need for clarification may arise (for some examples of such occasions, see Brown, 1986).

6. Almost all Outer and Expanding Circle varieties simplify the diphthongs and triphthongs of the British variety, e.g. *ei>e* as in "paid," *ou>o* as in "bowl," and *au>aw* as in "our."

7. Stressed and unstressed vowels are not distinguished, i.e. there is no reduction of vowel in the unstressed syllable.

8. In several varieties (e.g. GhE), *i:* and *i*, and *u:* and *u* are not distinguished, therefore, "sleep" and "slip" have identical pronunciation, and so have "pool" and "pull."

The grammatical differences in the Outer and Expanding Circle varieties combine with the differences in rhythmic patterns to cause serious problems occasionally in communication between speakers of Inner Circle and Other Circle varieties. However, as has been noted in the literature (Giles,

1973; Giles *et al.*, 1987), users of English in all the Circles arrive at an accommodation as they become more familiar with the variety in use among the interlocutors. Awareness of variety differences, thus, is highly desirable for successful communication across varieties. The media has started playing a bigger role in this venture, as multinational channels such as the BBC, Public Radio International (PRI), and CNN employ more and more local reporters with a variety of accents to inform worldwide audiences about local and regional events.

SOUNDS AND INTELLIGIBILITY

In view of such differences, the question naturally arises: how important is accent for intelligibility? Accent refers not only to the pronunciation of sounds, but also to stress and intonation, or to the rhythm of speech. Just like variety, accent also leads to controversies about which one is superior, desirable, and so on. As the British phonetician David Abercrombie observes (1951, p. 15):

> The accent bar is a little like a colour-bar—to many people, on the right side of the bar, it appears eminently reasonable. It is very difficult to believe, if you talk Received Pronunciation (RP) yourself, that it is not intrinsically superior to other accents.

In popular belief, there is a natural pairing of variety and accent—no distinction is made between the two. However, it is clear that a variety may tolerate many different accents, e.g. American English has distinct accents identifiable as New England, Southern, Mid-Western, and even some associated with particular cities, such as New York or Chicago, and particular groups of people, such as African-American or Mexican-American. More than the variation in articulation of sounds or even rhythm, attitudes toward particular accents may become a barrier in communication across varieties.

Attempts are being made to define a core for English used as a lingua franca, especially within the European context (see Jenkins, 2000). Reassuring as these attempts may be to those who look for a definite model for teaching and learning, and more importantly, for gate-keeping functions of the ELT profession, experience shows that one prescription for a core sound system for an idealized International English hardly proves to be a resounding success in all situations. Greater success in crosscultural communication is achieved with sensitivity to the variation in world Englishes, as has been demonstrated again and again by those who conduct negotiations in various fields, whether academic, diplomatic, financial, health, or media-related. Those who interact with other variety users accommodate to the variation they notice in each other's speech or writing and gradually learn to communicate more effectively. This experience is shared by a large number of expatriate workers and professionals all across East and West, North and South in this era of globalization.

Notes

1. The phonetics of stress in Outer Circle varieties such as Indian English are still being investigated. For two recent research reports on this topic, see Peng and Ann (2001) and Wiltshire and Moon (2003).
2. The brief description of sound system in various Englishes presented here is based on the following sources: Gargesh (2004), B. Kachru (1965, 1983a, 1985a, 1985b, 1986a, 2005a) for Indian English; Bao (2001), Brown (1986), and Platt and Weber (1980) for Singapore-Malaysian English; Llamzon (1997) and Bautista and Bolton (2004) for Philippine English; Rahman (1990) for Pakistani English; Simo-Bobda (1994a) for Cameroon English; and other sources listed in the References.

Further Reading

For the sound systems of various Outer and Expanding Circle varieties, see the following:

Bamgboṣe, A. (1992) Standard Nigerian English: issues of identification. In B. B. Kachru (ed.), *The Other Tongue: English across Cultures* (pp. 148–161). Urbana, IL: University of Illinois Press.

Craig, D. R. (1982) Toward a description of Caribbean English. In B. B. Kachru (ed.), *The Other Tongue: English across Cultures* (pp. 198–209). Urbana, IL: University of Illinois Press.

Kachru, B. B. (1983) *The Indianization of English: The English language in India.* Delhi and Oxford: Oxford University Press. [See pp. 26–32.]

Platt, J. and Weber, H. (1980) *English in Singapore and Malaysia: Status, Features, Functions.* Kuala Lumpur and Oxford: Oxford University Press. [See pp. 49–59.]

Zuraidah M. D. (2000) Malay + English → A Malay variety of English vowels and accents. In H. M. Said and K. S. Ng (eds), *English is an Asian Language: The Malaysian Context* (pp. 35–46). Sydney: Persatuan Bahasa Moden Malaysia and The Macquarie Library Pty Ltd.

Suggested Activities

1. Watch a Disney cartoon (e.g. *The Lion King*) and observe which accents have been used with which characters. Discuss what it means in terms of the perception of individuals with such accents. That is, accents associated with members of specific ethnic groups are labeled "crude," "uneducated," "vulgar," "sophisticated," "pleasant," etc. Analyze which accents the characters that are portrayed as "evil" in Disney movies use

and which accents are employed by characters that are shown to be "good."

2. Jenkins (2000, pp. 158–159) suggests the following lingua franca core for ELT. In your experience, are all these features necessary for intelligibility? Additionally, how successful are teachers in teaching— and learners in learning to make—all these contrasts within your community of teachers/learners?

Consonantal inventory

- rhotic *r* [as in General American English, rather than the quality of British *r*]
- intervocalic -*t*- as in bu*tt*er
- most substitutions of θ and $ð$ and *ɫ* permissible
- close approximation to core consonant sounds generally permissible [that is, *th* for θ, *l* for dark *r*, etc.]
- certain approximations not permissible [where contrasts may be lost]

Phonetic requirements

- aspiration following the fortis plosives *p, t, k*
- fortis/lenis differential effect [the effect of *p* vs. *b*, *t* vs. *d* and *k* vs. *g*] on preceding vowel length (generally the vowels preceding the voiced sounds *b, d, g* are longer than those preceding the voiceless *p, t, k*)

Consonant clusters

- initial clusters not simplified
- medial and final clusters simplified only according to L1 rules of elision

Vowel sounds

- maintenance of vowel length contrasts [e.g. as in *slip* and *sleep*]
- L2 regional qualities permissible if consistent, but ɜː [as in *bird*] to be preserved

One additional recommendation is:

- Nuclear stress production and placement and division of speech stream into word groups [as in "Did you buy a *tennis* racket or a *squash* racket?" as opposed to "Did you *buy* a tennis racket or did you *rent* one?"]

Chapter 6

Phrases and Sentences

INTRODUCTION

For the users of the Outer and Expanding Circle varieties, English is either a second language, or, if they happen to be multilingual, one of the languages in their linguistic repertoire. This, of course, is also true of immigrant populations in Britain, and some hyphenated Americans in the USA, that is, Arab-Americans, Indian-Americans, Korean-Americans, or Mexican-Americans. The varieties in the Outer and Expanding Circles are in constant contact with the languages of the regions in which they are used. Consequently they are influenced by the local language(s) in various areas of their grammars. This has resulted in specific characteristics in the grammar of these varieties. The differences relate to either extending or restricting the rules of the Inner Circle varieties of English. They have attracted sufficient attention in literature and thus deserve a description here.

GRAMMAR

The grammar of the Outer and Expanding Circle varieties is described below in three sections: the first deals with the grammar of nouns; the second with the grammar of verbs; and the third with the grammar of linkers. Constant comparisons are made with the grammars of the American/British Standard varieties, since they are codified in grammars (e.g. Quirk *et al.*, 1985) and dictionaries (e.g. Merriam Webster's, Random House, Longman's, and others) to make it easier to follow the discussion. This discussion is by no means exhaustive; varieties of English around the world are still under study and important findings are emerging as a result of descriptions and analyses of corpora (see, Greenbaum, 1990, 1991; Greenbaum and Nelson, 1996, and Nelson, 2004 for details of corpora collected and under analyses).

Noun

The grammar of the nouns deals with the dependency between articles and singular count nouns and the distinction between count/mass and singular/plural.

Articles and determiners: English articles belong to a category that is defined in relation to nouns. There is a relation of mutual dependency between articles and nouns in that the articles do not occur independently, and at least the count noun in the singular cannot occur without an article. For instance, *a* or *the*, though written as independent words, do not really have the privilege of occurring as independent words. Similarly, singular count nouns such as *boy*, *book*, *chair*, etc. can not occur in a sentence without an article or some other determiner such as *this, that, any, each*, etc.

There is nothing comparable to the articles of English in many of the languages spoken in different parts of Africa and Asia, although most languages have demonstratives such as *this, that*, etc. Furthermore, it is not quite clear to most teachers and learners of English in these regions as to what the semantic bases are for the use of articles in English. For instance, let us concentrate on the so-called indefinite article *a* and its phonologically determined variant *an*. It is not quite true that this article is exclusively used to signal a singular entity of the noun class known as "count" noun, e.g. *a book*. If that were the case, the following phrase ought to be ungrammatical, *an oppressive atmosphere* (since *atmosphere* is a mass noun), but it is not. It is also not true that *a(n)* is always used in the "first mention" of a noun in a connected text. If that were the case, the following sequence should be ungrammatical, because *a cell* in the second sentence follows *cells* in the first sentence, but it is not: *Cells are the building blocks of life. A cell is composed of a nucleus and cytoplasm.* Similarly, it is not true that the so-called definite article *the* is used to signal the definite and specific noun only. In fact, each of the articles in English is used to signal more than one meaning (see the discussion below), and the same meaning is signaled by more than one article (e.g. *a, the,* and the zero article, all three are used to signal the generic reference). Sometimes, the use of the article is purely grammatical, with no semantic consequence at all, e.g. the use of *a* in the predicate nominal such as *my father is a doctor.*

The article in English has three sets of functions: a set of purely grammatical functions; a set of semantic functions, including reference; and a set of pragmatic functions. The grammatical functions in themselves are quite complex, when the interlocking semantic and pragmatic functions are added to them, the description of the article system becomes even more complex. The grammatical functions of the articles are the following:

1. A count noun in the singular must be preceded by an article if not preceded by some other determiner (e.g. *A dog* is *a man's* best friend).
2. A predicate nominal in the singular must be preceded by the article *a* or *an* (e.g. My friend is *a student*).
3. Certain proper nouns must be preceded by the article *the* (e.g. *The Hague, The Rhine*).

The semantic functions are basically related to reference. These have to do with signaling the meanings of articles, i.e. definite/indefinite, specific/non-specific and generic/non-generic, reference. These will become clear if we consider the following examples in detail.

4. A: How was your weekend?
   B: Rather hectic. I had to go to **a movie** that my sister wanted to see on Saturday and then to a dinner on Sunday.
   A: How was **the movie**?

If we concentrated on the noun phrases in the bold type, *a movie* in B's utterance signals an indefinite reference in that B has no expectation that A has any idea as to which movie (s)he is referring to. *The movie* in A's response to B's statement, however, signals a definite reference in that A is now talking about the movie that B went to.

Note that although *a movie* signals an indefinite reference, B is making a specific reference, (s)he means that (s)he had to go to a specific movie (i.e. the movie that his/her sister wanted to see). This means that the indefinite does not always imply non-specific reference. In A's response, however, *the movie* is both definite and specific. The difference between non-specific and specific reference becomes clear in sentences such as the following.

5. a. He wanted to buy **some** books but couldn't find **any** worth buying.
   b. He wanted to buy **some** books but couldn't find **them** in the store.
   [The **some** in the above examples and throughout this discussion is the unstressed **some**.]

In the above examples, the non-specific reference is signaled by *some/any* and the specific by *some/them*.

These examples identify *a(n), the,* and *some* as the articles in English. Let us consider further examples to arrive at the complete set of articles:

6. A: Are bats birds?
   B: No, bats are mammals.
      Or
   B: A/the bat is a mammal.

In (6B), *bats, a bat, the bat* are all used to make a generic reference, i.e. to the species as a whole. In this case, it is clear that the so-called definite article is used to make a non-specific reference.

All the examples above have count nouns in them (note the implication of quantity in the use of *a(n)* with singular and *some* with plural). It is helpful to consider some examples with mass nouns as well:

7. A1: I understand you went to the store early this morning.
    B1: Yes. I needed (some) coffee, (some) sugar and (some) milk.
    A2: So you got everything you needed.
    B2: Oh, no, I forgot the milk!

In (7B1), either the zero article or the article *some* may be used to signal the indefinite non-specific meaning. In contrast, the definite specific meaning is signaled by *the milk* in (7B2).

The conventions of use of articles with nouns can be stated as follows:

8. *a(n)*: indefinite non-specific, or indefinite specific, or generic (with count nouns in the singular);
    the: definite specific (with count and mass nouns), or non-specific generic (with count nouns only);
    some: indefinite non-specific, or indefinite specific (with count nouns in the plural, with mass nouns);
    $\emptyset$: generic (with count nouns in the plural, with mass nouns).

The above description makes it clear that there is considerable overlap among the forms of articles and the meanings they signal. Of course, the generic reference is not signaled by the articles exclusively, the tense-aspect of the utterance is relevant, too. Compare *A tiger roars* vs. *A tiger is roaring* or *A tiger roared*; only the first one is a generic sentence, the other two are about a specific tiger that is in the consciousness of the speaker/writer.

There are two factors that complicate the learning of the above system of articles in areas where English is not acquired as the first language. First, in the Inner Circle varieties of English, either the indefinite or the definite article can be used to signal the generic reference, since the generic is a function of the non-specific and all the articles can signal this meaning. Second, in many languages of the world, the definite specific noun is not marked, it is usually the indefinite noun that is marked, and the generic is a function of the definite specific. This is true of all the major languages of South Asia, of Persian, and of several other languages of the world. Compare the translation equivalents of the Standard American or British English and their Hindi counterparts given below.

9. A: I want to buy **a book**, could you suggest some titles?
        muj^{h}e **ek kitaab** xariidnii hai, aap   kuc^h naam suj^{h}aaenge?
        to me **a book** to buy f is   you (h.) some names suggest will (h.)

B: (S)he got **a letter** from her friend today.
    aaj use dost kii **cit**ᵗʰ**ii** milii hai.
    today him/her friend of **letter** obtained is
C1: I just read **a poem** and **a short story** by Anita.
    maiN ne abʰii abʰii anitaa kii likʰii **ek kavitaa** aur **ek kahaanii** paṛʰii.
    I   ag. just   Anita of written **a poem** and **a story** read
C2: How did you like **the poem**?
    kavitaa kaisii lagii?
    poem how appealed
D: **A bat** is a mammal.
    camgaadaṛ stanpaayii hotaa hai.
    bat   mammal is

The noun phrases in bold types make it clear that in Hindi, the indefinite non-specific is consistently marked with a determiner such as *ek* (9A and 9C1), the indefinite non-specific (in 9B), the definite specific (9C2) and the generic (9D) are unmarked.

In view of such systematic differences, it is not surprising that the Outer and Expanding Circle varieties of English do not use articles in the same way that the Inner Circle varieties do. Since there is no one-to-one correlation between the forms (i.e. *a, the, some*) and the meanings they signal, it is difficult for learners of English to arrive at the principles underlying the use of articles. The picture is further complicated by the fact that depending upon speaker intentions, the choice of articles may vary in what appears to the learners as the same context. For example, both the following responses by B to A in (10) below are grammatical and appropriate:

10. A: I am thirsty.
    B: There is (some) orange juice in the fridge.

Except for the implication of quantity in the use of some as opposed to the zero article, there is no difference in referential meaning that is signaled by this choice.

Count/Mass: The above discussion may suggest that nouns are inherently either count or mass and the use of articles is determined by these properties of the nouns. Actually, this is not true. As has been stated earlier, there is a relation of mutual dependency between articles and nouns. In fact, according to Huddleston (1984), there are general usage rules that can be applied to all determiners and "[c]ountability has to do with a noun's potential for combining with various types of determiner. . ." (p. 246).

According to Allan (1980), there are eight different classes of nouns in English in view of (1) their potential for combining with the following types of determiners: the zero determiner; unit determiners such as *a(n)*, *one*; fuzzy quantifiers such as *several, about fifty*; the determiner *all* in the sense of "completely"; and (2) their potentiality for being marked as plural, either inflectionally or in terms of agreement features. According to

Huddleston (1984, p. 245), there are six classes of nouns exemplified by *equipment* (fully mass), *knowledge* (almost mass, but occur with *a*, e.g. *a good knowledge of Latin*), *clothes* (occur with fuzzy quantifiers such as *many, few,* hence are more count-like), *cattle* (occur with fuzzy quantifiers and large round numbers), *people* (collective noun, have plural forms, e.g. *peoples,* but are not fully countable in that these nouns do not occur in a singular form), and *dog* (fully count).

Thus, the English system of countability is complex. Note that the conventions of marking countability differ across languages. In English, mass nouns (*equipment, sugar*) are inherently singular, in Sinhalese and Swahili, they are treated as plural. In many languages, there is no distinction between a *shirt* and (*a pair of*) *trousers.*

In African, Caribbean, East, South, and Southeast Asian varieties of English, the complex system of marking count/mass distinction in English is simplified. Perceptually countable items such as *furniture, equipment,* and *luggage* are regularly used with a plural marker to denote more than one piece (Bokamba, 1992; Low and Brown, 2003; Shim, 1999). Also since neither the determiner nor the countability system is clearly described in any language learning/teaching texts, there is a great deal of variation in the Outer and Expanding Circle varieties in the usage of determiners and the categorization of nouns. In some varieties, such as Singaporean and Thai, inflectional marking of plural is not always consistent, partly as a result of phonological processes such as final consonant cluster simplification. The same is true of SME. According to Brown (1986, p. 6), in syllable final position the commonest consonants to be deleted are the alveolar stops /t, d/. Other consonants commonly omitted in SME final clusters are /s, z/.

Verb

The grammar of verbs deals with not only the tense-aspect distinctions, but also semantic categorization of verbs in terms of *stative/dynamic, factive/non-factive, volitional/non-volitional,* etc. These categorizations do not coincide in all the varieties of world Englishes.

Stative/Dynamic. According to Quirk *et al.* (1972), the distinction in terms of stativity is central to the grammar of verbs in English. Stativity of the verb interacts with the aspectual and mood systems of the English verbal construction. For instance, stative verbs do not occur in the progressive aspectual form; sentences such as the following are ungrammatical: **You are resembling your brother, *They were knowing all the answers.* Also, the following imperative sentences are strange: *?Know Russian! ?Resemble your mother!*

Many languages of the world, however, do not express the stative vs. dynamic meaning through verbs. It is, therefore, common in the Outer and Expanding Circle varieties of English to ignore the distinction between stative and dynamic verbs. Sentences such as the following are perfectly grammatical in, e.g. South Asian varieties: *He is having two cars*; *I was not knowing him then*; *She is not recognizing you* (B. Kachru, 1986a).

Factivity and volitionality: In addition to the stative/dynamic distinction mentioned above, there are other distinctions, partly semantic and partly grammatical, that are made in the verb system of human languages. For instance, English makes a distinction between *factive* and *non-factive* verbs (e.g. *Peter regrets that he was rude to Bill* vs. *Peter believes that he was rude to Bill*). Note that negating the main verb in case of the factive verb regret does not affect the interpretation that it was a fact that *he was rude to Bill*, but negating the non-factive *believe* negates the whole sentence (cf. *Peter did not regret that he was rude to Bill* (from the perspective of the speaker, Peter was, in fact, rude to Bill); *Peter did not believe that he was rude to Bill* (the speaker is not asserting that Peter, in fact, was rude to Bill)). Other languages may make a distinction between *volitional* and *non-volitional* verbs, i.e. verbs that assert that the subject was responsible for the action expressed by the main verb of the sentence, and verbs that do not imply such responsibility. Compare the English sentence *He lost the key* with its Hindi counterparts, *usne caabʰii kʰo dii* vs. *usse caabʰii kʰo gaii*. The first is in the active construction with the first causal or transitive verb *kʰo denaa*, the second is with the non-causal process verb *kʰo jaanaa*. In the first sentence, the agent is marked with the agentive postposition *ne*, in the second, the pronoun subject is marked with the instrumental postposition *se*. The first is equivalent to the English sentence *He (deliberately) lost the key*, and the second is equivalent to the English sentence *He (accidentally) lost the key*. In the Inner Circle varieties of English, responsibility can be assigned by either using adverbs such as *deliberately* or by stressing the subject, i.e. ***He*** *lost the key*.

The facts described above with regard to differences in verbal distinctions are true not only of Hindi, but of all major languages spoken in South Asia. This has led to the development of certain characteristic features in IE that lead to problems of interpretability in interactions with speakers of Inner Circle varieties of English (Gumperz, 1982b).

Verbalization strategies: The parts of speech categorization of words in English is not rigid; the same item may be a noun as well as a verb, e.g. *man*. This property of the English grammar is exploited creatively by various world Englishes. For instance, Ghanian English has uses such as *Your behavior tantamounts to insubordination* and *It doesn't worth the price* (Gyasi, 1991). Other Englishes utilize the productive derivational affixes of English for coining new verbs. According to Simo-Bobda (1994b), Cameroon English has verbs such as *titularise* "confirm a civil servant," and IE has *prepone* parallel to *postpone*.

Tense/Aspect: In East Asian as well as Southeast Asian languages such as Thai, verbs are not inflected for tense. The distinction between present and past time reference, for example, is expressed by adverbs. In several South

Asian languages, tense, aspect, and mood have complex interactions that are missing from the English tense/aspect system. Matters are further complicated by the fact that most English language teaching texts do not explain the semantic and pragmatic factors involved in the choice of a tense form. Speakers of the Inner Circle varieties acquire the tense-aspect system as they acquire the interactional norms of their community; learners of the Outer and Expanding Circle varieties obviously have little opportunity to do so. They base their system on the system they know best, that of their first language or, if they are multilingual, the languages in their repertoire. As a result, there is a great deal of variation in the use of the tense-aspect markers of English in the Outer and Expanding Circle varieties. For instance, it is common to come across definite past time adverbs with the present perfect (e.g. *I have written to him yesterday*) in IE; it is common for speakers from East and Southeast Asia to leave out the tense-markers and signal the time reference with time adverbs (e.g. *I talk to her yesterday*); it is common to signal the aspectual meaning with adverbs such as *already* ("completive") and *last time* ("formerly") in the Southeast Asian varieties, e.g. *Her fiancé at that time brought over some canned ribs, pork ribs, yes, about . . . twenty eight (of) cans of them. And then we return about fourteen of them* (Tay, 1993, p. 99). Once the past time has been established by the adverb *at that time*, the tense-marking becomes optional, and thus *brought* is tense-marked but *return* is not.

Gumperz (1982b) discusses two court cases in the USA involving a Filipino doctor and two Filipino nurses, respectively, in which the Filipino subjects were perceived as being untruthful. The doctor, in fact, was sued for perjury. If we look at the following exchanges, it becomes clear why the Filipinos were regarded with suspicion in the context of their testimony.

11. Q: Would you say that the two of you were close friends during that
          period of time?
     A: I would say that we are good friends but we are really not that close
          because I don't know her and we don't know each other that much.

According to Naylor (1980), quoted in Gumperz (1982b, pp. 173–174), the prosecution's case against the two Filipino nurses was based entirely on circumstantial evidence and hinged on the credibility of the nurses' testimony as compared with that of the experts. The answer in (11) above, according to the norms of Standard American English, was interpreted as false in view of the fact that the nurse under interrogation had earlier testified that in the course of going through the ordeal of the trial, the two nurses had become good friends. Phrased in the present tense, the answer in (11) above was thus obviously false according to the norms of American English.

In Filipino English (or FE), as in several other varieties of English, however, tense distinctions are not as important as aspectual distinctions. The influence of Filipino languages is invoked in Naylor (1980) to explain that FE does not make a distinction in present and past tenses. It is shown, for example, that Tagalog, a Filipino language, operates on a system of aspectual distinction in terms of the beginning and completion of actions rather than the time reference of the actions. Thus, Tagalog has the following distinctions:

12. Not begun: *kakain* "will eat"
    Begun: not completed *kumakain* "eats/is or was eating"
    Completed   *kumain* "ate/has or had eaten"

The nurses' failure to make a clear distinction between present and past naturally affected their credibility in the context of the courtroom.

The same phenomenon is noticeable in the transcript of the case against the Filipino doctor mentioned above. The following excerpts make this clear:

13. Q: Then I am to understand that you were really not aware at the time that you were working at Port Huename that a list of rules, or what we call the Navy Instructions existed governing the day to day conduct and operation of the hospital?
    A: I'm not aware.
    Q: You weren't aware of that?
    A: May be they have, but I was not told where to find it or where I could find it.

Note the first exchange when the question (Q) is in the past but the answer (A) is in the present, and the subsequent exchange for clarification.

Excerpt (14) below supports the claim that this is systematic:

14. Q: At the end when you released the child to the family, did you feel that the cause of the injuries was sunburn or thermofluid burn?
    A: I still feel it was due to sunburn.

The impression created by the exchange is that the person giving the answer still believes the cause to be sunburn. That, however, is not correct. By this time, the doctor undergoing the trial for perjury is aware of the fact the cause was child abuse. What he means to say is something like "I still feel I was justified in concluding that it was due to sunburn" (Gumperz, 1982b, p. 175). The use of the present tense in the answer, however, precludes any such interpretation in the context of the US court room.

In addition to the use of tenses, the Outer and Expanding Circle varieties differ from the Inner Circle varieties in the use of sequence of tenses. The sequence of tense phenomenon is almost always missing in the Outer and Expanding Circle varieties. In a narrative, tense forms seem to vary from present to past to future to present or past with dizzying frequency from the point of view of a speaker of Inner Circle variety. Nelson (1985) documents such usage in creative writing in Indian English. It has been shown in

Y. Kachru (1983) that the Indian languages do not have a grammatical constraint of sequence of tense. As such, the tense forms in successive sentences are determined by the natural sequence of events in time. As a narrative, the following, for example, is perfectly well-formed in Hindi as well as IE:

> 15. Last Wednesday, he said that he will be going to the City on Saturday and coming back on Sunday. So we will meet for dinner on Monday. I went to his room, and saw that he is not there.

In a long narrative or conversation with a speaker of an Inner Circle variety, this creates problems, especially when combined with prosodic clues that differ significantly from the Inner Circle variety (Mishra, 1982).

Modals: There is a preference for *would* instead of *will* in Outer Circle varieties such as African, Philippine, and South Asian. For example, Banjo (1997, p. 89) cites the following examples from a daily newspaper, *The Guardian*, of Nigeria:

> 16. At dawn, fog patches are expected which by mid-morning *would* give way to a partly cloudy and hazy afternoon. . . .
> 17. Applicant must be a Registered Nurse, ... Successful candidate *would* be involved in the treatment of staff and staff dependents, ...

In our small database of newspaper Englishes, we found examples such as the following. From *The Guardian*, Lagos, Nigeria (April 6, 2000):

> Since the past seven years, the telephone lines in Umualum Nekede have not been functioning, ... The unfortunate part of it is that the subscribers are still servicing the lines with the hope that NITEL territorial headquarters in Owerri *would* resuscitate them in due course.

From *The Manila Times*, Manila, the Philippines (June 17, 2003):

> Feken has suggested the passage of a municipal ordinance requiring inveterate chewers to tote or dangle from their necks portable spittoons, together with their betel quid pouches, to contain the messy sight caused by the phenomenon. "An empty sardine can *would* do," he said.

From *The Indian Express*, Delhi, India (June 30, 2005):

> Although the Parechu disaster seems to have been averted, it is high time that Chinese and the Indian governments cooperate and formulate a policy for joint water management . . . . If not, then it *would* be difficult for India, being the lower riparian state, to have any say in the use and control of water by China.

Select Syntactic Patterns

Some syntactic constructions that have attracted attention and have been contrasted across varieties are the following.

Question-answering systems: In the case of the Filipino doctor's problem in the US courts mentioned above (and exemplified in (12) and (13)), the difficulties with tense forms were further compounded by the use of a question-answering system that does not operate in American English. This is exemplified in (18) and (19) below.

18. Q1: Did you check to determine if dehydration was present?
    A1: Yes.
    Q2: What steps did you take to determine that? If it was there or absent?
    A2: When the child came, I initially examined the patient and I noted the moistness of the tongue, sunken eyes, the skin color, and everything was okay.
    Q3: Are you suggesting that there were no sunken eyes?
    A3: No.
    Q4: I think we better slow down a little bit more and make sure the record . . . did you observe sunken eyes?
    A4: No.

The statement in A2 suggests the presence of *sunken eyes* which is contradicted by the last clause *everything was okay*. Q3 attempts to obtain clarification, but fails because of A3 being *no*; it is only after Q4 which elicits A4 that the situation becomes clear. The third exchange illustrates the question-answering strategy which is based upon the implied assumption of the question "there were no sunken eyes?" and answers that assumption. This happens in excerpt (19), too:

19 Q: It is the testimony by LOG that you did not attend the briefing.
    A: Yes.
    Q: You did attend it?
    A: No.

Notice again that the *Yes* in the first exchange in (19) is in agreement with LOG's testimony, not an assertion that the doctor attended the briefing, but the questioner is baffled by this unfamiliar pattern of response.

Such linguistic behavior made the doctor appear to be unreliable and brought on the perjury trial. Later, when the linguistic basis for the utterances was explained to the jurors, the doctor was acquitted of the perjury charges.

This pattern of response is not restricted to the FE only. Other Outer and Expanding Circle varieties exhibit the same system, e.g. the African (Bokamba, 1982), the South Asian (e.g. B. Kachru, 1994a), the varieties of the Malay Archipelago (e.g. Lowenberg, 1984), and the variety developing in China (Li, 1995, p. 55). In fact, almost all studies of Inner Circle speaker interaction with speakers from other Circles mention the fact that Outer and Expanding Circle speakers' way of answering questions is confusing to the Inner Circle speakers of English.

Actually, in the Outer and Expanding Circle varieties, the system is the same as the Inner Circle varieties as far as the positive yes–no questions are concerned. The difficulties arise when the context demands a negatively-oriented yes–no question (e.g. *Isn't your car working?*). An example of the system utilized by these varieties can be seen in the following exchange (Bokamba, 1982, pp. 84–85):

20. a. Q: Hasn't the President left for Nairobi yet?
         A: Yes, the President hasn't left for Nairobi yet.
     b. Q: Didn't you see anyone at the compound?
         A: Yes, I didn't see anyone at the compound.

In each case, the expected answer in the Inner Circle varieties would be *No, the President . . .* and *No, I didn't. . . .*

According to Pope (1976), there are two types of question-answering systems that human languages have. In one, the answer follows the polarity of the question, i.e. if the question is in the positive, the answer confirming the assumption of the questioner is in the positive, and the answer disconfirming the assumption is in the negative. If, however, the question is in the negative, the answer confirming the assumption of the questioner is in the negative, and the answer disconfirming the assumption of the questioner is in the positive. This is called the **positive–negative system**. There is another system, which several languages spoken in various parts of the world follow, in which an answer confirming the assumption of the questioner is always in the positive to signal agreement, and in the negative to express disagreement. This is called the **agreement–disagreement system**. The difficulty that speakers of Inner Circle varieties face in interacting with those who use the agreement–disagreement system is that they are never sure how to interpret the *yes* or *no* of the other speaker, since the *yes* or *no* is not always followed by a full clause to clarify what the person answering the question is saying. We have already seen some examples of such confusion in the court case involving the Filipino doctor quoted above. Almost all speakers of Inner Circle varieties who have had extensive interaction with speakers of Outer and Expanding Circle varieties will be able to narrate incidents where the question-answering systems created difficulties in understanding one's conversational partner. The ones that use the *agreement–disagreement system* are, for example, varieties spoken in Africa (Bokamba, 1982, pp. 84–85), South Asia (B. Kachru, 1983a), Singapore and Malaysia (Platt and Weber, 1980, p. 80).

Tags: In addition to direct question, the other device that the Inner Circle varieties of English use to request confirmation are tags. Tags are used with question intonation along with statements, e.g. *You are coming to the party, aren't you?* The tags are formed following very general principles of tag formation, e.g. the subject of the sentence is copied with appropriate form of the pronoun, the tense and aspect are copied, and the polarity is reversed, e.g. *John hasn't arrived yet, has he?* Note the agreement between *John* and *he*, the repetition of *has* (present perfect) and the positive *has* instead of the negative *hasn't* of the statement part in the tag.

In the Outer and Expanding Circle varieties, the principles of tag formation are not the same. A general tag, *is(n't) it* or *no*, is used universally. For example, the following are grammatical in IE, SME, and several other varieties:

21. a. A: I want it at six o'clock.
       B: At six, is it? (Tongue, 1974, p. 42)
    b. A: You are not going home, is it? (Platt and Weber, 1980, p. 76)

In SME, the tag *is it* signals a request for confirmation or agreement. The tag *isn't it*, on the other hand, seems to signal a straightforward question.

Complementation: Many Outer and Expanding Circle varieties of English use adjective, noun, and verb complements differently from the Inner Circle varieties. The differences are attributable to two major grammatical features. In the Inner Circle varieties of English, complements are either full clauses or if reduced, either gerunds or infinitives. Not all varieties of all these choices are available in their grammars. Second, specific verbs, prepositions, and adjectives are associated with specific forms of complements. For instance, the verb *say* takes a full clausal complement, *enjoy* takes a gerund as a complement, and *want* takes an infinitive as a complement:

22. Josephine said that she liked watching surfers.
23. Sally enjoyed visiting Alaska.
24. Bill wanted to send some money to his friend.

In many languages, e.g. some of the major languages of South Asia, complements have only two forms: full clause and infinitive. In South Asian English, therefore, infinitives and gerunds are used differently. The examples cited below from Indian and Pakistani English illustrate this phenomenon (Baumgardner, 1987; Nihalani *et al.*, 1979; Whitworth, 1982; for a more recent description of verb complements in Indian English, see De Ersson and Shaw, 2003; the 'IE' and 'PE' indicate Indian and Pakistani varieties, respectively).

25. IE/PE They were not at all interested in democracy . . . and were only *interested to grab* power at any cost.
26. PE   It is believed that PIA (Pakistan International Airlines) *is prepared for filing* an insurance claim.

In English grammars, the adjective *interested* governs the gerund, and *prepared* governs the infinitive, respectively.

> 27. PE   According to him the government had not *succeeded to redress* the real problems of the people.
> 28. PE   He also *suggested to curtail* the number traveling through sea route by half.

Again, in the Inner Circle varieties, the verb *success* requires a preposition *in* and the gerund in the complement position; the verb *insist* requires a preposition *on* and a gerund in the complement position; the verb *suggest* as a mono-transitive requires a finite *that*-clause complement.

> 29. IE/PE   Meanwhile the police are *avoiding to enter* the campus where the culprits are stated to be hiding.
> 30. GhE   They *insisted to go* in spite of my advice.
> 31. PE/IE   He does not *hesitate from using* four-letter words.

The verb *avoid*, like the verb *success*, requires a gerund as complement, and the verb *hesitate* requires an infinitive. The verb *want* does not take a finite *that*-clause complement in the Inner Circle varieties of English, unlike the example in (32).

> 32. PE/IE   She said that her party *wanted that* we should not intervene in internal affairs of Afghanistan.

The verb *let* requires a bare infinitive in the Inner Circle varieties, but not in the South Asian varieties:

> 33. IE/PE   She said democratic forces would not *let* any conspiracy against the Nation *to succeed.*

Ditransitive verbs, such as *tell*, are used as though they were mono-transitive in the South Asian varieties:

> 34. IE/PE   The Minister *told that* the pay committee has recommended for a solid pay structure for employees of different categories.

Complements of nouns exhibit different usage patterns, too, as in the example in (35):

> 35. PE   Pakistan has no *control to influence* affairs inside Afghanistan.

Finally, purpose adverbials have the preposition *for* followed by a gerund instead of the infinitive:

> 36. IE/PE   He *went* to China *for learning* Chinese. (Baumgardner, 1987)

Since the complement types do not seem to be clearly linked to any semantic differences, and some verbs such as *like* govern both gerunds and infinitives (I like to swim and I like swimming), it is difficult for learners to acquire the complement system. Also, it is reasonable to expect variation in this area of English grammar.

Linkers

In the Outer and Expanding Circle varieties, various types of linkers are used in ways that are unfamiliar to the speakers of the Inner Circle varieties. The use of prepositions is discussed below. The use of conjunctions is discussed in the next chapter in relation to cohesion.

Prepositions: According to Quirk *et al.* (1972), the meaning of place prepositions in English can be described in terms of those that signal location at a point, along a line, on a surface, or in three-dimensional space. Also, prepositions signal location as well as motion. Whereas signaling location vs. motion is important in all language, signaling different dimensions may not be as important. For instance, it may not be important to distinguish between location at a point vs. on a surface. Also, the orientation may be always with reference to the person of the speaker rather than the reference point established in the utterance by the speaker. The semantic extensions of the place prepositions to time and other dimension may not follow exactly the same principles either. All these lead to difficulties in the use of prepositions in the Outer and Expanding Circle varieties, especially because not much systematic information is available about the prepositions in English. The use of prepositions is determined partly by their meaning and partly because of their formal grammatical requirement with no reference to their meaning. Some examples of the use of prepositions in the Other varieties are given below:

37. a. Singapore English (Tongue, 1974)
    i. We can give some thought *on* the matter.
    ii. The matter has been studied with a view *of* further reducing the risk of fire.
    b. Ghanian English (Gyasi, 1991, pp. 29–30)
    iii. The police are investigating *into* the case.
    iv. We will not be deprived *from* our rights.
    v. She has gone *to* abroad.
    vi. He has regretted *for* his hasty action.
    c. Indian English (Nihalani *et al.*, 1979)
    vii. We were discussing *about* politics.
    viii. He is very well adapted *on* his job.
    ix. He was accompanied *with* his best friend.
    x. I admire *for* his courage.

THEMATIC INFORMATION

The organization of information that the sentence conveys is also organized differently in the Outer and Expanding Circle varieties of English. This is obvious if we look at the devices utilized for expressing **focus** and **theme**.

Focus and theme. In the Inner Circle varieties of English, usually, the initial element in the sentence in the unmarked case signals the theme (the item being talked about), and the element that follows the main verb is in focus (information of interest about the item being talked about), e.g. in the following exchange, the italicized element is the theme, and the element in bold letters is the focus in the context of the question:

38. Q: Where did Sue go yesterday?
    A: *She* went to **the beach**.

In (38) "Sue's going somewhere" is being talked about, "the beach" represents the information of interest about Sue's destination.

In several of the Outer and Expanding Circle varieties, these conventions of signaling the theme and the focus are not utilized. Consider, for example, the sentences in 39 from different varieties:

39. a. Certain medicine we don'(t) stock in our dispensary.
    b. One subject they pay for seven dollars.
    c. And weekend you can spend with your brother.
    d. My daughter she is attending the University of Nairobi.
    e. Tswana, I learnt it in Pretoria.
    f. Me I am going to sleep.

Example sentences (39a–b) are from SME (Platt and Weber, 1980, p.73), sentence (39c) is from IE (Gumperz, 1982b, p. 34), sentence (39d) is from African English (Bokamba, 1982, p. 83), sentence (39e) is from South African Black English (Mesthrie, 1997, p. 127), and sentence (39f) is from Zambian English (Tripathi, 1990, p. 37). The front-shifting of direct object (in 39a) and prepositional object (in 39b) is for focusing. In (39c), the front-shifting seems to be for the purpose of definitization (Gumperz, 1982b, p. 34), which is consistent with thematization. The front-shifting in (39d–f) are for thematic purposes. Thematization or topicalization is widespread in the Outer and Expanding Circle Englishes. In all these varieties, the device of front-shifting is utilized both for thematization and focusing or emphasis.

CONCLUSION

Many more areas of English grammar can be more fully explored, and many more examples of use in the Outer and Expanding Circle varieties can be extracted from the published literature, but these few examples are sufficient to establish the fact the speakers of different varieties use English differently. The processes that lead to grammatical differences are aspects of acculturation and nativization of the language to express the meanings the users intend to convey. English can be said to be as much an Asian or an African language now as it is American, Australian, or British. In other words, English belongs to those who use it (Bautista, 1997; B. Kachru, 1997c; Newbrook, 1999; Said and Ng, 2000). This fact has to be appreciated before any progress can be made in the direction of successful crosscultural communication through English in the Three Circles.

Further Reading

Baumgardner, R. J. (ed.) (1996) *South Asian English: Structure, Use, and Users.* Urbana, IL: University of Illinois Press.
Bautista, Ma. L. S. (2000) *Defining Standard Philippine English: Its Status and Grammatical Features.* Manila: De LaSalle University Press.
Bolton, K. (2002) Chinese Englishes: From Canton jargon to global English. *World Englishes,* 21(2), 181–199.
Gough, D. (1996) Black English in South Africa. In V. de Klerk (ed.), *Focus on South Africa* (pp. 53–77). Amsterdam: John Benjamins.
McArthur, T. (1998) *The English Languages.* Cambridge: Cambridge University Press.

Suggested Activities

1. Watch *The Story of English,* part 4, from the beginning to 0465. Discuss how Scottish is different from British/American English.
2. Watch *The Story of English,* part 5. Discuss what Dillard says about the influence of Black English Vernacular on American English.
3. Watch *The Story of English,* part 7. Discuss the characteristics of Australian English.
4. Watch *The Story of English,* part 1, and discuss some/all of the world varieties of English represented in the episode.
5. Select readings from any two or more sets of English newspapers/magazines published in India, Japan, Malaysia, People's Republic of China, Singapore, Thailand, and other countries and note down any differences you notice in the use of articles, plural forms, verb tenses, prepositions, etc.
6. Collect instructions that come with products (cameras, computers, etc.) regarding their use from various countries (e.g. Japan, South Korea, Taiwan). Notice and discuss the English used in such texts.

Chapter 7

Words and Collocations

INTRODUCTION

In Chapter 6, it was mentioned that some of the characteristics of Outer and Expanding Circle varieties reflect the physical, social, and cultural contexts as well as the impact of language contact in their regions. The same is true of the lexicon or vocabulary of the Englishes used in the Asian contexts. Just as American English had to find words to talk about the various locational and sociocultural facts of the new world, Chinese, Indian, Japanese, Philippine, and Singaporean Englishes had to do the same in their respective sites. The Inner, Outer, and Expanding Circle English lexicons thus show variation just as their phonological and grammatical structures do.

In some Englishes, there has been a long tradition of compilation of vocabularies. For instance, Indian English lexicography goes back to the beginning of the nineteenth century and is comparable to the beginnings of American dictionary-making efforts (see B. Kachru, 2005b), though it is true that there is nothing comparable to the Webster's in any of the Outer or Expanding Circle varieties as yet (see, however, Cruz and Bautista, 1995; Lewis, 1991; Rao, 1954; Yule and Burnell, 1886). Currently, there are projects that aim at filling this gap, for instance, Southeast Asian and South Asian Regional Dictionary project described in Butler (1996, 1997a, 1997b), and projects described in Bautista (1996, 1997) and Pakir (1992). There are dictionaries, however, of South African and Caribbean Englishes that are comparable to Australian, Canadian, and New Zealand English dictionaries (e.g. Allison, 1996; Allsopp, 1996; Allsopp and Allsopp, 1996; Branford, 1978; Cassidy and LePage, 2003; Holm and Shilling 1982; Silva *et al.*, 1996; Winford, 1991).

One important fact that has to be kept in mind is that dictionaries, like grammars, are crucial in the description, codification, and standardization of language. That may not be the motivating factor of those who compile dictionaries or write grammars, but once a dictionary or a grammar comes into existence, one of the uses people make of it is to check their own or others' use of words or sentence patterns against the examples included in the dictionary or grammar. Dictionaries and grammars thus essentially become prescriptive in some sense though they may have been meant to be merely descriptive, and they also embody ideologies that may not always be evident (B. Kachru and Kahane, 1995; McArthur, 1986).

Butler (1997a) exemplifies the conflict between description vs. prescription in the context of dictionary making by suggesting that it should mirror the usage of a community in some broad sense, that is, if words are in widespread current use in some segment(s) of a community, it is not reasonable to leave them out. Instances of such listings are racist terms (such as "chink," "macaca," "nacho," "nigger"), which are definitely offensive to many segments of the community, but which nevertheless form part of the vocabulary in use in the wider community.

Another example comes from pronunciation in Australian English where the real effect of a dictionary is to provide support and assurance to people who may appeal to it for guidance. Such community "consensus" rules out the Australian pronunciation "filum," for *film*: Butler (1997a, p. 91) observes that the pronunciation "filum" will not be accepted as legitimate by Australian English speakers, at least not anytime soon.

ISSUES IN COMPILING DICTIONARIES

In the Outer and Expanding Circles, where external standards are in competition with the internal usages, the "right of a word" to be listed in the dictionary assumes importance (Butler, 1997a, p. 92). The assumption is that if a dictionary is a faithful recording of the usage of a community, then that "right" to be listed in the dictionary as a legitimate item is assigned by the range and depth of occurrence of a given word. However, the real problem arises in determining the range and depth of occurrence of a given word, especially in situations where users can be torn between two standards—a codified, well-established, external standard and a poorly documented, de facto, internal standard. In such situations, the "de facto" forms are not usually recognized by the sorts of people who might be expected to use a dictionary.

An interesting example is provided by Australia, where a dictionary of Australian English is a more recent development. Butler (1996) reports that *The Macquarie Dictionary* (1981) "presented in a very tangible form an image of the wholeness of Australian English," and that as a direct consequence the "false dichotomy" between "the Queen's English" and "Aussie slang" quickly disappeared.

THE ASIAN CONTEXT

Asian ELT professionals rely on American and British dictionaries of English such as Longman's, Merriam-Webster's, and Oxford. The teachers and learners are used to norms presented in these dictionaries and as mature users of the language, they rely on their prior experience. However, they are also aware of the local norms of usage and are familiar with words and expressions that even highly educated people in their own community use regularly. These local words and expressions, of course, are not always listed in the dictionaries they are familiar with. The dilemma that they face is whether to consider the local items legitimate and acceptable in educated English.

One way of deciding what is legitimate and acceptable is to follow the suggestion (Butler, 1997a) that local items that occur frequently in a wide range of domains and are used by speakers of all educational levels are legitimate and acceptable in that local variety of English. For instance, items such as *salvage* ("to kill in cold blood") and *studentry* "the student body" (Bautista, 1996) are part of Philippine English; *follow* "to accompany" and *weekend cars* "cars which can be driven only after 7 pm and before 7 am on weekdays, after 1 pm on Saturdays and the whole of Sundays and public holidays" (Ho, 1992) are in the lexicon of Singapore English; *boy* "waiter," *lathi-charge* "charge with baton by the police," and *cousin sister/brother* are part of Indian English (B. Kachru, 1983a).

There are, of course, items that are used by those who have minimal competence in English in the Outer and Expanding Circle contexts. Various conceptualizations have been adopted in the case of the variants in a particular variety that are sub-standard or non-standard. For example, some researchers have talked about a *lectal* range (e.g. Platt, 1977; Platt and Weber, 1980) and others have discussed a *cline* of bilingualism in English (e.g. B. Kachru, 1983b; Pakir 1991; Bamgbose, 1982). Platt and Weber (1980) describe three reference points on a continuum in the context of Singapore English: acrolect (educated variety), mesolect (colloquial), and basilect (uneducated non-standard). In the realm of cline of bilingualism, one end of the cline represents the educated variety whereas at the other end are varieties such as Nigerian Pidgin (Bamiro, 1991), *basilect* in Singapore (Lowenberg, 1991; Platt and Weber, 1980; Pakir, 1991), and *bazaar* English or *butler* English in India (B. Kachru, 1983a, 1994b; Hosali and Aitchison, 1986). Items that occur exclusively at the lower end of the cline or the lectal range may be excluded from the dictionary.

In addition to the above, there are items that occur infrequently, e.g. in literary texts in specific contexts. It has not been customary to consider such items worth listing in dictionaries (see Pakir, 1992 for discussions of these considerations in the context of Singapore English).

On the other hand, there are items that have restricted use, that is, they are used in specific registers. Good examples are items such as the following in Indian English: *collector* (in the administrative register for a government official who is responsible for revenue collection in a district), *sacred thread* (in the context of caste), *Vedanta* (a system of philosophy), and *satyagraha* "passive resistance" (political register). Such specialized terms which are widely used in their respective domains are normally included in any dictionary of the relevant variety.

Familiar items from "mother" (Inner Circle) English have undergone changes in the Other Circle varieties, e.g. *salvage* in Philippine English and *follow* in Singapore English. Items change their grammatical categorization, too, as is evident from the extensive use of collective nouns as countable in almost all Outer Circle varieties. Forms such as *furnitures, equipments, informations,* and *evidences* are attested in African, Philippine, Singapore, South Asian, and Southeast Asian varieties. As there is still a lingering resistance to indigenous norms in many parts of the English-using world, there is uneasiness about such "ungrammatical" usages. However, as Lowenberg (1992) has shown, Inner Circle Englishes are not always consistent in the treatment of collective nouns, either. The whole notion of countability is not very well grammaticized in English anyway, as has been demonstrated in Chapter 6.

PROCESSES OF NATIVIZATION

People in Africa, Asia, and other parts of the world often need to express themselves through the medium of English. Inner Circle Englishes, such as American and British, are not always adequate for such purposes. Words may be adapted to convey some meanings, but there are concepts that are not lexicalized in English. For example, class distinctions exist in Inner Circle English-speaking societies, but there is no institution comparable to caste. Meanings that need to be expressed in local contexts demand the nativization of English. Early examples of this process can be seen in British English as used by the British in India, and American English as it developed in North America. The British imported items such as *shampoo, chintz, brahmin, sacred cow,* and other items into the English language to represent new objects and concepts as a result of contact with India. In order to use English in the changed context of the North American continent, a large number of items were adopted from various sources in American English, including Native

American, Chinese, French, German, and Spanish (Mencken, 1936). Now, items such as *cayote, prairie, bayou, depot, canyon, corral, tornado, frankfurter, hamburger, kowtow,* and others are an integral part of American English and are a testimony to the acculturation of the language in the new context.

The examples cited above make it clear that borrowing items from an indigenous source language is one device that is used for nativization of a language in a new situation. Thus, Indian English has a sizable vocabulary borrowed from Indian languages, Singaporean English from Chinese and Malay, Philippine English from Tagalog and other local languages, Nigerian English from Yoruba, Igbo, and others, and so on. Such borrowings are not restricted only to items such as nouns, verbs, adjectives, etc. Rather, items that signal interactional meanings in conversational exchange and others that play a role in discourse may also be borrowed. One good example is that of the particle *la* in Singaporean-Malyasian English (Chan, 1991; Pakir, 1992; Platt and Ho, 1989; Wilma, 1987). Pakir (1992, p. 149) suggests the following tentative definition and usage note for the particle:

> Definition: Impossible at this point. Pragmatic meanings include code-marking, emotive-marking, contrast marking. It serves the functions of conveying obviousness, softening the harshness of an imperative or an explanation, dismissing the importance of an item on a list, deflecting compliments, etc.
> Etymology: Chinese languages found in Singapore, and Malay.
> Usage note: Use of *la* would indicate that solidarity and familiarity levels are high. All speakers of SgE use *la* in their informal conversation.

One other process is that of loan translation, i.e. translation of a local concept using English items, e.g. *chewing stick* for a twig that is chewed up at one end and used as a brush to clean one's teeth in African English (Bokamba, 1992, p. 137) or *sacred thread* "thread worn diagonally across the chest to signify initiation into adulthood by higher caste men" in Indian English.

As the above examples show, loan translations may lead to new collocations unfamiliar to Inner Circle users of English. New collocations occur even when no loan translation is involved; they are needed simply to express something that is novel from the perspective of the Inner Circle. African English has compounds such as *small room* "toilet" (Sey, 1973), *head-tie* "woman's head dress" (Bamgboṣe, 1992), and *bush meat* "game" (Bokamba, 1992); Indian English has items such as *dining leaf* "banana, lotus or other leaves that are used as disposable plates," *communal dining* "eating with people of different religious groups," *love marriage* "marrying someone of one's own choice as opposed to someone chosen by the family," and *pin drop silence* "silence so profound one can hear a pin drop" (B. Kachru, 1983b).

Lexical items that are used in rather restricted meanings in Inner Circle English acquire a wider semantic range in Outer and Expanding Circle

Englishes. This is especially true of kinship terms. In African Englishes (e.g. Zambian), *father* is not restricted to one's biological male parent but may be used for father's older brother, too (Tripathi, 1990). *Uncle, aunt, brother, sister, mother, grandmother,* and *grandfather* are used widely as terms of address to express solidarity or respect in many Englishes. That is why one comes across expressions such as the following in African Englishes: *I went to see my sister,* **same father same mother** (Chisanga, 1987, p. 190, quoted in Kamwangamalu, 2001, p. 53), and *My aunt Gladys, who is my father's* **womb-sister** . . . *The next minute he was drowned in a sea of belonging to uncles, aunts* . . . **brothers and sisters of the womb and not of the womb** (Dangaremgba, 1988, pp. 35–36, quoted in Kamwangamalu, 2001, p. 53). Some familiar vocabulary items acquire the opposite characteristic—they are used in a more restricted sense. The adjective *communal* has acquired a very special meaning in IE; it is used only in the context of religious communities.

Many words go through change in meaning in one variety such that users of other varieties may not understand them. For instance, in Nigerian English *travel* means to be away (Bamgboṣe, 1992), in Zambian English, *footing* means "walking" (Tripathi, 1990), in Cameroon English, *convocation* means "summons" (Simo-Bobda, 1994b), in Ghanian English, *hot drinks* means alcoholic drinks, and in Indian English, *bunglow* means a rather large one-story dwelling.

Many words change their membership in grammatical categories, e.g. adjectives used as verbs with verbal inflections: *Your behavior* **tantamounts** *to insubordination* or *It* **doesn't worth** *the price* (Gyasi, 1991).

In addition, most Englishes have new items that have been coined for various local purposes. Users of English in Singapore and Malaysia may characterize one as *actsy* "conceited, proud" (Butler, 1997a); in African English one may talk about *destooling* "removing from a position of power" a dictator; *detach* someone to indicate to second some official to another department; in Philippine English one may disapprove of someone's *blue-seal* "foreign girlfriend"; in Indian English a college student may boast of his/her *fight* meaning (s)he gave something his/her best shot.

Productive derivational processes may be used in ways that are not attested in Inner Circle Englishes, e.g. *installment* and *instalmentally* in Cameroon English or *prepone* in South Asian English. Compounding in novel ways is also very productive, e.g. *downpress* "oppress," *overstand* "understand" in Jamaican Rasta talk (Patrick, 1997, p. 49), *grey area* "area where people of all races live or work," and *Old Year's night* "New Year's Eve" in South African English (Silva, 1997, p. 171).

Increasingly most varieties use their own characteristic abbreviations, at least in speech, that are hard to process across varieties. Singapore-Malaysian Englishes have items such as *air con* "air conditioning," Philippine and Indian English have items such as *funda* "fundamental," Indian English has *chooch* "scooter, a three wheel motorized vehicle for passenger transportation," and Australian English has *mozzie* "mosquito," *pollie* "politician," and *footie* "football."

New idioms and metaphors are created not only by the creative writers but also in everyday speech in the multilingual contexts of Englishes. In Ghanaian English one says *Give me chance/way* in contexts where in American or British English one says *Excuse me* (e.g. in a narrow passage where people are crowded and one has to make one's way through them). In South Asian Englishes, one talks of *blackening one's face* to mean "suffer disgrace" and *sit on someone's head* to signal "to get someone to do something by persistence." In South African English one hears *I wrote it down in my head* to indicate "I made a mental note of it" and *Snakes started playing mini soccer in my spine* to signal "I became very excited." The expressions *beat someone with a cooking stick* means "to feed someone" and *to step with fur* means "to tread carefully" (Kamwangamalu, 2001).

Some metaphorical expressions lead to a highly creative process of giving rise to a large number of collocations, e.g. in South African English, the indigenous item *indaba* "a serious meeting involving community leaders" collocates with English nouns and yields compounds such as *indaba bid*, *indaba presentation*, *indaba gurus*, *bush indaba*, *education indaba*, and *diversity indaba*. The English item rainbow, having been reinterpreted to signal "the coming together of people from previously segregated groups" or "something that affects or benefits these people" yields collocations such as *rainbow nation*, *rainbow complacency*, *rainbow swimming pool*, *rainbow blanket*, *rainbow circle*, *rainbow gathering*, *rainbow-nation school*, *rainbow alienation*, *rainbow hand*, and *rainbow warrior*.

CONSIDERATIONS IN COMPILING REGIONAL DICTIONARIES

As most Englishes slowly drift toward an endonormative standard, the issues of grammars and dictionaries for such varieties become urgent for several reasons.

One major question related to that of education is: what should the teachers teach and learners acquire in school? In the absence of grammars and dictionaries of varieties, they have to rely on descriptions and dictionaries of American, Australian (to a lesser extent), or British English. Then there are the needs of professionals (including writers, journalists, and government officials) who may wish to consult a grammar or a dictionary to double-check the syntax or spelling of an item.

The Macquarie Dictionary is currently engaged in gathering corpora and devising criteria for inclusion or exclusion of vocabulary items for Southeast Asia and South Asia (Butler, 1997a). The criteria include occurrence in the corpus, frequency of an item, and opinion of local experts with regard to the item's status, i.e. is it used in "standard" regional English—both formal and informal—or is it restricted to informal colloquial language use only? The source materials on Asian Englishes in the ASIACORP being compiled include published texts for the local, not international, readers and they include mainly newspapers, some fiction and non-fiction, and some translated fiction. The aim is to produce a dictionary of about 50,000 entries with perhaps 150,000 lexical items to be of use to the average educated user of English in South and Southeast Asia. The educated speaker, of course, includes both mature users with high competency to students with limited competence. The dictionary does not aim to include all local usages, and be fully representative of all variation within a local variety even within a small geographical area, e.g. Singaporean English.

CONCLUSION

In some sense, vocabulary is the least important aspect of linguistic structure—it is not systematic in the sense that sounds or grammatical patterns are.

Nevertheless, words pack in the most expressive power of the language (for theoretical considerations in compiling a dictionary, see, Zgusta, 1980). If we just think of words such as *see, look, glance, gaze, stare, peep,* and *visualize,* it becomes clear how each one signals a different set of meanings not only in terms of what it literally indicates but what it conveys by way of speaker attitudes and intentions and the reaction each may produce in the hearer. It is no wonder in the varied contexts of Outer and Expanding Circles, world Englishes are creating varied lexical items, metaphors, and idioms to convey various meanings new to the Inner Circle Englishes (see, e.g. Dubey 1991 for characteristic use of vocabulary in Indian English newspapers). The processes described above represent one important aspect of the acculturation and nativization of English in the Other Circles. Regional dictionaries that list representative words from world Englishes will be of immense value to ensure successful communication across varieties.

Further Reading

Bautista, Ma. L. S. (1997a) The lexicon of Philippine English. In Ma. L. S. Bautista (ed.), *English Is an Asian language: The Philippine Context* (pp. 49–72). Sydney, Australia: Macquarie Library Pty Ltd.

Butler, S. (1997) World English in the Asian context: why a dictionary is important. In L. E. Smith and M. L. Forman (eds), *World Englishes 2000* (pp. 90–125). Honolulu: University of Hawaii Press.

Görlach, M. (1991) Lexicographical problems of new Englishes. In M. Görlach (ed.), *Englishes: Studies in Varieties of English 1984–1988* (pp. 36–68). Amsterdam and Philadelphia: John Benjamin.

Leitner, G. and Sieloff, I. (1998) Aboriginal words and concepts in Australian English. *World Englishes*, 17(2), 153–169.

Suggested Activities

1. Look up local news, classifieds, interviews with politicians and public figures, and letters to Editors published in newspapers of either your country/region or one of the Outer Circle countries (e.g. India, Nigeria, Singapore). Are there words that are not part of the "standard" variety of English used in your country/region? Are they listed in any dictionary? Under which conditions would you include them in English teaching materials used in your country/region?

2. a. Administer a questionnaire such as the following to participants in English language classes in your institution (college or university) to see how the items in the questionnaire are characterized by them. b. Depending upon the responses you get, write a brief description of the grammar of nouns in this variety, i.e. how nouns are classified in terms of the property of countability.

Questionnaire

Please answer the following questions in conjunction with the table on page 112:

Are the following well formed in your variety of English? If not, how would you change them to conform to your standards of grammatical sentences?

TABLE 7.1
Questionnaire

Sentence	Well formed	Not well formed	Corrected form
1. We bought some furnitures and are waiting for them to arrive.			
2. The chemistry lab needs more equipments than we have.			
3. When we arrived in New York from Bangkok, our luggages were missing.			
4. What evidences do they have that Bob is guilty?			
5. She gave Peter a good advice.			
6. His family are all very well educated.			
7. The Board of Trustees of our University decided that they will meet every month.			
8. The Working Committee are of the opinion that the party should start a movement to organize the workers.			

CONVERSATIONAL AND WRITING STYLES

INTRODUCTION

Part III of the book builds on the background information imparted in Chapters 1 through 7. Now that the readers are familiar with the spread and functions of English across languages and cultures and the resultant variation in grammatical structure of the language, it is reasonable to explore the areas and modes of language use.

Effective communication requires **competence** in language and **capacity** to utilize linguistic competence in expressing one's intended meaning (Widdowson, 1984). In this part of the book, we focus on how the capacity to use English in the oral and written modes differs across cultures. In Chapter 8, the focus is on conversation; in Chapter 9, on personal and business letters, and on expository and argumentative prose; and in Chapter 10, on creative literature.

It has already been pointed out that in many parts of the world, English is only one code in the linguistic repertoire of the local speech communities. It is, therefore, not used in all the functions that it is assigned in those communities where English is the only code. Nevertheless, in almost all parts of the world, English is used in the spoken as well as written modes, and for purposes that range from informal conversational interaction to formal diplomatic and commercial negotiations in the spoken mode, and from personal letters to various specialized genres in the written mode.

CONVERSATION

Conversational interactions in different varieties of English display different styles depending upon the sociocultural context in which they take place. In the multilingual and multicultural context of Outer and Expanding Circle varieties, English is used in conversational interactions in ways that do not meet with the expectations of the speakers of the Inner Circle varieties. The concepts that are necessary to discuss patterns of conversational interaction in the Outer and Expanding Circle varieties are discussed in some detail in Chapter 8. Concepts necessary to describe the styles of interaction through the written mode are dealt with in subsequent chapters (see Chapters 9 and 10).

WRITING

In many parts of the world, English is used not only in the spoken mode, but also in the written mode. It is true that written language is sometimes used for conveying factual information rather than for interaction. It cannot, however, be claimed that the written mode is not used for interactional purposes. An important function of personal letters, e-mail, and fax, for example, is interactional, although letters may convey factual information also. All writing may be claimed to be interactional; exposition, argumentation, persuasion, all presuppose addressee(s) who need to be informed, convinced, and persuaded.

Most of our discussion of the characteristics of the Outer and Expanding Circle varieties has so far focused on the spoken mode. However, a great deal of interaction between and among those who use English as a first language and those who use it as a second or additional language is carried on through the written mode. The domains in which writing is crucial include diplomacy, business, commerce, and cultural exchange. It is, therefore, not only useful but important to look at the nature of written communication in the Outer and Expanding Circle varieties, too.

SPOKEN VS. WRITTEN LANGUAGE

There are some obvious differences between spoken and written languages, and these have been the focus of a great deal of research (see, e.g. Chafe, 1982; Ochs, 1979, among others). In speech, rhythmic patterns and non-linguistic cues (e.g. gestures, body postures, tone of voice, etc.) provide as much information as the spoken words themselves. Also, as compared to spoken language, especially conversation, there is more time to plan what one wishes to say in writing. There are some non-linguistic cues that may be utilized in written communication as well, e.g. the color of the paper, ink, and envelope in letter writing, use of different type-faces, punctuation, icons, etc. in printing. However, written communication largely depends on the structure of the text and the use of language itself. As such, there is very little opportunity for "repair" (i.e. providing more information to make speaker intentions clear; Schegloff, 1979), especially because the writer and the reader of the text generally do not occupy the same time and space.

This has consequences for the use of language. In speech, there are false starts, hesitations, repetitions, etc. In the written mode, all these are usually edited out (see, however, Tannen, 1989 for instances of stylistic use of repetition in literary English). In speech, very many less precise expressions are used (e.g. *thing, sort, stuff*); in writing, there is greater pressure for precision. In speech, some meanings may be conveyed by pointing or glancing or by other devices, in writing, referential, sequential, and other linguistic relationships are conveyed by using explicit markers such as defining modifiers and linkers (cf. *I like this one* vs. *I like the white car with the blue interior; His car broke down, he can't come* vs. *His car broke down, therefore, he can't come*).

As in speech, reader expectations in terms of "cues" for interpretation are crucial in written communication; a failure to meet these expectations results in judgments of "incoherence," "fuzzy thinking," "lack of competence in the language," and so on. Whereas a speaker gets some feedback from his/her audience, a writer has no means of observing reader reactions. Consequently, the writer has to judge accurately what reader expectations have to be satisfied in order to achieve successful communication. It is worth remembering, however, that reader expectations may differ from culture to culture and from genre to genre (Hinds, 1987). This point is discussed in greater detail in Chapter 9. One advantage that a writer has over a speaker is the following: a speaker cannot help revealing, at least partially, his/her own feelings, attitudes, etc., but a writer does not necessarily have to be in that position.

TEXT TYPES

The Inner Circle varieties of English have developed a number of genres over a period of time. These include the familiar literary genres such as lyrics, novels, plays, literary criticism, etc., and the genres of legal, scientific, and technical writing of various types. In the Outer/Expanding Circle varieties of English, many genres have developed over a shorter span of time and in a multilingual and multicultural situation. The development of genres is related to the issue of literacy and its role in society.

In different literate cultures, different domains have been assigned to the spoken vs. the written mode. For instance, invitations for weddings, etc. are generally conveyed through writing in Western culture(s). In several cultures, including those of South Asia, invitations have to be, if at all possible, conveyed in person. Where circumstances prevent such personal contact, the written invitation should carry suitable phrasing to express the regret the person(s) extending the invitation feel(s) for their inability to do so. Thus, a wedding invitation sent by a relative from India to a person residing in the USA, for example, will end with a sentence such as "Please forgive me (us) for my (our) inability to extend this invitation in person."

In literate as well as non-literate cultures, different genres have developed with characteristic patterns of language use. These genres are generally well known to the users of the language. For instance, it takes very little effort to identify a sermon as opposed to a political speech in English. Similarly, in non-literate cultures, religious chants have very different characteristics as compared to folk songs. We, however, do not have a complete inventory of all the genres and their characteristics in all the cultures. As such, crosscultural comparison of speaking and writing conventions is still at a beginning stage.

INTERACTIONAL VS. TRANSACTIONAL TEXT

It is not our aim to discuss different text types in detail here. For our purposes, it is useful to distinguish three text types: interactional, transactional, and imaginative. The first two terms are from Brown and Yule (1983, p. 1). In interactional, we focus on letters and e-mail messages, both personal and business, and in transactional, we concentrate on the properties of expository and argumentative prose (Chapter 9). This selection is not haphazard; these are two very important text types, crucial for crosscultural communication through English. This, however, does not mean that the boundaries between interactional and transactional text types are equally clearly marked in all cultures, or in all contexts in the same culture. This will become clear when we discuss conventions of letter writing in Chapter 9. Imaginative texts deserve separate treatment, though, as mentioned before, the boundaries between text types are not watertight.

IMAGINATIVE TEXT

There is a long tradition of creative writing in the Outer Circle varieties of English. This body of writing has already been utilized in describing language variation, language contact, and the impact of culture on language (B.

Kachru, 1983a, 1992; Smith, 1981, 1987; Smith and Forman, 1997; Thumboo, 1992, among others). Attempts have also been made to demonstrate how this body of literature could be utilized for raising awareness of cultural interactional patterns in educating teachers and teacher trainees of English (e.g. Nelson, 1985; Tawake, 1993, 1995). Chapter 10 addresses these topics in some detail.

Chapter 8

Conversational Interaction

INTRODUCTION

Conversation is an activity relevant to all domains of human interaction. It is through conversation that social structure is instituted and maintained, and humans enact their social roles through conversation more than any other behavior. It is not very surprising that conversation analysis as a subfield of research had its beginnings in the works of sociologists, who established that conversation, in turn, has its own structure.

In order to describe the structure of conversation in the Outer and Expanding Circle varieties of English, we need a vocabulary to refer to activities that take place in face-to-face verbal interaction. We discuss the required concepts first; subsequently, we point out some of the observed crosscultural differences in the organization of conversation.

Two types of activities take place in conversation: the first relates to how the interaction is managed; the second relates to what is being conveyed or negotiated between the participants. The first has been termed interactive acts (Widdowson, 1979, p. 138). The second type of activity involves those aspects of conversational interaction that are discussed under the notions of speech acts, the Gricean cooperative principle, and politeness as discussed in Chapter 2. All these are relevant to a discussion of conversational styles in the new varieties of English. In addition, issues of identity play a major role in any interaction that involves participants from varied backgrounds.

ORGANIZATION OF CONVERSATIONAL INTERACTION

When two people engage in a conversation, both do not usually speak at the same time. Normally, first one speaks and then the other. This way of organizing speaking has been called "turn-taking" (Duncan and Fiske, 1977). Schegloff (1968, p. 1076) describes the general rule of conversational exchange in American English as "one party at a time." Normally, when a speaker completes a "turn," (s)he indicates the completion by displaying a "turn signal," which is accomplished through the occurrence of "cues" (Duncan, 1980, p. 69) such as intonation, the utterance of expressions such as "you know," "or something," etc., termination of a gesture, a lengthening of the final syllable, or a stressed syllable in the last part of the utterance, etc.

Another concept useful in describing conversation is that of "floor" (Edelsky, 1981). Floor refers to the right to begin to talk, or make a first statement. Turn-taking mechanisms determine when the next speaker takes the floor in a conversational exchange. Floor has some duration in an interaction and is related to topical content, so that normally the floor is occupied by the participant who controls the topic. The participant who initiates and continues to talk about the topic of conversation has the primary floor, and others, who may contribute to subtopics within the conversation, have the secondary floor (Edelsky, 1981). Speakers utilize sets of specific devices and strategies to gain the right to speak (or, to acquire the floor), hold onto their turn in order to talk about the topic or subtopic of their speech (or, to maintain the floor), and signal to their conversational partner to take his/her turn (or, to relinquish the floor).

While one participant speaks, the other participant usually indicates that (s)he is attending to the speaker's utterances by giving backchannel (Yngve, 1970) cues such as "uh-huh," "yeah", "right," etc. Some backchannel cues overlap with a speaker's turn, others signal as "moves" by functioning as requests for turn, and thereby interrupt the current speaker's turn. This happens in some situations. In other situations, however, more than one participant engages in simultaneous talk without causing any interruption and discomfort in face-to-face interaction. In addition to signaling attention, backchannel cues encourage the speaker to continue to speak by indicating that (s)he still has the floor (see pp. 122–123).

Conventions of turn-taking, frequency of and overlap in backchannel cues, simultaneous talk, and acquiring, maintaining, and relinquishing the floor, all differ from culture to culture, and are being investigated. We will look at some of these differences in the following pages.

CROSSCULTURAL DIFFERENCES

Every language and culture has particular conventions, characteristic sets of strategies, and specific devices for the management of conversational interaction (see, Valentine, 1988, 1991, 1995, 2001 for such strategies and devices in Indian English). These, as they relate to speech acts, Gricean maxims of cooperation, and notions of politeness, were discussed in Chapter 2. They also involve patterns of turn-taking, acquiring, maintaining, and relinquishing the floor, giving backchannel cues, interrupting a speaker or talking simultaneously, and other aspects of interaction management. Since speech acts, Gricean maxims, and politeness have already been discussed in some detail in Chapter 2, we will focus on the organization and management of conversation here.

Turn

The term *turn* indicates both the opportunity to assume the role of speaker and what is said by him/her as a speaker (Schegloff, 1968; Schegloff and Sacks, 1973). Sacks *et al.* (1974) propose a system of turn-taking in conversation that regulates conversational exchanges.

It has already been mentioned (see p. 120) that the convention regarding turn-taking in American English is "one party at a time." This is true of the British and other Inner Circle varieties of English in general. Children are taught not to interrupt and wait for their turn to speak in multi-party conversations even within the family domain. In some speech communities, such as the Hindi speech community in India, the Japanese speech community, and some communities in the Middle East and Eastern Europe, the "one party at a time" rule does not hold. In conversations where more than two participants are involved, the turn-taking behavior is not rigid. Interruptions and simultaneous talk may be quite common in these situations. This is discussed in greater detail on pp. 123–125.

Floor

Sacks (1972) defines *floor* as a *ticket*, a right to make a first statement during a conversation. Edelsky (1981) points out the distinction between a turn and a floor by demonstrating that a turn may not constitute a floor, as in the following example:

A: Did you hear the news?
B: What?
C: Bill is back in town!

In the above exchange, B takes a turn, but not the floor, which still belongs to A, who maintains it in the third line. Other researchers who have contributed to the development of the concept are Erickson (1982), who demonstrates the close relationship between floor and topic of conversation, and Philips (1983) and Tannen (1981), in addition to Erickson, who point out the socioculturally patterned ways of floor allocation.

Hayashi (1988, p. 273), building on this body of research, defines the concept of floor "with respect to: (1) who is orienting his/her attention to the on-going conversational content, (2) who the central figure(s) of the on-going conversation is/are, and (3) to whom and where the communicative territory belongs." Hayashi (1991) further claims that floor is not static, it is constructed creatively in mutual interaction by participants in conversation and thus is part of their communicative competence.

There are conventions regarding who can initiate the topic of conversation, who can join or leave an ongoing conversational interaction, demand the floor or grab the floor, and who must yield or relinquish the floor. It has been observed in American English cross-sex conversations that men are more successful in initiating and maintaining topics than women, and men also tend to demand the floor more frequently than women (Fishman, 1983). In conversations between age-different participants in India, the older participants have the right to initiate conversation, maintain the floor, and yield the floor. Any attempt to interrupt or demand the floor on part of a younger participant is considered rude and insulting behavior. In traditional Western European communities, children were admonished that they were meant to be seen, not heard. In many cultures, in certain contexts, only older males have the right to speak, and therefore, they initiate, maintain, and control the floor.

It is not always necessary for any (segment of a) conversation to have a single floor. In most conversational interactions, several speakers create and maintain a collaborative floor. In conversation involving many participants, there may be more than one floor at the same time and different participants may move in and out while making their contributions to them.

Backchannel

Backchannel is an important device in maintaining the flow of conversation. The backchannel cues signal that the listener is attending to the speaker, and additionally, may signal agreement, approval, surprise, etc. Backchannel cues can overlap with a speaker turn and not lead to an interruption. However, the frequency with which such support is given to a conversational partner differs across speech communities. As compared to speakers of American English, Japanese speakers give many more backchannel cues and have a greater number of devices for signaling hearer attentiveness (Hayashi, 1987, 1988; LoCastro, 1987). In a study conducted by White (1989), Japanese dyads used backchannel cues for every 14 words of speech. American dyads used backchannel cues for every 37 words. The most backchannel cues were used by Japanese dyads, followed by the crosscultural dyads, and the least number were used by the American dyads. In addition, the backchannel cues in Japanese, unlike in American English, may last a long time, as long as three to four seconds (Hayashi, 1988).

Speakers of languages that are socialized in the patterns of providing frequent and longer backchannel cues may use the same strategy in interacting with other English speakers, which may be disconcerting to the Inner Circle English speakers. This is true of interaction between Indian and Anglo-American interlocutors, for instance, especially in telephone conversations.

Simultaneous Talk

It has already been mentioned that although backchannel cues overlap with talk, they are not perceived as interruptions. Talk by another participant that overlaps for a considerable period with a current speaker, however, is perceived as an interruption in American and British Englishes. In order to discuss simultaneous talk, we need to discuss rhythmicity and synchronization of talk by different participants briefly.

Rhythmic coordination: This refers to patterning in speech and non-verbal body movements, both within the speaker and between speakers, that participants in conversation exhibit in interaction. Research has shown that a sense of smooth and successful verbal interaction results from the participants' coordination of their rhythmic patterning. Research has also shown that styles of rhythmic patterning and their association with particular kinds of speech activity are culture-specific.

Simultaneous talk does not lead to interruption when the participants in a conversation synchronize their speech and non-verbal motions in the same movement (Erickson, 1982). There may be no way to teach people how to be in sync with each other, but sync behavior is observable and it should be possible to analyze it so that participants can become sensitive to orienting themselves to each other in conversation (Hall, 1984).

Sync talk: One noticeable difference between American and Japanese conversation is the phenomenon of sync talk (Hayashi, 1988). Sync talk is characterized by overlapping speech and synchronized hand movements, head nods, body postures, etc. among the participants in a conversation. All these simultaneous actions are coordinated rhythmically and are in sync (Hayashi, 1988, 1996).

In single floor conversational interaction, there is a marked difference between the American and the Japanese speakers. Americans do not engage in sync talk as frequently as the Japanese do, and even when do, they synchronize in a far less active manner. Their hand movements, head nods, etc. are much less pronounced than the Japanese. According to Hayashi (1988, pp. 280–281):

> A very typical aspect of Japanese conversational interaction is the extraordinary frequency of simultaneous talk. The simultaneous talk varies from one word or phrase to more than two sentences, and the simultaneous talk sometimes involves three or even four people . . . It is often difficult to judge who holds the floor in Japanese casual conversation even if the participants acknowledge that one particular person holds a floor, because the sync phenomenon makes the interaction "floorless" on the surface. The verbal simultaneous talk, however, does not necessarily produce interactional conflict among Japanese participants, especially when other forms of communicative behavior are appropriately in sync, because sync talk creates ensemble and comfortable moments.

In contrast, American speakers tend to avoid overlapping speech and are more conscious of the rule "one speaker at a time." They "tend to direct simultaneous talk into negotiation and competition, while Japanese speakers often convert simultaneous talk into rhythmic sync talk to create ensemble" (Hayashi, 1988, p. 283).

High involvement style. It is important to remember that overlap or simultaneous talk is attested in American English also. Tannen (1984) makes a distinction between a *high involvement style* in which supportive simultaneous talk, skirting of inter-turn pauses, and rapid speech are used as devices to indicate interest and rapport. In contrast, in what she terms high-considerateness style, the rate of speech is slow, interactants wait for their turn, and the end of a turn is signaled by a pause. The latter style does not tolerate simultaneous talk, which is perceived as interruption. Generally, in less intimate domains, Eurocentric cultures tend to perceive simultaneous talk as interruptions and a speaker thus interrupted tends to fall silent out of frustration.

In a recent study, FitzGerald (2003) has posited six different styles of interaction in relation to cultural groupings that are summarized here. She cautions that there were insufficient data for some groups, but feels relatively more comfortable with claims in relation to Eastern European and East and Southeast Asian groupings.

The six styles of interaction according to FitzGerald (2003, pp. 166–169) are as follows:

1. Institutional/Exacting: English-speaking cultures/Northern and Western Europe. In this style, high value is placed on individual

autonomy and non-imposition on others, brevity, explicitness, linearity, and orientation to a definite goal.

2. Spontaneous/Argumentative: Eastern Europe: This style places high value on sincerity, spontaneity, and closeness, therefore it is blunt and direct.

3. Involved/Expressive: Southern Europe/Latin America: This style highly values warm, emotional expressiveness, and concern with according positive face to others, therefore, it is affective and contextual, and tolerates overlap. The interaction is collaborative rather than competitive with overlap and is tangential and digressive in its organization.

4. Elaborate/Dramatic: Middle Eastern: In this style, high value is placed on harmonious relation and positive face, achieved by affective, contextual style stressing form rather than content. The interaction is marked by sweeping generalizations, overgeneralizations, dramatic embellishment, expressive metaphors, rhythmical repetition of words, and parallel structure to persuade others, which is the main purpose of communication.

5. Bureaucratic/Contextual: South Asian: High value is placed on harmonious relations and positive face; the interaction is marked by affective, contextual style, taking turns with formal bureaucratic language, repetition, and preference for inductive organization. Normally both sides of an issue are considered and agreement and disagreement are included in the same turn.

6. Succint/Subdued: East and Southeast Asia: This style highly values harmony, modesty, conformity, and positive face; these are achieved by masking negative emotions and avoiding unpleasantness. The talk is status-oriented, deferential, indirect; and people are expected to infer meanings. The turns are short and talk concise except when inductive organization of information and conciliatory approach is involved. Talk is not highly valued; people feel a great deal of comfort with silence.

Rhetorical Strategies

In addition to the interaction management strategies discussed above, rhetorical strategies, or how what one says is organized, also differ in various Englishes. Young (1982, p. 76) points out the different rhetorical strategies of interaction between American and Chinese interlocutors in professional settings by citing the following example. Following a talk given by a Chinese visiting professor of nutrition from Beijing, an American in the audience raised a question. The following exchange took place:

American: How does the Nutritional Institute decide what topics to study? How do you decide what topic to do research on?

Chinese: **Because**, now, period get change. It's different from past time. In past time, we emphasize how to solve practical problems. Nutrition must know how to solve some deficiency diseases. In our country, we have some nutritional diseases, such as x,y,z. But, now it is important that we must do some basic research. **So**, *we must take into account fundamental problems. We must concentrate our research to study some fundamental research.*

American listeners, and readers of the above transcription of the exchange, usually feel frustrated as they process statements that do not seem to answer the question. The Chinese professor is, of course, following the rhetorical strategy he is familiar with. One must first provide the background, which generally consists of the history of the endeavor, and then slowly unfold the main point of what one is trying to convey. The linkers in bold face above (**Because** and **So**), are the markers of this transition; the statement in italics constitutes the answer to the question, which comes at the end.

Young (1982) has a number of examples of this pattern of interaction in settings related to business and finance; many of these contain both the linkers and most of them contain *so* to mark the transition to the crux of the matter as mentioned above.

Valentine (1995) discusses the strategies used to indicate agreement or disagreement by speakers of Indian English in interaction. She observes that it is unexpected to have a sequence such as *no, . . . but yeah*, which occurs in Indian English data (Valentine, 1995, pp. 243–244; the f preceding A, B, C below indicates a female speaker):

1. fA: Do you think it (wife abuse) is common?
    fB: In India? In rural families this is common.
    fC: **No, it's common.** Very much common even in very literate families.

There are cases where direct disagreement is expressed and is followed by backing down by the previous speaker in the speech of both male and female speakers:

2. fA: So in your family were you treated differently from your brothers in other ways?
    fB: **No, not in other ways, but yeah yes I was.** They didn't allow me.

This strategy is also attested in conversations in Hindi; however, the occurrence of the negative particle *na* in Hindi seems to signal a strategy to indicate confirmation in Hindi rather than that of disagreement.

Items from local languages are transferred into Englishes in various parts of the world not only to designate local objects or concepts, but also to affirm in-group membership and solidarity. The following excerpt from a conversation between two Maori speakers of English illustrates such transfer (Stubbe and Holmes, 1999, pp. 255–256):

> Rewi: Tikitiki//well we're\across the river from there and
> Ngata: /**ae** ["yes"]\\
> Rewi: if we wanted to go to Tikitiki we had to go right around to Ruatoria and
>   back out again
> Ngata: that's right yeah oh well we actually went right around to Ruatoria and
>   down we didn't cross across ++ **te awa rere haere te- too koutou taniwha i
>   teeraa waa** ["the river flowed over the taniwha (a legendary monster which
>   resides in deep water) there"]
> Rewi: in winter **eh**

The use of *ae* to indicate agreement, switch to Maori in Ngata's second turn, and Rewi's use of the particle *eh* to elicit confirmation are all devices that affirm the two interlocutors' in-group membership and solidarity.

Similar strategies are employed by the two Malaysian young women in the following piece of conversation (Baskaran, 1994, p. 28):

> Khadijah: *Eh* Mala, where on earth you went ah? I searching, searching all over
>   the place for you—no sign till one o'clock, so I *pun* got hungry, I went for *makan.*
> Mala: You were *makaning* where? My sister, she said she saw you near Globes—
>   when we were searching for parking space. . . . Went roun(d) and roun(d)
>   nearly six times *pun* [also], no place. That's why so late *lah!*
> Khadijah: So you ate or not?
> Mala: Not yet *lah*—just nibbled some "kari paps" [curry puffs] at about eleven,
>   so not really hungry.

There are several items from the Malay language in the above excerpt; the particles *eh* and *lah* are especially noteworthy as they perform several functions in SME (see the discussion in, e.g. Pakir, 1992; Platt and Ho, 1989; Wong, 2004).

IMPLICATIONS FOR CROSSCULTURAL CONVERSATION

Since rhythmicity in interaction is acquired within the context of one's own culture, it is difficult to suggest any education or training that could prepare people for synchronized, harmonious conversational interaction. It is, however, possible to sensitize people to observe and minimize conditions that lead to a sense of discomfort in verbal interactions. For example, Americans who have to interact with the Japanese may be made aware of Japanese sync talk so that they do not feel uncomfortable by what they perceive to be interruptions. Also, they may feel more comfortable giving more backchannel cues, and adjusting the rate and type of their body movements. Similarly, the Japanese who need to interact with the Americans may be made aware of the turn-taking rule, so that they feel less uncomfortable in reducing the frequency of backchannel cues and making less elaborate body movements to create the ensemble effect.

Similarly, although rhetorical strategies are acquired along with other conventions of conversation, professionals who interact frequently across cultures accommodate to different strategies as they become familiar with patterns of interaction. Given enough exposure and sensitivity to diverse cultural conventions, it is possible to create an environment of negotiation and cooperation.

SPEECH ACTS, COOPERATIVE PRINCIPLES, AND POLITENESS

Recent research has shown that there are differences in the aspects of speech acts, cooperative principles, and politeness across cultures. For instance, it is not clear that all cultures have speech acts that conform to what are known as "thanking" and "complimenting" in the Inner Circle Englishes. Thus, speech act genres may differ across languages and cultures. All cultures do not attach the same value to the maxim of quantity, *be brief*. In some cultures, several opening exchanges may be necessary to establish the context of even a casual conversational interaction. It is also not clear that the notion of *face* is the same across cultures. For instance, some cultures may attach a great deal of importance to negative face, i.e. freedom of action and freedom from imposition, whereas others may attach more value to positive face, i.e. the positive, consistent self-image claimed by an interlocutor for himself/herself. All these need to be clarified in order to define styles of interaction.

Speech Acts

It has been established by research that there is no set of speech acts and no set of strategies for performing speech acts such that all languages and cultures share them (Y. Kachru, 1991, 1992, 1993b, 1998a; Wierzbicka, 1985). This, however, does not necessarily mean that there is no universal set of speech acts and strategies, only that given a universal set, most languages and cultures select particular subsets for their communicative needs and purposes.

One example may make this clear. There is a speech genre *saugandh khaanaa* or *qasam khaanaa*, which is roughly translatable as "to swear." It is, however, different from the English item "swear" in that it only shares the following meanings with it: "to assert, promise, agree to, or confirm on oath." The other, more negative meanings of the English item are not shared by the Hindi item. Another difference is that one can "swear" by anything dear or valuable to one, e.g. one's own self, one's kin, and, of course, the *Bhagvadgiitaa* (one of the sacred texts of Hindusim) or God. It has the illocutionary force of persuasion, challenge, promise, or entreaty, depending upon the context. Two examples of how it is used in Indian English with the illocutionary forces of assertion and persuasion, respectively, are given below:

3. "He, brother, what is it all about?"
   "Nothing. I think it's about the quarrel between Ramaji and Subbaji. You know about the Cornerstone?"
   "But, *on my mother's soul,* I thought they were going to the court?" (Rao, 1978b, p. 17)

The context is that one villager, named Dattopant, is trying to find out what the bailiff's drum meant from another villager, named Sonopant. He "swears" in order to convince Sonopant that he had a certain piece of information which he thought was true.

In the second example, an older sister is scolding a younger brother for arguing with her:

4. ". . . And Ramu," she cried desperately, "I have enough of quarrelling all the time.
   In the name of our holy mother can't you leave me alone!" (Rao, 1978b, p. 88)

The expression *holy mother* in the above example does not refer to any deity; it refers to the female (biological) parent of the siblings. The sister is trying to persuade her brother to drop the topic they have been arguing about.

The two examples make it clear that the cultural meaning of *saugandh khaanaa* is very different from "to swear" in the Inner Circle English-speaking contexts. The two instances of swearing are interpretable only in the context of a society or culture that shares the specific meanings with South Asian society and culture (Y. Kachru, 1997d, 1998b). For a description of swearing in the Arabic-speaking culture and society see Abd el-Jawad (2000).

The strategies adopted for identical or similar speech acts, for example, expressing gratitude or regret, may differ, depending upon the context. In many cultures, there are no verbal expressions equivalent to "thank you" or "sorry" of Inner Circle Englishes. In Indian languages, elders may bless a child instead of saying "thank you" for rendering some service. Research has shown that in Hebrew (Blum-Kulka, 1989), and in the variety of Mandarin Chinese spoken in Taiwan, a more direct strategy for making requests is adopted as compared to American English (Lee-Wong, 1994). The same is true of Indian English (K. Sridhar, 1991; see also, Y. Kachru, 1998a).

In many cultures, certain speech acts are performed by silence—a total absence of talk. For instance, according to Nwoye (1985), in Igbo society the most appropriate way of expressing sympathy to the bereaved following a loved one's death is to leave them alone for at least four days, then visit them by going straight to them in their home, stand before them for a short time and sit down for a while with other mourners in mutual silence. When the visitors feel they have stayed long enough, they again stand before the bereaved so that their presence is noted, and leave as silently as they came. In this case, not saying anything says everything: that they share the grief and sympathize. In Igbo society, it is felt to be inappropriate to increase the bereaved person's sorrow by talking about the loss suffered. Thus, the silent presence rather than any verbal expression signals the offering of condolence.

The Cooperative Principle

In general, in the Inner Circle Englishes, in conversational exchanges and even more so in written communication, it is expected that the speaker/ writer will come directly to the point of interaction after greeting the interlocutor. In many cultures some prefacing is required to satisfy the demands of a polite exchange (see Chapter 3). For example, in making a request, one may begin by saying something like, "I am sorry to trouble you . . .," or "Is it permissible for me to ask a favor of you . . ." even if the purpose of interaction is just elicitation of some ordinary piece of information. This may be perceived as a violation of the Gricean maxim of quantity by a speaker of American English, but will be perceived as polite by South Asian speakers of English. Cultures differ as to what is perceived as being cooperative in social interaction.

In the Inner Circle, talk is highly valued and pauses between turns are short. Any long pause in conversation creates awkwardness and silence is frequently interpreted as either a signal of disagreement or hostility. In contrast, in many cultures, silence is highly valued and there may be long pauses between turns or even in responding to a question. For instance, Yamada (1992, pp. 81–82) in her analysis of American and Japanese business discourse reports that an average pause in Japanese meetings is 8.2 seconds long; in the American ones, only 4.6 seconds. More specifically, long pauses in Japanese occur consistently between all topics; in American, only one between topics. The average pause-time to shift topics in Japanese business meetings is 6.5 seconds; in American, it is 1.7 seconds.

In interactions between an elder and a young person in South Asia, silence on the part of the younger person is interpreted as signaling agreement or acceptance of whatever the elder says. There is a saying in Sanskrit that means silence is a sign of acceptance. Thus, observing silence is one way of observing the cooperative principle.

Politeness

Recent research in politeness across languages has raised questions that relate to many of the theoretical notions discussed in Chapter 2. For example, Matsumoto (1989) questions the adequacy of the theoretical notion of "face" as postulated by Brown and Levinson (1987) to account for the politeness phenomena in Japanese conversational interactions. In her study, it has been argued that since the Japanese culture values group harmony over individual rights, positive face considerations play a greater role in determining politeness than negative face considerations. For example, it would be very unlikely that an American parent, when introduced to a son/daughter's professor at a university would request him/her to "keep an eye on him/her." This would be considered an unreasonable expectation on the part of the parent and an imposition of unjustifiable responsibility on the professor. Such a request would be considered a threat to the professor's negative face. In contrast, a request of this kind would be considered entirely appropriate in Japanese as well as South Asian contexts, since the parent by making such a request displays a high degree of regard and confidence in the professor. A teacher is like a parent and has both the authority to "discipline" a child and the obligation to make sure the child does not go astray. The request, by affirming the teacher's societal status and rank, satisfies the positive face wants of the interlocutor, and hence is perfectly polite. This would be true in many other cultures, too. As far as the son/daughter is concerned, (s)he may be offended by the parents' lack of confidence in him/her in the American context; in the Asian context, it will be interpreted as the usual parental concern and no reflection on the child's maturity.

Liao (1997, pp. 105–108) contrasts the linguistic strategies used by American and Taiwanese bosses to tell an employee his/her job performance has been unsatisfactory. An American boss will use statements such as the following: *I am concerned about your performance; I have been extremely concerned about your work performance lately; I don't feel that you're working to your full potential.* A Taiwanese boss, in contrast will prefer statements such as the following: *I don't like your performance; I am not pleased with your performance; I am not satisfied with your performance.* Liao goes on to observe that over 50 percent of American English speakers give constructive instructions to employees to improve their job performance, and over 50 percent of Taiwanese English speakers do not do so.

Takahashi and Beebe (1993) contrast the feedback the teachers may give to students who give wrong answers to questions. They conducted a study in which the task set before American subjects (Group 1), Japanese subjects using their variety of English (Group 2), and Japanese subjects using the Japanese language (Group 3) required each member of the three groups to come up with patterns of correction in the following situation: You are a professor in a history class. During the class discussion, one of the students gives an account of a famous historical event with the wrong date. The patterns that emerged were as follows (pp. 140 ff.):

Group 1 patterns:
- That was very good but I believe that took place in 1945.
- That was a great account of event X. Everything was in line except the date. It was 1942, not 1943.
- Excellent description, Henry! I like the way you outlined the events. Now when did all that take place?

Group 2 patterns:
- I think that date is not correct.
- The date is wrong.
- In 1945.

Group patterns:
- Wait a second. The date is incorrect. It's 1603.
- The date you just mentioned is incorrect. Please check it by the next class.

In the use of positive remarks, the three varieties ranked Group 1> Group 2>Group 3, and in the use of softeners (i.e. expressions that mitigate the effect of statements), the ranking was Group 1>Group 2>Group 3. The explanation the researchers suggest are threefold: the nature of teacher–student relationship in the Japanese society; distrust of verbal expression; and the hint of untruthfulness in positive remarks when the answer is wrong.

It is obvious that more than face is involved in what is considered appropriate polite speech in the Japanese classroom context. It has been claimed that the Japanese distrust talk, they believe that *If the bird had not sung, it would not have been shot* (Yamada, 1992). In the Japanese context the cultural values of when direct criticism is appropriate, and what is perceived as insincere and therefore uncooperative, takes precedence over face considerations.

ISSUES OF IDENTITY

In addition to the factors mentioned so far, in any interaction participants project, maintain, or negotiate their identities. While accommodating to their interlocutors, speakers adopt "accommodative processes" that relate to the different ways in which they manipulate language "to maintain integrity, distance or identity" (Giles and Coupland, 1991, p. 66) with them. A great deal of research is available in how, for example, gender identity or ethnic identity is signaled in conversations (e.g. Stubbe and Holmes, 1999; Valentine, 2001). Y. Kachru and Nelson (2006, Ch. 19) discuss in some detail the linguistic devices used for establishing or indicating identity in conversations.

Some of the rhetorical strategies discussed in this chapter perform the same function: participants engaged in conversation may adhere to shared strategies of signaling politeness, for example, or adopt the norms they have grown up with which may not be familiar to their interlocutors. In the first case, the participants are deferring to their interlocutors; in the second case, they are projecting their identity as distinct from their interlocutors either to distance themselves, or to draw the interlocutors into their own group and make them a part of their in-group. It takes a great deal of familiarity to interpret the intentions of speakers from different sociocultural backgrounds.

CONCLUSION

It is clear that communicative success depends on various aspects of conversational interaction, some related to the content, others to the organization of conversation. Various aspects of language use and organizational structure combine to create the stylistic effects that either lead to success, or failure, or a total break down in communication. What is true of communication across languages and cultures is true of varieties of a language and subgroups within a culture. For example, Tannen (1984) has shown clearly that the New York Jewish style of casual conversation is not generalizable as an American conversational style.

Further Reading

Lee-Wong, S. M. (1994) Imperatives in requests: direct or impolite—Observations from Chinese. *Pragmatics*, 4, 491–515.
Matsumoto, Y. (1989) Politeness and conversational universals: observations from Japanese. *Multilingua*, 8, 207–221.

Sridhar, K. K. (1991) Speech acts in an indigenized variety: sociocultural values and language variation. In J. Cheshire (ed.), *English around the World: Sociolinguistic Perspectives* (pp. 308–318). Cambridge: Cambridge University Press.

Suggested Activities

1. I have an urgent letter that needs to be mailed. I cannot go out to mail the letter and would like to persuade my roommate to do it for me. I may pronounce any of the utterances below to make a request of my roommate. Rank them on a scale of politeness (note that there is no rigid rank order such that each expression is ranked either lower or higher in comparison to each of the other expressions though some are ranked either lower or higher in comparison to others). Then discuss what factors influenced your ranking, e.g. imagined context of situation in terms of setting, participants, etc., or, if you are from Outer or Expanding Circle of English, your intuition about what you would say in your language(s) in the same situation:

   Mail the letter for me.

   Would you mind mailing the letter for me?

   Could you mail the letter for me?

   Could you do me a favor and mail this letter?

   Please mail the letter for me.

   I will be very grateful if you could mail the letter for me.

   I would really appreciate it if you mail the letter for me.

   It would be very kind of you to mail the letter for me.

   I wish you would mail the letter for me.

   I need to have the letter mailed immediately, and also have to be here to receive a very important phone call.

2. Record two short segments of conversation or take extracts from published literature on conversation (e.g. from Dautermann, 1995; Stubbe and Holmes, 1999; Tannen, 1981). Compare them in terms of (a) who claims turns and how; (b) who claims the floor, and how; (c) which backchannel cues are used; and (d) how agreement and disagreement are expressed. Correlate your analysis to determine if the conversation is an instance of successful interaction or not, and the reasoning behind your determination.

Chapter 9

Interaction in Writing

INTRODUCTION

There are different conventions that govern the structure of writing in various world Englishes. As the famous African writer Chinua Achebe observes: "Most African writers write out of an African experience and of commitment to an African destiny. For them that destiny does not include a future European identity for which the present is but an apprenticeship" (Jussawalla and Dasenbrock, 1992, p. 34).

Writing from one's own experience means that conventions of writing differ across varieties (Y. Kachru, 1999, 2001c). It has an effect on the language one uses, even the words one feels comfortable using. For instance, the Philippine writer Jose (1997, p. 168) emphasizes using material that writers know "firsthand" and asserts, "I have expunged the word 'summer' from my writing unless it is in the context of four seasons . . . Because there is no summer in this country. We have a dry season, wet season, rainy season, dusty season, but never, never 'summer.'" It also affects how writers structure what they write and how they present information or argue a point. We have already seen how grammars differ across varieties (Chapter 6); in this chapter we will consider how genres and structures of texts in the written mode differ in world Englishes.

As examples of writing, it may be useful to focus on a few genres as it is impossible to treat all different purposes of writing in one short chapter. It is reasonable to assume that in the contemporary world, two types of writing are within the experiential range of almost all educated persons—the genre of personal and professional letters, and that of academic writing. These are discussed in some detail below.

LETTERS

Letters are essentially composed of three parts: salutation or addressing the recipient of the letter, the message, and the signature of the writer. There are other optional elements that may or may not be specified, e.g. recipient's and writer's addresses, date and place of origin of the letter, subject matter of the letter, etc. All these are governed by strict conventions.

Differences in Politeness Strategies

In Inner Circle Englishes, the formulas for writing letters are observed strictly. For example, the salutation and signature in business vs. personal letters are paired as follows: *Dear sir. Sincerely, Yours faithfully* vs. *Dear First Name/Mr. Surname: Yours sincerely.* However, according to Bamgboṣe (1982, p. 110, fn. 3), in Nigerian English, ". . . one has little choice but to mix formulas . . . since it will be considered impolite to address an older person by his surname, and positively disrespectful, if not impudent, to use his first name." Thus, even a personal letter in Nigerian English may begin with *Dear sir*, and the signature may be *Yours sincerely.*

In South Asia, where there are elaborate rules for using names and codified expressions to address one's parents, teachers, and other highly respected members of society such as authors, editors, etc., as opposed to one's intimate friends and younger people, *Dear + Kinship Term* (*Father, Uncle,* etc.) or *Dear + Title + Surname* is not felt to be respectful enough. Hence, insertion of *Respected* after *Dear* is very common. Also, a variety of expressions are common before the signature of the writer, e.g. yours *sincerely/affectionately/obediently/faithfully, respectfully yours, your most obedient servant,* etc. Intimate friends and younger people may be addressed by their first names; the names of younger members of an intimate circle must be preceded by appropriate terms of blessings, e.g. *chiranjiiv* "one with eternal life," *aayushmatii* "one with long life (f.)," *saubhaagyavatii* "one with good fortune (f.)," etc. More often than not, such blessings become part of personal letters in IE.

In business letters, it is generally considered inappropriate in the Inner Circle varieties to inquire about the recipient's and his/her family's health. After greetings, one is expected to come directly to the main point of the letter. In many Outer and Expanding Circle varieties, it is considered impolite not to inquire about the addressee's and his/her family's health. Even a slight acquaintance in a business context is enough to elicit a response in other Circles that is associated with more "intimate" domains in the American or British culture. Also, it is considered uncivilized to come directly to the point of the letter without showing some concern for the addressee or some offer of reciprocity.

Most personal letters in many Outer and Expanding Circle varieties begin and end with a great deal of salutation (if addressed to an elder) or blessings (if addressed to a younger person) and invoking of God's Grace for the preservation of the addressee. Users of Inner Circle varieties of English, if unfamiliar with the cultures of these variety users, find these practices archaic, ridiculous, or insincere, and refuse to take them seriously. Similarly, users of the Other Circle varieties often consider the letters written by users of Inner Circle varieties offensive, aggressive, or indifferent. One example of a strategy that many Outer and Expanding Circle writers may use is the insistence on compliance when an invitation is issued. Al-Khatib (2001, p. 190) cites the following letter written by a Jordanian to an Inner Circle friend to visit her in Jordan:

1. Dear Mary,
    How are you? How is your work? How is the family? I hope you are in good health when you receive my letter. I want to invite you to Jordan. *By the way, I am still waiting for you to come and visit us here as you promised me before. Everybody around is willing to see you because I keep talking about you to my friends. I'm sure that you will have lots of fun when you visit the various ancient places in Jordan . . . and spending marvelous beautiful nights in our country. I'll be waiting for you. Please come soon, and don't make me get angry with you. . . .* [emphasis in the original]

According to Al-Khatib (2001, p. 190) while the Jordanian notion of politeness suggests that the insistence of the writer is a marker of her seriousness and sincerity, an American respondent reported, "I feel pressured. I would like a less direct invitation."

In some cases, the choice of lexical items may lead to grave misunderstandings, as is exemplified by the following by a female subject to her female friend (Al-Khatib, 2001, p. 194):

2. My sweetheart, I want you to be with me in these nice days. So, please come to visit me, and you will stay with me in my own room.

The writer informed the friend that she was about to get married and then invited her to spend the last few days of her status as an unmarried woman relatively free of responsibilities with her. It is normal in Jordanian Arabic to use terms of endearment (e.g. *my love x*) for one's friends, and these may be repeated at the beginning of each paragraph to show solidarity between the writer and the addressee. Additionally, the offer to share her room conveys the generosity of the writer—she is willing to put up with personal loss of space for her friend. Obviously, this strategy of showing intimacy by using strong terms of endearment does not work in all Englishes; the reaction of an American female respondent was (Al-Khatib, 2001, p. 194), "I would be offended by sweetheart because it is used in romantic relationships. I would also be concerned about staying with her after such an implication."

Al-Khatib (2001), on the basis of a large body of elicited data, provides a detailed discussion of sociocultural norms and discourse strategies that characterize Jordanian English letters and that differ from Inner Circle English letters.

A few examples of letters written in the same domain may make such differences clear. Consider the following letters of request to a couple of linguists. Letter (3), written by a male, requests some information from a female addressee; letters (4) and (5), written by males, request copies of a paper presented at a professional meeting by the male addressee:

3.   Madam,

          . . .
          Now coming to the crux of the matter, . . . I request you *very humbly to enlighten me* of the following points.
          . . .
          So, *with folded hands* I request you to help me by supplying the needed information and names of any devotees and fans of E. I am writing to B. S. today. *If you want anything from my side just let me know.* Waiting *very anxiously* for your reply,

                                                                                 Yours sincerely,

4.   Dear R,

          I was unable to attend the LSA meeting in LA this year. *Please help me get over the irreparable loss and guilt feelings* at having missed your paper, by sending me a copy.
          And have a healthy, productive and prosperous (in linguistics) 1993.
                                                                                 Yours sincerely,

5.   Dear R,

          I was unable to attend your recent paper at the LSA meeting and would greatly appreciate it if you could send me a copy. I am also working on quirky subjects, but with Spanish and Italian, and would like to see how you have approached the problem in Kashmiri.
          Thank you very much.
                                                                                 Sincerely,

It is probably not too difficult to guess which letter was written by an American scholar (by the way, the expression *quirky subjects* refers to the topic of non-nominative subjects in syntax). For those who are not familiar with the Outer and Expanding Circle varieties of English, it would be difficult to guess who the writers of letters in (3) and (4) are. The first letter is written by an Indian, and the second by an Austrian.

There are several points to note about these letters. First, note that the Indian letter is much longer and contains only the item *Madam* as salutation. The item *Dear* is left out. Some writers may feel uncomfortable addressing any unfamiliar female addressee with a term of endearment, though, obviously, the term *Dear* in formal letters is simply formulaic in English. Second, the writer expresses humility twice, and offers reciprocal favor to the addressee. The Austrian letter acknowledges loss to the writer in having missed the presentation of the scholarly paper, but there are no expressions of humility or reciprocity. Obviously, neither the Indian nor the European writer feels it is polite to make a request without making the benefactor feel good about himself/herself. In addition, the Indian writer feels it is appropriate to express humility as a seeker of favor, and offer to reciprocate the favor. These characteristics of the letters are in tune with the cultural values attached to humility and reciprocity in Indian culture, and catering to the positive face wants of the individual in the European culture. This may be a violation of the Gricean maxim "Be brief" from the point of view of some Inner Circle readers; neither the Indian nor the Austrian feels (s)he has been excessively wordy.

The American letter in (5) is very straightforward; it follows the Gricean maxims and meets the expectations of an American reader. Being straightforward and coming directly to the point are markers of politeness in American interactions. The face threatening act of request has been softened by an explanation: the seeker of the favor is working on similar problems in other languages and would benefit from the addressee's work.

Differences in Formality

Some style differences are related to politeness, others are to what is considered a cultured, formal, high style in different cultures. This difference is illustrated by fragments of sales letters written by American, British, and Indian firms (Frank, 1988). The letters were written and sent to the same recipient, a speaker of American English, by companies in Britain, India, and the USA engaged in the publication of "Who's Who Directories" (Frank, 1988, p. 26). The fragment in (6) is from an Indian, (7) from a British, and (8) from an American company:

6. We come back upon the correspondence resting with the inclusion of your biographical note in the forthcoming volume of our "Biography International" and thank you much indeed for your esteemed cooperation in sending to us the same.

7. Your name has been put forward for biographical and pictorial inclusion in the Twelfth Edition of Men of Achievement, and you are respectfully invited to complete the questionnaire overleaf and return it to our editors

so that they can prepare your detailed biography and send you a typescript for proofing.

8. Enclosed is a copy of your sketch as it appears in the 44th edition. Please proofread it carefully. Make any necessary additions and corrections. Then, even if no changes are needed, sign the sketch where indicated and return it to me *within the next 15 days.*

The long sentence in (6) seems overly complicated to Inner Circle readers, whose expectations are satisfied by a simple statement such as "Thank you for your response to our invitation." The notion of "high style" in the Indian context, however, is not satisfied by such "bald" statements. A comparison of the three fragments is instructive: in the American style of writing, it is appropriate to use direct imperatives with the conventional politeness marker please. In the British style, however, more indirect request strategies are considered appropriate, e.g. *you are . . . invited,* and an extra politeness marker is used, *respectfully.* In the Indian letter, *thank you* is followed by two intensifiers, *much* and *indeed,* and a modifier, *esteemed,* is used before *cooperation* to express an extremely deferential attitude toward the addressee. One other noticeable feature is the linking of the two clauses with *and*; to an Inner Circle reader, it appears strange to introduce the two unrelated episodes—the correspondence regarding a biographical note with the addressee, and expression of gratitude by the writer of the letter—in this manner. From the Indian point of view, the reference to the correspondence implies receipt of a biographical note from the addressee, for which thanking is appropriate, and the two are thus related (see Y. Kachru. 1983, 1985a, 1985b, 1985c, 1987, 1988, 1992 for a discussion of the style features of Indian English writing).

Differences of Emphasis

An English translation of a letter originally written in Japanese, illustrates the Japanese conventions of business letter writing (Jenkins and Hinds, 1987, .349):

9. Dear sir,

In Japan, fall has deepened, and the trees have begun turning colors. As exchange students, we believe you are busy studying every day.

Well, getting right into it. We are carrying out the 1984 business evaluation with the material described below. We hope that you will please fill out the enclosed evaluation card and send it to us.

We believe that this will cause you some inconvenience, but since winter in coming near, we will hope that you will take care of yourself.

Sincerely,

The Japanese letter reflects the dominant cultural value of emphasis on what Jenkins and Hinds (1987) term "space," i.e. the relationship between the reader and the writer. The opening situates the letter in a shared season, and its implication for the addressee. The transition is provided by the first sentence of the second paragraph, which is followed by the request. The third paragraph acknowledges the "imposition" made by the request and attempts to establish the desired harmonious relationship by expressing concern about the addressee's well-being.

The Indian and Japanese letters show a consideration for form, i.e. appropriate signals of awareness of the addressee as a person and his/her face needs, whereas the American letter demonstrates the emphasis on content, i.e. coming directly to the point of the written interaction.

ACADEMIC WRITING

Similar to the formulas of letter writing, there are well-established conventions in most literate cultures for writing academic prose. Academic writing can be and has been studied utilizing several different approaches. We will discuss two of these approaches, those of contrastive rhetoric and genre analysis, and show their relevance to looking at writing in world Englishes in this chapter. Although these two approaches have been applied in the study of writing in world Englishes to some extent, the majority of work, especially in contrastive rhetoric, has been in the ESL (English as a Second Language)/EFL context (for a recent survey of approaches to ESL/EFL writing research, see Silva and Brice, 2004).

According to the contrastive rhetoric approach, initiated by Kaplan (1966), different cultures and traditions have different text types that are identifiable on the basis of their linguistic and organizational features. It is helpful to see what is meant by text types before contrasting the rhetorical organization of text types across cultures.

Werlich (1976) lists the following text types for English and classifies them into subjective and objective text forms:

Descriptive text forms (impressionistic description—subjective and technical description—objective);

Narrative text forms (the narrative—personal; the report—objective; and the news story—objective but related to the writer's personal view);

Expository text forms (the expository essay—personal; the definition—objective; the explication—objective; the summary—objective; summarizing minutes—objective, text interpretation);

Argumentative text forms (the comment—personal; scientific argumentation);

Instructive text forms (instructions—with reference to personal authority; directions, rules, regulations, statutes—with reference to impersonal authority).

On the other hand, in Hindi, the text types are said to be of the following types: **descriptive, narrative, deliberative,** and **personal.** Deliberative essays include argumentation, and personal refers to the stance the writer takes— the topic may be description, narration, deliberation, argumentation, or any combination of these.

The two types that are vital for academic purposes are expository and argumentative writing. In the Inner Circle Englishes, expository prose is expected to express "straight, linear progression of thought" (Kaplan, 1966; see also, Connor and Kaplan 1987). In many cultures, however, alternate techniques of presentation are preferred (Y. Kachru, 1995a). Recent research has shown that Japanese (Hinds, 1980, 1982; Miner, 1972) prefer a structure that may be characterized as "association and iteration in a progressive flow" (Miner, 1972), whereas Hindi and IE (Y. Kachru, 1983, 1988, 1995a, 1995b, 1997a) both prefer a direct and a spiral structure.

More recent research points out that "as a measure of rhetorical effectiveness the logocentrism of Western tradition is the exception rather than the rule; both oral and literate culture traditions of non-European cultures challenge the straight-edged geometry of Western rhetoric" (Lisle and Mano, 1997, p. 16). They document evidence for this assertion by citing observations about several non-Western traditions. This point is elaborated on pp. 155–156. Here the focus is on the structure of texts.

Macro and Micro Structure

Writing in different languages and varieties differs in macro structure as well as micro structure. That is, there are differences in how the text as a whole is organized (macro structure), and how each element of the text is organized (micro structure).

In terms of micro structures, it has been observed that Outer and Expanding Circle varieties prefer grammatical devices that are different from the ones preferred by the Inner Circle varieties to signal relationships between elements of a text. A few examples will make this clear. First, we will look at some examples to see how inter- and intra-sentential relationships are expressed in the Outer and Expanding Circle varieties. This is the domain of *cohesion* (Halliday and Hasan, 1976). In addition, we will discuss the macro structure of texts in terms of the concept of *coherence* (Brown and Yule, 1983, p. 223 ff.). Examples will be presented to show the characteristics of overall textual structure in the Outer and Expanding Circle varieties in terms of **thematization** and **staging,** in addition to **paragraph** structure. Subsequently, we will look at different concepts of argumentative-persuasive writing in different cultures and their impact on writing in world Englishes. Finally, we will briefly discuss the genre analysis model of analyzing academic writing (Bhatia, 1993; Swales, 1990).

Micro structure

A great many facts regarding the grammatical differences between the old and the new varieties of English have already been discussed in Chapter 6. This section, therefore, deals with intra- and inter-sentential linking devices that are crucial for text construction.

Cohesion: The following excerpts from letters to editors of prominent English language newspapers from India and Singapore illustrate the differing norms of expressing cohesive relationships in these varieties:

10. *Though* the intention of the government was good *but* in reality administration of public schools has collapsed *for* the negligence of the education department. (Letter to the Editor, *The Assam Tribune*, March 24, 2000)

11. They *should not have been appointed* as Cabinet Ministers in the first place until they *are exonerated* of the charge by the trial court. (*The Hindu*, March 25, 2000)

12. These laws might have proved useful and efficient, *but, nevertheless,* they are counterproductive to our goal of becoming a civil society. (*Straits Times*, April 6, 2000)

The following properties of the three examples cited above are worth noting:

1. the use of a correlative construction (*though . . . but*) for expressing the concessive relationship, and *for* to signal a causal relationship, in example (10);
2. the lack of tense agreement in (11); and
3. the use of both *but* and *nevertheless* in (12) to signal the adversative meaning.

Additional examples of cohesive ties not attested in Inner Circle Englishes are as follows:

13. The position has belonged to *such* actresses *who* came to personify, at any given moment, the popular ideal of physical beauty . . . (*India Today*, September 30, 1983, p. 39)

14. They are brought up in *such* an atmosphere *where* they are not encouraged to express themselves upon such subjects in front of others. (Singh and Altbach, 1974, pp. 194–195)

In the sentences in (13) and (14) above, *such* has been used as a correlative of *who* and *where*, which extends the convention of use of this linking device in the grammar of English. Notice that it is not the case that *such* is *not* used as a correlative in American or British English; it is so used, for example, in *such . . . that* (as in *they made such a racket that everyone woke up*). However, there is no correlative item in relative clause constructions in these varieties. The sentences in (13) and (14) do not conform to the conventions of Inner Circle Englishes; they will do so only if the item *such* is deleted. The convention followed in the use of *such* above comes from the Indian languages where relative clause constructions require both a relative and a correlative marker.

Another example from Japanese writing in English supports the statement made above that users of Outer and Expanding Circle varieties make characteristic use of linking items:

15. A dramatist may entertain various points of view which, reinforcing or qualifying one another, incorporate themselves into a coherent moral vision. Informed as it is by such a vision, his play is a far more complex thing than it appears to a casual reader. It is a self-contained organism, each component part of which is carefully integrated into the total pattern. The raison d'etre of a character or an incident, therefore, must be determined on the basis of the meaning of the play as a whole. To try to explain the character of Cleopatra, for instance, from her action and speeches alone would be to lose sight of her magnificent stature and reduce her to a mere royal whore. Every scene in which she does not appear, every character with whom she has no connection on the story level, is also instrumental in building up in our minds a dramatic image of her. Similarly, it would be quite beside the point to comment to Cordelia's "pride and sullenness" on the sole basis of certain speeches assigned to her in the play. A play is not "decadent", *therefore*, simply, because it deals with an immoral theme, or because certain characters in it might be regarded as morally reprehensible in real life. The problem of "decadence" should be discussed only in rela-tion to the full moral texture of the play. [Italics added] (T. S., *ECJ*, p. 102)

Let us focus on the use of *therefore* in the fourth line from the bottom in the quote in (15). The first three sentences make a general statement about the moral vision of a dramatist as expressed in a play through its various components, including the characters. This is further elaborated and exemplified in the next three sentences. It is not clear why the item *therefore* occurs in the next sentence, which is a general statement about what the basis should be for judging a play "decadent." In fact, nothing about decadence has been mentioned in the paragraph prior to this point. A careful look at the total text reveals that the item *therefore* has been used to link up the concluding lines of the paragraph under focus with the two paragraphs that precede it. Typically, in the Inner Circle varieties of English, items such as *therefore* are not used to renew links with elements that are not in the immediately preceding text, but have occurred elsewhere in the text.

Further examples of innovative use of linking devices from educated Fijian, Singaporean, and Thai Englishes are given below:

16. a. I am impressed with the cleanliness of the city, something which contrasts markedly with much of Suva our capital, *let alone* the various towns of Fiji.
    b. . . . some of the vendors at the swap meet know where to get it. I'm told that some of *these* go from place to place.

Both the above excerpts are from essays by an educated Fijian. Note the use of *let alone* in (16a), and *these* in (16b). In the Inner Circle varieties, (16a) would have to be rephrased to express the intended meaning that even the capital, not to mention the other towns in Fiji, lacks the standards of cleanliness observed in Honolulu. In (16b), the item *these* will normally be replaced by *them*. The following observations about Singaporean English point to the use of certain cohesive devices of English in a way unfamiliar to most speakers of Inner Circle varieties (the items under focus are italicized):

17. a. A letter recommending the abolition of fireworks during Chinese New Year gave reasons for the recommendation, adding "*on the other hand*, people may need peace and quiet". (Tongue, 1979, p. 59)
    b. Minister X called on Muslim parents to give their children a balanced education covering religious studies *as well as* science and technology subjects. (Tongue, 1979, p. 59)
    c. He is somewhat unusual barrister as he is qualified in law *as well as* in economics. (Tongue, 1979, p. 60)

According to Tongue, in Singaporean English, *on the other hand*, is used in the sense of *furthermore*, and *as well as* is used in a manner that is opposite of the way it is used in British English. In British English, the unexpected information precedes the expected, in Singaporean, the order of new vs. old information is reversed, as is clear from the examples in (17b) and (17c) above. The unexpected information in (17b) is that Minister X wanted Muslim children to be educated in science and technology as well as religious studies, and in (17c), the barrister is unusual because he is qualified in economics in addition to law.

There is no compelling evidence to conclude that such usage provides evidence for "fossilization" (à la Selinker, 1972) or lack of competence in English. In the examples quoted above, the use of the linking devices is patterned on the conventions of the first languages, i.e. the Indian languages and Japanese. The other examples provide instances of similar phenomena. Such use "makes sense" to the users of these varieties. It is difficult for an Indian or a Japanese speaker/writer of English to see why such uses seem to be "incoherent" to a speaker of the American or British variety.

Such innovative use of cohesive devices for linking elements is not a characteristic of the English used by the Fijians, Indians, Japanese, Singaporeans, and Thais alone. Recent research in the learning of English by the speakers of Spanish and Chinese suggests that this phenomenon is quite common. For instance, it has been observed that Spanish speakers make fewer "errors" in the use of the article *the* but a great number of "errors" in the use of the article *a(n)*. A careful examination of the total texts produced by Spanish learners makes it clear that they use the English articles in contexts where they would use parallel Spanish articles when they speak or write Spanish. The context for the use of the definite article matches in the two languages, hence there are fewer "errors" in the use of *the*. The use of the indefinite article, however, does not match across languages, hence there are more "errors" in the use of *a(n)* (work by Roger Anderson referred to in Schachter and Celce-Murcia, 1983).

Chinese and Japanese learners of English come up with sentences such as the following: *There are so many Taiwan people live around the lake.* At first glance, this seems like an "error" in relative clause construction; the relative marker *who* seems to be missing. Schachter and Rutherford (1983), however, convincingly argue that sentences such as the one above represent attempts at constructing a topic-comment structure following conventions of Chinese and Japanese.

Macro structure

Although cohesion is necessary for text construction, it is not sufficient for the purpose. In addition to grammatical cohesion, there are other properties that are crucial for the perception of a text as coherent. These are discussed below.

Coherence. Although the use of appropriate linking devices such as articles and conjunctions help achieve coherence, they are not essential for coherence. This is clear if we compare examples such as the following:

18. A: Why are you so upset?
    B: Because my travel agent goofed again, I can't leave for my vacation tomorrow.

19. A: Why are you so upset?
    B: I was planning to leave in the morning, but the garage says my car won't be ready till the evening.

It is clear to any English-speaker that the utterance by B in (19) is answering A's question in the same way as in (18), although in (19), B is not answering A's question directly. In (18), the *Why* is directly answered by a *Because*. In (19), there is no such obvious linking device. Note that it is not the linking device itself that makes the answer by B in (18) coherent. If B were to say something like *Because the earth is a planet*, this would not be considered a coherent reply in the normal context of the use of English for interaction. Nevertheless, the linker does provide the necessary clue for the interpretation of what follows. In contrast, what makes (19) coherent is the fact that A can draw some inferences from B's reply, e.g. the reasons for B being upset are his/her disappointment at having to delay his/her vacation, the inconvenience of changing reservations at the destination, etc.

Such inferences are based upon a number of extra-linguistic factors. Some of the factors are related to our "knowledge of the world" in a general sense, others to the specific sociocultural contexts of particular speech communities. Since the relationship of the concept "knowledge of the world" to our understanding and interpreting texts is clear, it is more useful here to concentrate on the sociocultural contexts of texts. Consider the following example from American English:

20. In reaction to the spreading fear, Americans are arming themselves with guns as though they still lived in *frontier days*. "It is the *Matt Dillon syndrome*", says Jack Wright, Jr., a criminologist at Loyola University in New Orleans. "People believe the police can't protect them." They are buying guard dogs and supplies of *Mace*. [Italics added] (E. M., *Time*, March 23, 1981, p. 16)

The quote above is from an article in *Time* magazine about the crime situation in the USA. Fluent speakers or readers of English from other parts of the world, if not familiar with the history and contemporary life in the US when the text was produced, will not be able to interpret the text in (20). The italicized items in (20) will have no clear referents for such readers.

Consider another example from Indian English:

21. Large wedding expenses, at all social levels, are intended to assure the *social welfare* of the family's children and to enhance the family's reputation. Family elders, especially the women, commonly believe that their economic resources can be expended in no better way than for these purposes. They argue that *economic capital* is not worth much unless it can be translated into *social capital*. Economists and planners have deplored these expenditures, vast in their totality, that do not help to increase economic productivity. Members of a family, however, typically feel that no investment deserves higher priority than investment in the *social security* of their children. (Mamdelbaum, 1970, p. 652)

The collocations *social welfare* and *social security* have special meanings in British and American English. It is not quite clear to speakers of these varieties, and to several others, what these concepts have to do with large wedding expenses. It is the sociocultural context of "wedding in India" that gives meaning to these terms and also to the collocations *economic capital* and *social capital.* Fluent speakers or readers of English will be able to "understand" the above texts at one level (high comprehensibility); however, they will have no real "interpretation" of these texts (interpretability) unless they are familiar with the larger social and cultural institutions and situations in the whole of South Asia.

The examples quoted above are from journalistic and scholarly writings. A number of examples of similar nature can be quoted to show that the background knowledge hearers and readers bring to bear upon what they hear/read plays a crucial role in the interpretation of texts. In an important sense, texts do not have meaning, hearers/readers assign meanings to them. That does not mean that speakers/writers do not have anything to do with how texts are to be interpreted. They utilize the conventions of the language *and* the conventions of the speech community to structure the text in such a way that those who share their background are able to come up with the intended interpretation. A great deal of recent research in discourse analysis examines the regularities in interaction and the structure of texts and proposes several abstract constructs to clarify the processes of text construction and interpretation. Some of these are discussed in the following pages.

It has already been demonstrated in the foregoing discussion that sociocultural knowledge plays an important role in the interpretation of texts. It is clear that it also plays an important role in the structure of texts. Speakers/writers make some assumption about what they can take for granted as the "common ground" (Stalnaker, 1978, p. 321), or "non-controversial" information (Grice, 1981) between their audience and themselves. These *presuppositions* (Grice, 1981; Stalnaker, 1978) or *pragmatic presuppositions* (Givón, 1979, p. 50; 1989, Ch. 4) are signaled in linguistic and discourse structure. In the following pages, the discourse structural devices are discussed in some detail.

Thematization: In English, the initial element in the sentence is normally the theme (Halliday, 1967–1968). Besides this structural position, there are several grammatical processes that thematize certain elements that do not normally occur in the initial position. Some of these are simple word-order adjustments, and others are more complex ones. For example, they involve picking out items, which were under focus in the preceding text, so that the speaker could treat them as the point of departure for the subsequent text. It is as though the speaker presents what (s)he wants to say from a particular perspective. What is true of speaker is equally true of writer. The speaker/writer perspective has important consequences for the structure of sentences, paragraphs, and other units of discourse. An example will make this clear. Consider the following text:

22. *The first half-decade of the 1970's* represents the pioneer years in the serious study of vernacular literature. *During these years,* the accelerating process

of decolonization encouraged *nationalist inquiry* into the dynamics of cultural relations between the Philippines and its past colonial masters. *In the process*, the impulse was towards re-examination of our *cultural heritage* from the past. *The resulting rediscovery of the hitherto neglected native tradition* has led to a fresh and enlightened appreciation of the attempts of our vernacular writer to assert through their works a vision of their society and its future. [Italic added] (Lumbera, 1978, p. 65)

The title of the essay, "Philippine Vernacular Literature" provides a point of departure for the entire text. The opening sentence thematizes a time expression, *The first half-decade of the 1970's,* and the subsequent sentence maintains the thematic unity by thematizing the time adverbial, *During these years.* In the two following sentences, there is a shift in the perspective, what is being thematized in these two sentences is that which was under focus in the preceding sentences. For example, *the process* in the initial adverbial in the third sentence refers back to *nationalist inquiry* in the preceding sentence, and the *resulting rediscovery of . . . tradition* in the last sentence refers back to the *cultural heritage* in the preceding sentence. Thus, the writer adopts a staging strategy that leads the reader through a temporal setting to a process to its result: an appreciation of the vernacular literature of the Philippines.

A distinction in terms of **global** and **local topic**, analogous to the distinction in terms of **speaker's topic** and **discourse topic** in conversations (Brown and Yule, 1983, pp. 87–94), may be useful. The overall topic of the essay is identified in its title; there are several related topics, such as the time period, cultural heritage of the past, the colonial experience, and the rediscovery of the indigenous culture, that are relevant in the discussion of the global topic. Thematization in one or more successive paragraphs may pick up these subtopics and establish local topics for parts of a paragraph, a whole paragraph, or a number of paragraphs. In the paragraph quoted above, more than one local topic has been picked up, the relationship between them, however, has been clearly established. Hence, in spite of a multiplicity of local topics, the paragraph seems coherent to the reader.

Different languages and cultures adopt different staging strategies to structure texts. Although it is probably not the case that there are as many conventions of staging as there are languages, recent research with texts suggests that there is certainly more than one convention of staging and that different languages prefer different conventions from within the options that are available. Our perception of whether a text—spoken or written—is coherent or not partially depends upon our familiarity with the staging strategies adopted by the speaker/writer.

Consider the following example:

23. Among the literary genres, it is *the novel* which has been used most effectively as a vivid reflector of certain given conditions in a particular

society. *Its form* lends itself quite well to an all-encompassing view of society as projected by the novelist bent on capturing that texture of lived life. As pointed out by Ian Watt in his *Rise of the Novel, the novel* could arise only when philosophy started to debunk the myth of the universals and in its place affirm the view that reality was composed of concrete and ever-changing patterns of experience. Hence, preoccupation with *recognizable characters* and situations set against such particularized time and place, became a distinguishing trait of the novel. Occupying a pivotal role is *the novel's hero* no longer endowed with supernatural qualities; he is seen as a man among men, a product of his society and in some contemporary western novels (the works of Kafka, Hemingway, or Faulkner) reduced to a pitiful victim of society. [Italics added] (Reyes, 1978, p. 72)

There are several characteristics of this paragraph that are worth discussing. The following are especially notable: the focusing device used in the first sentence to establish *the novel* into the consciousness of the reader, maintenance of thematic unity by referring back to the novel through the device of making *its form* the subject in the second and *the novel* in the third sentence, and the change of theme in the fourth sentence. The staging strategy up to the fourth sentence is successful and there is little difficulty in keeping up with the text. The sudden shift in the fourth and fifth sentences, however, is difficult to process for most readers of the paragraph. It is obvious that *the novel's hero* is being thematized in the fifth sentence as signaled by the structure of the clause, but the only item in the preceding text to which this item could be related is *recognizable characters*. Unfortunately, this noun phrase is buried in a conjoined phrase functioning as a prepositional object not under focus in the clause; it goes almost unnoticed at first reading. Obviously, the staging strategy at this point is not successful at least from the point of view of users of several varieties of English. All the items in italic letters are potential exponents of local topics in view of the global topic of the text. Thematization of *the novel's hero* without adequate preparation, however, creates problems for readers who are not used to sudden topic-shifts. From the point of view of these readers, the paragraph in (23), as compared with the paragraph in (22), seems to be less coherent.

Example (23) above is the opening paragraph of an essay in a Filipino publication and has been identified as a piece of *formal* writing. Obviously, the above paragraph represents writing in educated Filipino English, and the staging strategy is acceptable in this variety.

Filipino English is not the only variety in which sudden changes in perspective are tolerated. Y. Kachru (1983) has several examples from IE to illustrate the same phenomenon. One of the examples discussed in Y. Kachru (1983) is reproduced below to illustrate the staging strategy in IE:

24. Several such *"Indian" themes* have emerged to form recurrent patterns in Indo-Anglian fiction, and the patterns are more easily discernible today

than they were even ten years ago. The novels laid in the nineteen-thirties and 'forties invariably touch upon *the national movement for political independence.* . . . This is not a situation unique to Indo-Anglian fiction, because novels in other Indian languages also testify to their intense concern with *the national movement.* But *the phenomenon* assumes greater significance in English because this is one of the few pan-Indian experiences of our time and English remains the only pan-Indian language of modern India. *Northrop Frye has noted the "alliance of time and the western man" as the defining characteristics of the novel as distinct from other genres of literature.* . . . *The concern of the Indo-Anglian novel today is the "ultra-historical" modern man whose individuality and personal life are shaped by factors of history.* (Mukherjee, 1971, p. 26)

The opening line of the paragraph makes it clear that the author is talking about themes in novels written in IE. The focus is on *the national movement for political independence* in the second sentence which is alternately thematized and focused upon in the following sentences. The sentence beginning with *Northrop Frye* and subsequent sentences, however, do not maintain the same theme or focus; the focus shifts to a certain type of man without making it clear as to how this type of *man* is related to *the national movement for political independence.* The paragraph itself, as a result of such shifts in perspectives may strike us as being incoherent to Inner Circle readers. However, if the entire section in which the paragraph quoted above occurs is considered, the text is perfectly coherent.

It is helpful to look at a complete text and see how different groups of readers with different expectations react to it. Vavrus (1991) conducted a study to see if the evaluation of a text written by an Outer Circle writer by candidates in a Masters in Arts in Teaching English as a Second Language (MATESL) program would be influenced by the context for which the text was written. The piece, written by a Nigerian student and reproduced below in (25), was published in *The Africa Reporter*, a magazine published by African students in the USA. It is interesting to note that it received good ratings from the African readers, but not from the American readers. Note that the text is six paragraphs long:

25.   Academics in Chains

Paul Baran in his famous article on "The Commitment of the Intellectual" outlined on the expected role an intellectual must play particularly in the present-day society where there is the tendency towards misrule, abuse of power, corruption, tyranny, misery and mass poverty, and affluence of the few to the detriment of the rest of us. Paul Baran must have had in mind the role of the intellectual as the conscience of the nation, as the last bastion of hope, the voice of courage and reason that will speak against oppression and exploitation, against all vices that abound in the contemporary society.

However, a critical look at the expectations of our academics today and the realities in our contemporary political situation indicates that our intellectuals are in chains. Chains, though not visibly seen but are easily apprehended by the existing conditions in our citadels of learning, in the increasing atomization of not only academicians but also of democratic forces in the country, in the emergence of a culture of intolerance now quickly eating deep into the embers of our national life, in the precarious state of affairs that now characterizes learning, now defined in terms of certificate acquisition instead of knowledge comprehension, and in the increasing destitution and frustration of products of our educational institutions which are the mirror of future societal progress.

Nigerians do not need the services of any fortune teller for them to understand that the glamour of learning is no longer there, that those days when people dreamt of making it through their degrees acquired from the universities are over; when it was a pride to be a graduate, when learning was characterized by excellence, flexibility and dedication.

Today, the story is different. It is no longer fun to be a graduate; no longer news to make a first class, it is no longer a joy to read, write, study and research into knowledge. Gone are the days when lecturers were respected. Their rewards are in "heaven" even though they have responsibilities on earth.

Our universities had always been hot-beds of radicalism. Hence they must be cowed, and harassed. Their basic freedom to associate is trampled upon as the nation increasingly moves towards intolerance. Something informs me that our educational system which is a product of the economic condition in our society would witness increasing retardation, regression, malfunctioning and depression in the near future. The realities of the moment have shown that there is no way Africans can sustain a high degree of excellence when our educational institutions are under-funded and under-staffed. Worse, the few available manpower are treated shabbily.

The culture of learning is slowly being killed by those who run our educational systems as Emirate-systems, dividing our countries into council and district headquarters serving local champions and prejudiced warlords. What we need is greater tolerance, flexibility, consensus, fairness and justice in the running of African educational systems. (Vavrus, 1991, pp. 194–195)

American MATESL candidates were asked to evaluate the text from two perspectives: one group was asked to evaluate it as something intended for an American audience and the other was asked to evaluate it as something intended for an African audience. Both the groups expressed their dissatisfaction with the text with comments such as the following (Vavrus, 1991, pp. 190–191):

26. Though the topic is eloquently discussed, there are omissions in terms of logic—who? how? why? Also the style is rather grandiose and editorial for a magazine article.

    I really didn't understand what the person was trying to say. What was the point of the essay? The vocabulary was flowery. The sentences were too long—almost continuous.

> The lack of development was difficult for me. I'm not sure what the point was . . . the writer seemed to feel no need to explicitly demonstrate the validity of an opinion through reasoning.

> These are the kinds of essays I don't like grading—at first they seem well-written and sophisticated. But on closer inspection there are bizarre expressions, logical connections that aren't, and dramatic vocabulary (see paragraph 2). In short, the writer's ideas outrun his ability to effectively express them in English.

> This sounds like a bad translation.

Writing in English in the Outer Circle has often been characterized in these terms (see B. Kachru 1986a; Y. Kachru, 1988, among others). The notion of "high style" and "form," discussed in this chapter in the context of formal letters, are relevant for writing of other types of prose, too. This is particularly true of the African, Indian, and Japanese contexts, though the exponents of "high" style may not be the same in all these English-using communities.

Paragraph: In addition to the global organization, smaller units of organization, such as a paragraph, also follow different conventions of structuring in different varieties of English. In the American variety at least, a great deal of emphasis is placed upon "direct, linear progression of thought" (Kaplan, 1966) in expository writing. That is to say, the changes in perspective described in the Filipino and Indian English examples above are judged to be unacceptable in American English expository prose. The emphasis is on establishing a theme, developing it, and arriving at a conclusion without digressing from it (Kaplan, 1966).

Other languages, however, do not have the same preference for paragraph structure. According to Clyne (1983), German tolerates a great deal of digression and abrupt endings. Similarly, Y. Kachru (1983) and Pandharipande (1983) describe the paragraph structure in Hindi expository and Marathi argumentative prose as "spiral" and "circular" respectively. Hinds (1983, p. 80) describes the paragraph structure in Japanese expository writing as *ki-shoo-ten-ketsu* which is explained as follows: "First, begin the argument; . . . Next, develop that; . . . At the point where this argument is finished, turn the idea to a subtheme where there is a connection, but not a directly connected association [to the major theme]; . . . Last, bring all of this together and reach a conclusion." The conclusion need not be decisive, all it needs to do is to indicate a doubt or ask a question.

On the basis of preliminary studies, it has been suggested that in Persian, the paragraph in expository writing has the following characteristics (Katchen, 1982, pp. 178–179): with regard to general structure, essays may or may not contain introductory and concluding material and may not contain topic sentences. At the level of paragraph, clear topic sentences are uncommon, and there is a predominance of paired parallels or binary structure. These parallel structures are not only of general statement followed by specific statement or of a statement followed by a contrastive statement. They are also of the type where the new information at the end of a previous sentence becomes the given at the beginning of the next sentence.

What has been said above is true of expository and argumentative paragraphs; the same may not be true of paragraphs in narratives or other genres. A useful summary of the discussion of the paragraph as a unit of discourse appears in Brown and Yule (1983, pp. 95–100).

Whatever value may be attached to the direct, hierarchical structure for expository prose in the American variety, it is clear that it is not shared by many other literate cultures. This fact has to be appreciated for success in crosscultural communication through this channel (Y. Kachru, 1997b).

ARGUMENTATIVE TEXT

In the field of academic writing, a type of text that is highly valued is the argumentative. Argumentative pieces have been characterized either in terms of linguistic structure of sentences in the text, or speech acts of utterances. According to the grammatical structural approach (Werlich, 1976), the dominant sentence type in an argumentative piece is quality-attributing sentences (e.g. *The problem is complex*); clause expansion types are causal, concessive, and nominal; sequence type is contrastive; text structuring is deductive, inductive, and dialectical; and tense form is present. According to Biber (1986) argumentative texts contain infinitives, suasive verbs (e.g. *command, demand*), conditional clauses, split auxiliaries, and prediction, necessity, and possibility modals.

In terms of speech acts, Aston (1977) assigns two types of values to speech acts in an argumentative text: an illocutionary value and an interactional value. He further maintains that argumentative texts are characterized by representatives in terms of illocutionary acts, and the interactional relationships between acts are of four types: explanation, evaluation, instances, and meta-statements. Tirkkonen-Condit (1985) draws upon van Dijk (1980), Kummer (1972), and Aston (1977), and suggests the following view of argumentative text: it has a superstructure—the schematic form that organizes the global meaning of a text; it is a problem-solving process; and its goal is to convince the audience of the points made in the text (see Teo, 1995, pp. 17–39 for a detailed discussion of this model).

In the same tradition of study of academic writing, Meyer (1997, p. 19) suggests that

> perhaps the most interesting group of relevant lexemes are speech-act verbs and nouns (*argue, assumption, explanation, describe, recommendation*) which explicate

the pragmatic status of linguistic acts performed, mentioned or reported in a text. . . . It is obvious that they play a central role in the structure of technical texts. What is more, they signal one aspect of text structure . . . that is both typical of and common to all technical discourse . . . and that is manifested in a wide variety of expressions . . . It is at these words that we look for information on what the authors are doing in their texts, and what they ascribe to other authors. And this is often more revealing to the expert than the references to subject matter proper.

Varieties, however, differ in how argumentation and persuasion is viewed in their context of writing. One additional point worth keeping in mind is that text types such as narrative, argumentative-persuasive, expressive, etc., are not absolute categories. For instance, Parret (1987, p. 165) observes that there is overlap between argumentation and narration: "nobody can deny that argumentation and narrativity overlap in many sequences of discourse as well as of everyday language. . . ." Hatim (1991, p. 190) notes "texts are multifunctional, normally displaying features of more than one type, and constantly shifting from one type to another." According to Beaugrande and Dressler (1981, p. 183), the major difficulty in text typology is that "many actualized instances do not manifest complete or exact characteristics of an ideal type." Biber (1986, p. 390) supports this conclusion, "the identity of the salient text-type distinctions in English is an unresolved issue." It has been suggested that, in view of the difficulty of identifying text types, the notion of text type be seen as an abstraction.

In the Inner Circle academic circles, the purpose of argumentative-persuasive text is to convince the audience of the acceptability of one's position. It is, therefore, important to state one's thesis explicitly and marshal arguments to support that in a direct manner.

This, however, is not the model that other cultures follow. For instance, Chinese students are said to be taught to devote the opening paragraph of an essay to statements of universal truth; only after that is it appropriate to broach the topic of the paper (Lisle and Mano, 1997, p. 16). In the Japanese and Korean traditions, an essay consists of at least one tangentially related sub-topic "brought up with few overt transition markers" (Hinds, 1987, p. 150).

In Arabic rhetoric, verbal artistry and emotional impact are the primary measures of persuasive power: rhythm, sound, repetition, and emphatic assertion carry more weight than factual evidence, and organization may depend more on metaphor and association than on linear logic (Lisle and Mano, 1997, p. 17). This is supported by Sa'adeddin (1989, pp. 38–39), who makes a distinction between two different modes of text development: aural and visual. The former is characterized by recurrent and plain lexis, exaggeration, repetition of syntactic structures, loose packaging of infor-mation, a lack of apparent coherence, etc.—that is, a style that signals informality and solidarity, highly valued in the Arabic tradition. The latter, on the other hand, has the features of linearization, progressive development of a thesis, logical coherence, and syntactic cohesiveness, all of which are highly valued in the Western tradition.

Indirection and circumlocutory rhetoric are a part of African discourse strategy, as well. "By 'stalking' the issues, the speaker demonstrates skill and arouses hearers' interest. The person who gets directly to the issues is said to have little imagination and even less flair for rhetorical style" (Asante, 1987, p. 51).

A standard textbook on grammar and composition in Hindi published by the National Council of Educational Research and Training, India (Vyas *et al.*, 1972, p. 209), mentions the following categories of essays: descriptive, narrative, deliberative, explanatory, and imaginative, and further reduces these to three groups: descriptive (including narrative), deliberative (including explanatory), and imaginative. Argumentation is one subtype of deliberation or explanation; it is not a distinct category. The advice given to students in Vyas *et al.* (1972, p. 209; emphasis added) is as follows:

> For elaboration [i.e. the body of the essay], material should be categorized carefully to facilitate the sequential presentation of points. Everything that is said must be proved by arguments, facts, events, or quotation [i.e. citing authority] and they should be arranged in such a form that *readers can easily arrive at the conclusion desired by the writer.*

The purpose is not to *provide solutions* and *convince* the audience of their rightness; rather, it is to *lead* the readers to find the right solutions. Thus, deliberative essays are indirect by design.

World Englishes provide a rich data source for the study of cultural differences in what is meant by argumentation and persuasion across different traditions of literacy.

GENRE ANALYSIS

Genre is a highly structured and conventionalized communicative event, and most people have no difficulty in identifying the genre that a text belongs to when they come across it. Within the oral tradition, even small children can tell the difference between nursery rhymes and fairy tales. Most readers of newspapers are aware of the difference between news reports and opinion pieces. Academic communities have felt a need for a variety of genres and members of the professional, or academic, community have greater knowledge of the conventional purpose(s), construction, and use of specific genres than those who are non-specialists. Greater knowledge makes it possible for specialists to exploit the conventions for private intents.

Writers have freedom to use linguistic resources in any way they like; however, they must conform to certain standard practices within the boundaries of a particular genre.

Bhatia (1993, pp. 23–24) describes the following seven steps for a comprehensive analysis, "depending upon the purpose of the analysis, the aspect of genre one wants to focus upon, and the background knowledge one already has of the nature of the genre in question."

1. *Placing the given text in a situational context*: First, one identifies a genre-text (a typical example of the genre) intuitively in a situational context by calling upon one's prior experience, the internal clues in the text, and one's encyclopedic knowledge. The non-specialist may have to acquire the necessary knowledge by surveying available literature.

2. *Surveying existing literature*: This may involve surveying pertinent literature in the areas of linguistic, sociocultural, genre, and other types of analyses and acquiring knowledge of related speech community.

3. *Refining the situational/contextual analysis*: The intuitive placement of a text in a situational context needs to be refined by (a) defining the participant roles and relationships; (b) defining the historical, social, cultural, philosophic, and/or occupational placement of the relevant community; (c) identifying the surrounding texts and linguistic traditions that form the background of the text, and (d) "identifying the topic/subject/extra-textual reality which the text is trying to represent, change or use, and the relationship of the text to that reality" (p. 23).

4. *Selecting the corpus*: Selection of the right kind and size of corpus requires (a) defining the genre/sub-genre according to its communicative purposes, situational context(s), and distinctive textual characteristics; and (b) an explicit statement of the criteria based on which the text is assigned to the genre/subgenre.

5. *Studying the institutional context*: The institutional context of the use of the genre is important, since "rules and conventions (linguistic, social, cultural, academic, and/or professional) that govern the use of language in such institutional settings . . . are most often implicitly understood and unconsciously followed by the participants in the communication situation" (p. 24).

6. *Levels of linguistic analysis*: The analyst has to decide at which level of analysis the most characteristic or significant linguistic features occur. The levels are those of lexico-grammatical features, text-patterning, or textualization (the way a linguistic device is used in a restricted sense, e.g. past participles in a scientific article (p. 26)), and structural

interpretation of the text genre (e.g. the four-move cognitive structure of research article introduction discussed by Swales: establishing the research field, summarizing pervious research, preparing for present research, and introducing the present research, cited on p. 30).

7. *Specialist information in genre analysis*: Finally, the analysts need to establish their findings against reactions from one or more expert informants. The expert reaction confirms the findings, brings validity to the insights gained, and adds psychological reality to the analysis (p. 34).

Bhatia cautions that the steps are not to be followed strictly in order. The analysis may reveal patterns, but they are not to be taken as prescriptive norms. Genre analysis is pattern-seeking rather than pattern-imposing.

One set of examples may make the process of analysis clear. The research article abstract is a well-established genre and familiar to academics in general irrespective of their disciplinary affiliations. An abstract answers four questions for the readers of the article: what is the purpose of the research, what was done, what were the findings, and what is to be concluded from the findings. Bhatia proposes four *moves* of analysis to correspond with the four elements identified above (1993, pp. 78–79): introducing purpose, describing methodology, summarizing results, and presenting conclusions.

Two examples of academic paper abstracts are presented below to illustrate the structure of an abstract proposed in the above account:

27. This paper provides a description of the pragmatics of language use in Egyptian English newspaper editorials. Editorials are defined as "acts of passing judgment", and Searle's (1979) taxonomy of illocutionary acts is used to compare editorials from Egyptian, American, and Egyptian Arabic newspapers. The results show that Egyptian English conforms neither to the American English nor to Egyptian Arabic patterns with regard to the use of representatives and declaratives. It uses more declaratives and fewer representatives than American English, but fewer declaratives and more representatives than Egyptian Arabic. Qualitative as well as quantitative differences in the usage of the illocutionary acts are discussed, and it is hypothesized that American English places more emphasis on Grice's (1975) maxim of quantity, while Egyptian English places more emphasis on the maxim of quality. (Reynolds, 1993, p. 35)

The first sentence describes the purpose of the study, *This paper provides a description of the pragmatics of language use in Egyptian English newspaper editorials.* The first half of the second sentence—*Editorials are defined as "acts of passing judgment"*—defines the editorial, which is extra background knowledge. The second half answers the question, what was done: *Searle's (1979) taxonomy of illocutionary acts is used to compare editorials from Egyptian, American, and Egyptian*

Arabic newspapers. The next two sentences describe the findings: *The results show that Egyptian English conforms neither to the American English nor to Egyptian Arabic patterns with regard to the use of representatives and declaratives. It uses more declaratives and fewer representatives than American English, but fewer declaratives and more representatives than Egyptian Arabic.* The last sentence suggests what can be concluded from the research and its findings: *Qualitative as well as quantitative differences in the usage of the illocutionary acts are discussed, and it is hypothesized that American English places more emphasis on Grice's (1975) maxim of quantity, while Egyptian English places more emphasis on the maxim of quality.* Thus, the above abstract seems to closely conform to the generic structure suggested in Bhatia (1993), except for one creative element—the definition of an editorial.

Now consider a second example of another research paper:

28.   This article attempts to provide a precise definition for topic and to derive most of the properties of topic from this definition. The main assumption is that the topic-comment construction is a syntactic device employed to fulfill certain discourse functions. Topic is always related to a position inside the comment. Since topic has no independent thematic role but always depends on an element inside the comment for its thematic role, it has no syntactic function of its own. This dependence relationship is subject to locality constraints. (Shi, 2000, p. 383)

The first sentence of the abstract states the purpose of the research study: *This article attempts to provide a precise definition for topic and to derive most of the properties of topic from this definition.* The second and the third sentences propose a hypothesis: *The main assumption is that the topic-comment construction is a syntactic device employed to fulfill certain discourse functions. Topic is always related to a position inside the comment.* Although there is no explicit statement about a methodology, i.e. what was done, it is implied that the methodology of research will involve testing the proposed hypothesis. The next sentence draws a conclusion from confirmation, again implied, of the hypothesis: *Since topic has no independent thematic role but always depends on an element inside the comment for its thematic role, it has no syntactic function of its own.* And the last sentence reports another related research finding: *This dependence relationship is subject to locality constraints.*

One example of a study that explores the crosscultural generic difference in book blurbs is Kathpalia (1997). The study attempts to determine if there are culture-specific differences in how patrons are encouraged to buy books. She examines this genre in books published by "international publishers" and those published in Singapore by local publishers.

According to Kathpalia (1997, p. 417), blurbs comprise six basic moves: *headlines* followed by *justifying the book; appraising the book; establishing credentials; endorsement(s);* and *targeting the market,* in this order. Each of the moves has a specific function. The opening moves of *headlines* and *justifying the book* attract readers and convince them that the book conforms to the conventions of the discipline but at the same time is innovative. *Appraising the book* provides a brief synopsis and evaluation of the book. *Establishing credentials* and *endorsements* validate the book by displaying the writer's authority to write the book and citing supporting evidence from well-known reviewers. Finally, *targeting the market* specifies the market for which the book is suitable.

Kathpalia's study found two major sorts of differences between the books published by international publishers and those published by publishers in Singapore, or local books. First, both sets of blurb-writers follow the general conventions of book blurbs. However, there are differences in the favored moves and the distribution of moves across scholarly and popular books. For instance, *justifying the book, appraising the book* and *targeting the market* are favored both in scholarly and non-fictional local trade book blurbs, whereas *establishing credentials* and *endorsements* are rare, even in scholarly book blurbs.

Local book blurbs follow the sequence of moves faithfully and often consist of one-, two- or three-move structures, with *appraising the book* as the central or criterial move. Thus, the moves are *justifying the book, appraising the book, targeting the market* or *establishing credentials* or *endorsements*. Among the few structural deviations to be found is one in which *targeting the market* appears as the initial move.

Kathpalia describes other differences in the exploitation of linguistic patterns that international and local book blurbs seem to prefer. One of the salient differences is in the use of linguistic devices to achieve a specific purpose. In international book blurbs evaluation of the book is ubiquitous and not confined to the *evaluation* move. This is achieved by choosing appropriate lexical items and expressions (e.g. *invaluable, direct, uncluttered,* etc., in (29)). Local book blurbs focus on the *Evaluation* move and concentrate all such expressions in the sub-move that specifies the caliber of the book (see the italicized final part of (30)).

29.   International book blurb
      The *invaluable* reference for the SPSSTM user provides information in a
      direct, uncluttered manner. Meyer's *user-friendly* approach makes infor-
      mation *quickly* accessible to students in statistics and social-science
      methodology courses. . . .

30.   Local book blurb
      Adopting an integrated, multidisciplinary approach to the political geography
      of the Indian Ocean, this study analyses the Law of the Sea, evaluates the
      national legislation of those Indian Ocean littoral states which have pro-
      claimed their maritime limits over offshore waters, . . . *Apart from the well written
      text, perhaps the most important aspects of the work is the exceptional series of beautifully
      drawn maps and diagrams accompanied by detailed captions and commentaries, a
      unique collection worthy of publication on its own.*

These examples reveal that within the generic structure, there is considerable freedom to express one's intents as in the abstracts to academic papers and to choose how to verbalize which moves, as in the book blurbs. Not all the moves are essential in a genre, and conventions across disciplines and cultures may differ as to which ones are vital for achieving which purpose. For more and varied examples of genre analysis, see Bhatia (1996, 1997).

CONCLUSION

The discussion in this chapter makes it clear that speaking and writing are creative activities as all linguistic acts are, and they are based on individual experience situated in a context. The context is bound to reflect itself in written texts as much as in oral performances (Y. Kachru 2001a, 2001b). The processes described above represent one important aspect of the acculturation and nativization of English in the Other Circles. It is perfectly legitimate to make all writers aware of the rhetorical patterns preferred in Inner Circle Englishes; it is equally legitimate and desirable to make English educators aware of the different rhetorical conventions of world majority learners and users of English (Y. Kachru, 1997b). Just as we welcome diversity in dress, food, and various artifacts and fine arts, we should be prepared to appreciate diversity reflected in the medium that expresses so many different messages. It is axiomatic that no language is more or less logical than another; similarly, no rhetorical pattern is more or less logical or ideal.

Further Reading

Bhatia, V. K. (1996) Nativization of job applications in South Asia. In R. Baumgardner (ed.), *South Asian English: Structure, Use, and Users* (pp. 158–173). Urbana, IL: University of Illinois Press.
Frenck, S. and Min, S. J. (2001) Culture, reader and textual intelligibility. In E. Thumboo (ed.), *The Three Circles of English* (pp. 19–34). Singapore: UniPress.
Hinds, J. (1987) Reader versus writer responsibility: a new typology. In U. Connor and R. B. Kaplan (eds), *Writing across Languages: Analysis of L2 Text* (pp. 141–152). Reading, MA: Addison-Wesley.
Nwoye, G. O. (1992) Obituary announcements as communicative events in Nigerian English. *World Englishes*, 11(1), 15–27.

Suggested Activities

1. Read the following news item from the *Daily Nation* published from Nairobi, Kenya, and note down the differences you observe between

news reporting in this daily and the daily papers with which you are familiar. Also note down any linguistic features with which you are unfamiliar.

TWO ANGRY HUSBANDS SLIT THEIR THROATS
by Odhiambo-Orlale

Two men tried to take their lives by slitting their throats in separate incidents at the weekend.

The attempted suicides occurred in Kisumu and Nyeri.

In the first case, a 32-year-old father stormed into the Kisumu market on Friday afternoon, bought a Bible and a kitchen knife and tried to kill himself after a quarrel.

The drama occurred outside the market shortly after the man had attempted to see his wife at the Kisumu Medical Training centre where she is a student.

The man, who lives in the town, went to the centre to discuss a problem with his wife.

He sent somebody to call her from the hostels while he remained outside at the main gate. When she came, they had a short talk and the woman walked back to the halls of residence.

The man's attempts to convince her to return and see him at the gate were unsuccessful.

All the students sent by him to ask her to return told him she would not do so until he took to her their only child.

The 32-year-old husband, furious at the snub, walked to the municipal market where he bought a Bible and a knife.

He tried to commit suicide by slitting his throat but was rescued by wananchi. They took him to the New Nyanza General Hospital, which is next to the centre, and admitted in serious condition.

2. "ESP [English for Specific Purposes] is generally practiced on the basic assumption that it is both desirable and feasible to delimit the language to be learned to match a specification of learner requirements. But is such a delimitation desirable? . . . ESP could be interpreted as a device for keeping people in their place" (Widdowson, 1984, p. 190).

You have experienced the teaching of academic English. Do you agree with this observation in the quote above? What bearing does Y. Kachru (1995b) have on this issue?

Briefly, Y. Kachru (1995b) argues that the learners and users of English in the Outer Circle acquire discoursal rules for regulating interpersonal relations on the one hand, and how humans express their own requirements and understand what others are doing on the other hand, within their own particular cultural context from a very early age; that is, even before they acquire mastery of a language, and possibly continue to do so over one's entire lifetime. The varieties of

English differ in the details of such discoursal rules, and the only reasonable course of action for ELT enterprise is to encourage individual creativity while imparting received conventions of academic writing. It is the tension between the conventions and the innovative spirit of writers that produces good writing, whether in academic disciplines or in creative literature.

Chapter 10

Contextualizing World Englishes Literatures

English
is my mother tongue.
A mother tongue is not
not a foreign lan lan lang
language
l/anguish
anguish
-a foreign anguish. . . .

I have no mother
tongue
no mother to tongue
no tongue to mother
to mother
tongue
me.

Marlene Nourbese Philip
(1989; born in Tobago, now living in Canada)

I search for my tongue. . . .
You ask me what I mean
by saying I have lost my tongue
I ask you, what would you do
if you had two tongues in your mouth,
and lost the first one, the mother tongue,
and could not really know the other.
the foreign tongue.
You could not use them both together
even if you thought that way;
And if you lived in a place where you had to
speak a foreign tongue—

your mother tongue would rot,
rot and die in your mouth
unitl you had to spit it out.
                    Sujata Bhatt (1988; Gujarati speaker
                    from India, now living in the USA)

INTRODUCTION

The previous chapters have demonstrated that conventions of language use
are different in different regions of the English-using world. Chapters 8 and
9 have suggested ways of informing ourselves about these conventions by
drawing upon research findings in conversational styles and rhetorical
practices. In this chapter we would like to explore the possibility of utilizing
another resource for familiarizing ourselves with world Englishes. The
resource is creative literature produced by Outer and Expanding Circle
writers within or outside these Circles. These have been termed "contact
literatures" (B. Kachru, 1986c) and we will use this term throughout this
chapter instead of the more cumbersome "Outer and Expanding Circle
English literatures."

It has been suggested that globalization is creating new, hybrid forms of
culture, language, and political organization (Graddol, 1997). In fact, trade
and commerce and conquests have been creating hybrid forms of culture,
language, and political organizations for centuries. The influence of Indian
culture and traditions all over Southeast Asia in the pre-Islamic period left a
permanent mark of Sanskrit and Pali on languages and art forms of
Cambodia, Indonesia, Thailand, and other countries in the region. The effect
of Buddhism is discernible all over Asia, including China. The impact of
Persian language and aesthetics in South Asia has resulted in a rich heritage.
The influence of Greek and Latin languages and Roman and Greek thought
gives Europe its common cultural heritage and political institutions. The
English language owes a great deal to the impact of Romance languages, and
most East Asian languages and cultures have been enriched by Chinese
thought, language, and writing system.

What is different about the spread of English in the later half of the
twentieth century is the worldwide influence of one language and its
consequences. Some writers feel the agony of using a medium for expressing
themselves that did not originate from the same source as they did, as do the
poets quoted at the beginning of this chapter (see also, Ngũgĩ, 1981, 1986,
1991). On the other hand, there are writers, such as Chinua Achebe, Raja
Rao, and Salman Rushdie, who celebrate the medium as it transforms itself
by undergoing the processes of acculturation and nativization under the
impact of their creative energies (see, Achebe, 1965; Rao, 1978a; Rushdie,
1991). Not only have the English language and European cultures and

traditions become part of the cultural heritage of the whole world, the world cultures and multiple languages have left their imprint on the English language and given rise to multiple canons of literature in the Three Circles.

The writers of contact literatures from the Caribbean, India, the Philippines, West Africa, Southeast Asia, or wherever, as Thumboo observes (1985, p. 215), come from "powerful traditions marked by particular linguistic, literary and aesthetic pre-occupations that constitute what can be conveniently called a literary ecology. When the ex-Empire writes back, this ecology is implicit in varying degrees."

WHY LITERARY TEXT?

Contact literatures have by now earned a prominent place in world literatures, as is obvious from the numerous prestigious awards such works have won. These include: (1) the **Nobel Prize** in literature to Wole Soyinka (Nigeria) in 1986, Derek Alton Walcott (Trinidad) in 1992, V. S. Naipaul (of Indian origin, born in Trinidad, resident of Britain) in 2001; (2) the **Booker Prize** to Keri Hulme (Maori writer, New Zealand) in 1985, Chinua Achebe (Nigeria) in 1987, Ben Okri (Nigeria) in 1991, Micahel Ondaatje (born in Sri Lanka, living in Canada) in 1992, Salman Rushdie (born in India, resident of Britain) in 1995, Arundhati Roy (India) in 1997, Kiran Desai (born in India, residing in the USA) in 2006; (3) the **Betty Trask Award** to Hari Kunzru (of Indian origin, living in Britain) in 2002; (4) the **Neustadt Prize** to Raja Rao (born in India, living in the USA) in 1988; and (5) the **Pulitzer Prize** to Jhumpa Lahiri (of Indian origin, born in London, living in the USA) in 2000.

With the success of writers such as the ones mentioned above, attempts are being made to adopt them within the literary traditions of the Anglo-American literature. As Ashcroft *et al.* (1989, p. 7) observe:

> [T]hrough the literary canon, the body of British texts which all too frequently still acts as a touchstone of taste and value, and through RS-English (Received Standard English), which asserts the English of south-east England as a universal norm, the weigh of antiquity continues to dominate the cultural productions in much of the post-colonial world. This *cultural hegemony* has been maintained through canonical assumptions about literary activity, and through attitudes to post-colonial literatures which identify them as isolated national off-shoots of English literature, and which therefore relegate them to marginal and subordinate positions. *More recently, as the range and strength of these literatures has become undeniable, a process of incorporation has begun in which, employing Eurocentric standards of judgment, the centre has sought to claim those works and writers of which it approves as British.* (Italic added)

However, appropriating contact literatures within the canon of Anglo-American literature is not easy; the genres, literary and linguistic devices of particular eco-systems seep into the literary works that have no precedence and no interpretation within the Anglo-American canon (Thumboo, 1985). According to Thumboo (1985, p. 219) the language [i.e. English] is re-tooled to "reflect the subtlety of thought and the shades of meaning to the extent realizable in the language of one's own eco-system." Ashcroft *et al.* make the same point when they observe (1989, p. 10):

> The gap which opens between the experience of place and the language available to describe it forms a classic and all-pervasive feature of post-colonial texts. . . . So, for example, an Indian writer like Raja Rao or a Nigerian writer such as Chinua Achebe has needed to transform the language, to use it in a different way in its new context.

The controversies regarding the canonicity of these literatures notwithstanding (see B. Kachru, 2005a, for a discussion of this point), they are now considered eminently suitable for incorporation into English curricula in the Inner Circle and are thus exploitable for teaching English literatures and world Englishes in other contexts, too. In fact, colleges and universities around the world by now have begun introducing selections from several authors of repute from Africa, the Caribbean, the Philippines, South Asia, and Southeast Asia.

There are advantages to using literary works in English language teaching, as has been discussed in B. Kachru (1986e). They are a valuable source of sociocultural knowledge not easily recoverable from grammars, dictionaries, and textbooks. First, the material is readily available. Second, the works are produced by highly competent users of English from these Circles; they are of value as aesthetic objects in their own right. Additionally, in order to be perceived as "rooted in the culture" of their places of origin, they must represent "authentic" lifestyles, including styles of interaction. Thus, the **cultural themes** and patterns of verbal interactions contained in these works are of considerable value to scholars, researchers, and students of world Englishes (B. Kachru, 1986e; Tawake, 1990, 1993). We will discuss their relevance to our enterprise in terms of the following categories, discussed with examples below.

CULTURAL THEMES

There are several cultural themes that recur in literatures in English, or as Ashcroft *et al.* (1989, p. 217, n 3) label them, "english literatures."[1] The themes are related to the following domains: interpersonal (e.g. "parent–child," "wife–husband," "friends," "colleagues," "groups," "networks"); institutional (e.g. "school," "job," "profession," "politics"); value-related (e.g. "loyalty," "fidelity," "devotion to family"); and belief-related (e.g. "spirituality," "God," "heaven," "rebirth," "salvation").

To take one example out of the above list, the dynamics of family relationships are not identical across cultures, which is clear if one compares
fiction by writers such as Achebe (Nigeria), Lim (Southeast Asia), Desai
(India), and Hulme (New Zealand, Maori writer). For instance, Tawake
(1993, p. 325) claims that in one of the possible readings of the novel, *The Bone
People* (Hulme 1985), the work may be interpreted, to start with, as dealing
with a theme of disconnection from family. She then notes that "family in the
Maori context involves broader networks of connections than it does in typical
Western contexts." An added dimension is that what binds people in a family
is "their attachment to the land and their common heritage" (p. 330). From
this point of view, the three main characters have undergone disconnections,
but together form a new network: "in a meld of Maori-Caucasian blood lines,
they establish a family of the future" (p. 330). Courtright (2001) found that
for the culture-different readers of Desai's short story, *A Devoted Son* (1978),
the nature of the relationship between the father and the son was a mystery.
They had difficulty in interpreting the Western-educated physician son's
treatment of his old and ailing father in the story.

A close reading of the verbal behavior of characters in works of fiction
yields valuable insights into the cultural themes crucial for interpretation.
One example is provided in Y. Kachru (1993b), where the following excerpt
(Singh, 1959, p. 17) reflects the cultural context and lets the readers discover
the similarities and differences between what they are familiar with and the
"unfamiliar" being presented in the text:[2]

1. "This heat has given me a headache," he complained and stood up. "I am
   going to bed."
   "Yes, you must be tired," agreed his mother. "Champak, press his head,
   he will sleep better."
   "I will," replied Champak, standing up. She bent her head to receive her
   mother-in-law's blessing. "*Sat Sri Akal.*"
   "*Sat Sri Akal,*" replied Sabhrai lightly touching Champak's shoulder.
   "*Sat Sri Akal,*" said Sher Singh.
   "Live in plenty. Live a long age," replied Sabhrai taking her son's hand
   and kissing it. "Sleep well."

All the words in the above communicative event are from English, except for
the greeting *Sat Sri Akal.* The context is also familiar, situated in the family
domain, a son declaring he is going to bed and uttering a greeting before
retiring and his mother giving a response appropriate within the sociocultural tradition of the place. Other elements of the text, however, may not
be as easily *interpretable.* Some of the obvious "unfamiliar" contextual factors
may be the fact of the mother-in-law's presence on the scene, the command
that the mother-in-law issues to the daughter-in-law to "press" the son's head,
and the daughter-in-law and the son receiving the elder's "blessing" before
retiring for the night. A further not-so-obvious cultural feature is the mother's

response to son's words as compared to her gesture following the daughter-in-law's utterance. Indian readers of the novel with literary sensibility would wonder about the relationship between the mother-in-law and the daughter-in-law just based upon the two sets of exchanges. And they would be proven right: later in the novel it becomes clear that the mother-in-law is not very fond of the daughter-in-law: "Sabhrai, who had never particularly cared for Champak, stroked her head" (p. 189).

At the level of language, the greeting *Sat Sri Akal* identifies the family as belonging to the Sikh community, and the son's expression followed by mother's blessings "Live in plenty" "Live a long age" represent the traditional pattern of such exchanges in South Asia (Y. Kachru, 1995b). Other features of the interchange require relevant background knowledge for interpretation. The command to her daughter-in-law, "Press his head," is normal in that in the joint family, where the married sons live with their parents, the daughters-in-law are treated no different from the daughters—they are expected to obey their parents-in-law in the same way as the daughters are. Thus, the institution of family as it functions in India and the patterns of interaction that are attested in that context may not be familiar to all readers.

The above example illustrates the conversational styles in the intimate domain in one culture. The speech acts, styles of writing, and verbal repertoire of users of English differ from region to region and are represented in works of literature as the following two examples show. The first has its source in a work of fiction from Africa, the second from a piece of poetry from Southeast Asia:

2. From Saro-Wiwa (1989, p. 76):
   Chief Minster: I want to see the Chairman of the Corporation.
   Security Guard: Why for?
   Chief Minister: It's private.
   Security Guard: Private, ehn?
   Chief Minister: Yes.
   Security Guard: Wetting be dis place? Not office? Dis na office. If you wan see Sherman for private you just go to his house. Dis na office time.

The use of pidgin in the Security Guard's speech is for characterization purposes: he is not very well educated and does not command the acrolect. A full interpretation of the passage demands acquiring knowledge of the entire verbal repertoire of Nigerians and the state of education and institutional set up in Nigeria.

3. From Mohd Haji Salleh's *Time and Its People*, quoted in Thumboo (1985, p. 216):
   no I shall never wade this river
   of music to the upper bank of dryness

the flute and heart-stringed ukelele
soak a slow rhythm into me.
how can I ever dry myself
from a keroncong.
a sad song.

The genre of *keroncong,* according to Thumboo (1985), is a genre of Malay tradition that rests on feelings of sweet-sadness, not something momentary as in the "Ode to Melancholy," but as an appropriate state of being, inspired and annotated by a sense of the brevity of life.

Similarly, Lim's *Lost Name Woman* expresses the fractured identity of an immigrant (the *lost name* woman), who has lost her family since she moved away from her place, her extended family, and her ancestors in the home country. The successive generations carrying out the duties toward the dead ancestors, i.e. performing the rites that are supposed to keep the ancestors satiated in their afterlife, are not a certainty in the new place with the new identity. The stanzas of the poem locate the woman in several states in the USA and mention her wearing jeans, drinking soda, frizzing her hair and speaking English, and end with the last two lines quoted here (Lim, 1998, p. 42):

Woman with the lost name,
Who will feed you when you die?

The superficial images of dress and hair styles, drinks, and speech, should not detract from the fact that there is a wealth of cultural traditions, family loyalties, rituals, notions of duty and obligation that lie behind the 18 lines of the poem.

At another level of interpretation, as Lim herself observes (1994, p. 27): "the experience expressed in this poem is an analogue for the precarious situation of the English-speaking Asian woman writer. In 'marrying' the English language, the engendering of self occurs as the consciousness of alienation from a native culture." An exhaustive interpretation of the poem leads one to the rich cultural heritage of Asia in general and China in particular on the one hand, and the condition of the writers of contact literatures on the other hand.

Non-verbal behavior patterns, such as gestures, body postures, and gaze patterns, are part of the sign system that humans use to convey meanings in interaction. English literatures in the Three Circles contain interesting and revealing information about these signs that are meaningful and open to misinterpretation by readers from a different culture. For instance, in many cultures, including those of Asia, Africa, and Native America, children and young people are expected to keep their head and eyes lowered and maintain silence while the elders, including teachers, speak to them. In Anglo-

American culture, not looking at the person with whom one is interacting is considered a sign of deviousness on the part of the person who avoids looking at the speaker. Detailed discussions of gestures and their meanings across cultures are available in, e.g. Adams (1987), Hall (1959), McNeil (2000), Molcho (1985), Morris (1978), Payatos (1988), and Wolfgang (1984).

Writing in literate societies is part of verbal behavior and is also governed by conventions (Ferdman *et al.*, 1994; Freebody and Welch, 1993; Heath, 1983; Y. Kachru, 1997a, 1997b, 1997c; Scribner and Cole 1981). First, according to research in literacy, the aims, domains, genres, and rhetorical strategies of literacy practices differ in various societies (Y. Kachru, 2001a, 2001b, 2001c). Second, conventions that govern writing in any particular domain and in any specific genre are to a large extent culture-specific as are the rhetorical strategies (see Chapter 9).

Literary genres across cultures differ, as has been mentioned above, though language and cultural contact have resulted in cross-fertilization and hybrid forms of genres in many world literatures. Examples are Japanese haiku in English, Western-style fiction and lyrics, and Persian genres of *ghazals* and *masnavis* in South Asian literatures (see Russell, 1999 for accounts of these literary forms). For the purposes of this book, what is fascinating is the experimentation and acculturation of the English language in literatures around the world.

EXPONENTS OF CREATIVITY

The rhetorical strategies that creative writers adopt in their use of English is illustrated by Achebe in two versions of the same content (quoted in B. Kachru, 1986a (1990 edition), p. 162). Achebe states that the following examples "will give some idea of how I approach the use of English":

4. a. I want one of my sons to join these people and be my eyes there. If there is nothing in it you will come back. But if there is something then you will bring back my share. The world is like a mask, dancing. If you want to see it well, you do not stand in one place. My spirit tells me that those who do not befriend the white man today will be saying, "had we known," tomorrow.

Achebe goes on to say, "supposing I had put it another way. Like this, for instance":

4. b. I am sending you as my representative among these people—just to be on the safe side in case the new religion develops. One has to move with the times or else one is left behind. I have a hunch that those who fail to come to terms with the white man may well regret their lack of foresight.

Although the version in (4b) is closer to the Inner Circle Standard English version in terms of rhetorical strategies, Achebe asserts: "The material is the same. But the form of the one is in character and the other is not." That is, the version in (4a) is closer to the rhetorical strategies of the Nigerian character.

Rao (1963, pp. vii–viii) had made similar observations earlier, explaining his instinctive use of the rhetorical strategies of Kannada in his novel, *Kanthapura*:

5.   There is no village in India, however mean, that has not a rich sthala-purana or legendary history of its own . . . The Puranas are endless and innumerable. We have neither punctuation nor the treacherous "ats" and "ons" to bother us—we tell one interminable tale. Episode follows episode, and when our thoughts stop our breath stops, and we move on to another thought. This was and still is the ordinary style of our story telling. I have tried to follow it myself in this story.

Tutuola of West Africa shares the same style of story telling by bending all Inner Circle norms of punctuation and rhythm in prose (Taiwo, 1976, p. 76):

6.   When he tried all his power for several times and failed and again at that moment the smell of the gun powder of the enemies' gun which were shooting repeatedly was rushing to our noses by the breeze and this made us fear more, so my brother lifted me again a very short distance, but when I saw that he was falling several times, then I told him to leave me on the road and run away for his life perhaps he might be safe so that he would be taking care of our mother as she had no other sons more than both of us . . .

Some of this 'retooling' of language is spontaneous, but some is conscious and achieved with effort, as is clear from another African writer, Okara's (1964, p. 137) statement:

In order to capture the vivid images of African speech, I had to eschew the habit of expressing my thoughts first in English. It was difficult at first, but I had to learn. I had to study each probable Ijaw expression. I used to discover a situation in which it was used in order to bring out the nearest meaning in English.

The results are a stylistic success, as is evident from the following passage (Okara, 1964, p. 26):

7.   It was the day's ending and Okolo by a window stood. Okolo stood looking at the sun behind the tree tops falling. The river was flowing, reflecting the fininishing sun, like a dying away memory. It was like an idol's face, no one knowing what is behind. Okolo at the palm trees looked. They were like women with hair hanging down, dancing, possessed. Egrets, like white

flower petals strung slackly across the river, swaying up and down, were returning home. And, on the river, canoes were crawling home with bent backs and tired hands, paddling.

The excerpts above illustrate rhetorical strategies; in addition, speakers and writers have employed many devices at the levels of lexicon, idioms, and metaphors to express their creative potential (see Chapter 7).

TEACHING ENGLISH LITERATURES IN VARIOUS CONTEXTS

We have argued above for the relevance of literary works for the study of language and culture. The question naturally arises as to the best way of approaching the teaching of literature in language classes.

There are various methods one could adopt. One would be to read, say, short stories by a number of authors from different regions and compare their language use and their techniques of plot construction, characterization, etc. This would be more or less in the tradition of literary studies.

Another way may be to ask the participants in a class to "think aloud" as they read the material and record it (Black, 1995). These think-aloud protocols then may be analyzed by the readers and teachers together to see where the readers had difficulty with intelligibility, comprehensibility, and interpretability. Think-aloud protocols have been used in research for various purposes (e.g. in translation, in reading and teaching literature in second languages; see Davis and Bistodeau (1993) on second language reading, Jääskeläinen (2002) for a bibliography on translation; and Ericsson and Simon (1993) on the methodology of protocol analysis). Some work has been done in the area of world Englishes also employing this methodology.

Courtright (2001) utilized this methodology to investigate the process of reading and interpreting literary works in English by culturally different readers. The methodology essentially consists of "getting people who are doing something to verbalize their thoughts and feelings as they do whatever they are doing" (Patton, 2002). She selected Chinua Achebe, from Nigeria, and Anita Desai, from India, both well-known Outer Circle writers. She used their short stories, *The Madman* (Achebe) and *A Devoted Son* (Desai), as the study texts to elicit "think-aloud" protocols from six readers. Two Nigerian and two Indian consultants worked with Courtright to scrutinize the texts for their "[sociocultura] representatives, critical acceptability, and the multilingual creativity" (p. 46), and two readers from the USA also read the stories. All of them recorded their reactions to what they were reading as they went along. The stories were marked into units, usually of paragraph length, and the readers were asked to comment aloud on each unit as they read.

First, they told "what they understood of the section," then what they felt its "significance" was in the course of the whole text so far, and finally, "they asked any questions they had about any aspect of the text" (p. 51). Courtright says that "[t]he first two tasks correspond roughly to Smith's levels of comprehensibility and interpretability, while the third . . . may involve aspects of any level of Intelligibility" (p. 51) (See Chapter 4 for a discussion of these concepts.)

Readers' responses included, for example, an Indian reader who related scenes in Achebe's *The Madman* such as "a small village market" to familiar comparable scenes in India, and a US reader who said, "I found myself wanting to understand the story more than I was able to." The US reader commented:

> So much was assumed concerning the cultural taboos of running naked into the occult part of the market. Granted, I can figure out that it's not a bright thing to do, but I felt like there was so much more meaning attached to it than I was able to glean. (p. 128)

However, the reader did enjoy the challenge of trying to make sense of another culture.

This method of helping readers become aware of what they are reading, how they are making sense, or failing to make sense of what they are reading, may be very helpful in developing a critical appreciation of the specific texts under focus, or literary texts in general. It may also help them become aware of literature of their own tradition and looking at the familiar literary works with a new perspective.

CONCLUSION

It is true that not every classroom can teach all English literatures, simply because there is not enough time to provide the background sociocultural information of all the contexts to make the literary works intelligible, comprehensible, and interpretable. But, that does not mean that a judicious selection of texts from various Englishes to raise awareness and consciousness of linguistic and stylistic innovations and cultural themes is an impossible task. In fact, exposure to a few new contexts can go a long way toward opening up the horizons and sensitizing participants to other traditions and texts of literary creativity.

Notes

1. They explain the lower case letter in *english* as follows: "We prefer to see the use of the lower case as a sign of the subversion of the claims to status and privilege to which English usage clings."
2. Y. Kachru (1993b) discusses a part of the excerpt given here, beginning with "She bent her head . . ."

Further Reading

Kachru, B. B. (1995b) Transcultural creativity in world Englishes and literary canons. In G. Cook and B. Seidelhofer (eds), *Principles and Practice in Applied Linguistics: Studies in Honor of H. G. Widdowson* (pp. 271–287). Oxford: Oxford University Press.
Thumboo, E. (1992) The literary dimensions of the spread of English. In B. B. Kachru (ed.), *The Other Tongue: English across Cultures* (2nd edn.) (pp. 255–282). Urbana, IL: University of Illinois Press.

Suggested Activities

1. Ashcroft *et al.* (1989, pp. 8–10) claim that "[a] major feature of post-colonial literatures is the concern with place and displacement." They argue that "a valid and active sense of self" may have been affected by "dislocations" caused by forced migration, enslavement, "voluntary" movement as indentured labor, etc. It may have also been shattered by cultural disparagement and oppression of the indigenous peoples and cultures by a self-proclaimed superior race or culture. The resulting "alienation of vision and the crisis in self-image" finds expression in "the construction of 'place.'" They further suggest that "[t]he gap which opens between the experience of place and the language available to describe it forms a classic and all-pervasive feature of post-colonial texts." That is why "an Indian writer like Raja Rao or a Nigerian writer such as Chinua Achebe have needed to transform the language, to use it in a different way in its new context." Read a literary text from the Outer or Expanding Circle, or one written by a "minority" writer from the Inner Circle, and see if you can justify the claims made above.
2. Look up the full text of the poem quoted from Philip (1989) or Bhatt (1988) or any other that you prefer, and analyze to see if they are comfortable with their bi/multilingualism.

Conclusion: World Englishes: Legacy and Relevance

INTRODUCTION

The preceding chapters present a brief account of the spread and functions of English in the current context of a postcolonial and rapidly globalizing world. The spread of a natural human language across the countries and regions of the planet has resulted in variation as a consequence of nativization and acculturation of the language in various communities as has been discussed extensively in linguistic literature. These processes have affected the grammatical structure and the use of language according to local needs and conventions. Grammatical variation manifests itself in sounds, rhythm, words, processes of word formation, phrases, sentence patterns, idioms and metaphors, and discourse structures and strategies. Linguistic literature is replete with examples of language contact and convergence and their consequences for languages of wider communication such as Arabic, Latin, Persian, and Sanskrit throughout the ages. We have provided examples of such innovations and creativity with reference to Englishes in the earlier chapters. Use of English in various contexts manifests in varied genres, conventions of politeness, code-mixing and switching, and new canons of literary creativity—all the resources of multilingual, multicultural contexts are now part of the heritage of world Englishes.

ATTITUDES AND IDEOLOGIES

This enrichment, however, comes with a cost in terms of attitudes and ideologies. The preceding chapters have not dealt with such issues, not because they are not important, but because the focus of the book has been on raising awareness about the exponents of variation so that people from different parts of the world using the same medium—English—may be able to accommodate to each others' ways of using their own varieties for achieving common goals. In this concluding chapter, a few of the salient issues raised by attitudes and ideologies are discussed briefly. This is reasonable in view of the fact that interactions are never free from attitudes and ideologies. Concerns that arise due to attitudes and ideologies fall into two major categories: first, the place of Englishes in language policy and planning in the Three Circles, their educational, linguistic, and societal implications, and their standardization and codification;[1] and second, as the Englishes assume positions previously occupied by local languages in educational, professional, and other domains, the ideological questions of preserving linguistic diversity and linguistic human rights (see p. 180).

The learners of English worldwide constitute the largest group of language learners in the history of humanity. The estimates vary, but it is claimed that more than a billion learners are enrolled in English classes throughout the world.[2] This means that all the nations with learners have to make decisions with regard to when, how, and what kind of English is to be taught. Additionally, they have to decide what relationship the teaching of English should or could have with the teaching of other, indigenous languages. This is the area of language policy and planning—the educational context of the enterprise—that we are most concerned with. No doubt the educational context is impacted by what decisions are made in other contexts, such as administration, business, commerce, legal institutions, and media; these come into any discussion in the context of language education.

In the era of globalization and rapid diffusion of knowledge, all the nations are aware of the need to prepare their citizens to perform in ways that would ensure their prosperity and eminence in the world. In order to be competitive, they have to be able to function well in multinational industrial enterprises, international trade, diplomacy, and scientific-technological areas of expertise. They have to be innovative and contribute to the knowledge-base of the world. In order to achieve these goals, they need to be able to utilize the most widely used medium, English. International bodies such as the United Nations (UN), Asia-Pacific Economic Cooperation (APEC), Association of South East Asian Nations (ASEAN), European Union (EU), International Monetary Fund (IMF), South Asian Association for Regional Cooperation (SAARC), World Trade Organization (WTO), and others conduct their business overwhelmingly through English; the main medium of information technology is English; and more knowledge is created and distributed via publications through the medium of English as compared to any other language internationally. It is no wonder that most governments and educational institutions in the world are gradually implementing policies that would require children to acquire literacy in English at the level of primary or middle school education (see, e.g. the NCERT document (2000) for trends in India, and MEXT document (2003) for action plans in Japan, listed in the References).

Issues in Education

Such decisions, however, bring in a host of issues in education that are being debated widely all across the Three Circles.[3] Within the Inner Circle, the debates are in relation to immersion in English vs. bilingual education leading to maintenance of primary languages of the immigrant groups, and putting immigrant children in ESL vs. mainstream classes in the USA, UK, Australia, Canada, and New Zealand.[4] In the Outer and Expanding Circles, arguments rage about mother tongue vs. "other" tongue education, methodologies, appropriate textbooks, and models of English to be used in educational settings.[5] In the Expanding Circle, the external models, especially American and British English still continue to enjoy their favored status.[6] Australia is making a push for a bigger slice of the ELT pie, and there are controversies with regard to "importing" teachers from the USA and the UK when pools of indigenous teachers trained in ELT (both ESL and EFL— English as a Foreign Language) are available in Outer and Expanding Circle countries, e.g. in China, Japan, Europe, and other regions.[7]

A whole set of issues has been identified and studied in connection with ELT. In addition to teaching materials and methods, the processes and practices in producing supporting material, e.g. encyclopedias, handbooks, theoretical formulations in second or n-th language acquisition research, etc., have been dealt with in published literature (see, e.g. B. Kachru, 2005a, especially Ch. 6). Biases and prejudices in favor of the so-called "native speaker" have been focused upon and challenged (Ferguson, 1982), and arguments have been presented to show how "genetic" nativeness is being challenged by "functional" nativeness (B. Kachru, 1997b, p. 217) in all the Circles. The question of whether world Englishes should be introduced in ELT contexts—either in the MATESL curriculum or in the English language classrooms—has been discussed in studies such as Brown (1995) and Brown and Peterson (1997). Ideas about what it means to be the user of a language and what variation in performance signifies are being shaped and reshaped as phenomena such as code-mixing/switching and multilinguals' creativity are studied.[8] The challenges faced by a narrow view of "ownership" of English extend to the areas of literary canons and canonicity in addition to the nature of the language.[9] The impact of the spread of English education extends to theories of language and literacy, the nature of monolingualism vs.

bi/multilingualism, monoculturalism vs. multiculturalism, and cognitive bases of language acquisition.[10]

All the issues raised in the field of ELT mentioned above are of crucial relevance to research in world Englishes, and publications in the area demonstrate this clearly (B. Kachru *et al.*, 2006).

Issues of Ideology

In the context of the current profile of the language in the world, English sometimes evokes the image of Hydra—the multiple-headed monster of Greek mythology—at least in some people's minds (Bailey, 1992). Topics such as linguistic imperialism, linguistic hegemony, and linguistic human rights have already attracted a great deal of attention from linguists, sociologists, and political scientists interested in language issues in the context of English. The facts of diffusion of English are seen from the perspectives of imperial power of Britain and later, hegemonic power of the USA—the two Inner Circle English-speaking nations whose political and economic dominance played a major role in the spread of English.[11] Critical appraisal of ELT practices (as in Norton and Toohey, 2004) and voices advocating safeguarding linguistic diversity and protecting linguistic human rights to check and reverse the ceding of domains of use to English by numerous languages of the world are getting louder.[12] Teachers of English from Outer and Expanding Circles are making their voices heard, questioning the dominance of the "native speaker."[13]

ENGLISH IN HUMAN KNOWLEDGE AND INTERACTION

All these issues and questions are natural and the continuing debate on them advance our understanding of the complexities of the current status of world Englishes. However, in all these controversies and debates what gets lost is the crucial point about the nature of language as an integral part of human knowledge. As the Judge of the High Court of Judicature, Bombay (now, Mumbai), V. M. Tarkunde (Foreword, Shah, 1968, p. vi) observed almost four decades ago: "A little thought would show that whereas a nation may have a language, a language has no nationality." English as a field of knowledge now belongs to those who know it and use it. The main topics of the previous chapters thus still remain central to many of the practical concerns of users of English. As Sledd (1993, p. 275) observed, if English is to retain its use as a world language, "it has to be various" since it exists in the minds of its diverse users.

It is crucial for the increasingly globalizing communities to make sure that their interactions using various Englishes across cultures and communities are effective in realizing the goals of such interactions. As regards the apprehension that linguistic diversity of the world will be affected adversely by the ascendancy of English, it is worth keeping in mind the following comments by McArthur (1993, p. 235):

> [I]t is uncertain to suppose that one language medium could ever neutralize the diversities of the world—and on further reflection it is clear that the spread of English to date has never succeeded in neutralizing the diversities—and attendant tensions—of the peoples of Kachru's INNER circle. English currently reflects the background and attitudes of all the groups who have ever used it; the class tensions inside England; the ethnic tensions among English, Scots, Welsh and Irish (which are far from being resolved); the residual conflict between Catholic and Protestant, Jew and Goy; the established rivalry between Britain and America; stresses between English and other languages, as for example with French in Canada and Spanish in the United States; race tensions between black and white in Africa, the Caribbean, the United States and the United Kingdom—and, at the end of the list but by no means insignificant, the built-in Eurocentric bias among the mainly white societies of ENL [English as a National Language] nations, setting them apart from the other cultural blocks of Islam, Hinduism, Japan, and so forth.

It is true that numerous languages whose functional domains are shrinking to just the family and the community are losing the battle of survival, but that is not necessarily caused by Englishes in the Outer and Expanding Circle. In an overwhelmingly large number of cases, it is the regional, or state, or national languages that are taking over the public domains of language use as universal education spreads and populations that relied on their local languages for most of their purposes gain horizontal mobility in space and vertical mobility in economic status (see B. Kachru et al., 2008, for the situation of minor and minority languages in South Asia). It is difficult to see how this process can be halted or reversed unless the entire economic and sociopolitical systems of the world change.

The same is true of the Inner Circle; parents favor the language in education that they think would be an asset to their children in achieving upward mobility. That does not devalue the heritage languages; they may still be cultivated for ethnic identity and pride.[14]

CONCLUSION

In the near future, the demand for English in education and its use in the international arena is destined to grow. It is not certain how long this trend will last, but there does not seem to be any indication that the world is moving toward multiple linguistic mediums rapidly. What is clear, however, is that all users of English, no matter which Circle they come from, have to develop sensitivity to more than one variety of English. All agencies involved in English education, including the ELT profession, have to realize that accommodating variation is the key to success in communication across cultures in varied contexts of use of language for achieving common goals (Savignon and Berns, 1984). Attempts to promote constructs such as English as lingua franca, no matter how well intentioned, are bound to end up as prescribing another unitary norm ignoring Sledd's "variousness" mentioned above.[15] The selection of topics and their treatment in this volume is a small attempt in drawing attention to the factors that may facilitate adaptations to changing contexts of Englishes.

We have hinted at many different areas that enter the subject matter of this book. The topics raised here—those of policy and planning as relevant to societal use of language, reconciling linguistic human rights with variation in language on the one hand and the need to standardize and codify in the current sociopolitical and economic world order on the other hand, and bringing the insights from studies in literacy and cognitive bases of language acquisition to bear upon language education—all these are within the concerns of world Englishes research.

The claims that studies in world Englishes prefer an "elitist" approach that includes idealized "national" Englishes and that it ignores pidgins, creoles and so-called "substandard" dialects are based on misconceptions and unfamiliarity with the breadth of studies in the field (see the titles collected in Bolton and Kachru 2006, 2007). Human societies have always preferred certain languages over others as markers of various kinds of status—religious, social, political, economic, functional—and standardization has always played a key role in education. What is needed is the approach of world Englishes that does not devalue any variation. It attempts to study the functions of varieties in their contexts and how they empower their users to realize certain goals. This approach is reflected in Romaine's observations (1997 [2006], p. 151), that trying to impose one's standards on others "under the guise of concern about the unity of the English language, preserving intelligibility, providing access to native speaker norms, and other pseudo-scientific arguments" merely reinforces an artificial barrier between an Other Circle characterized as "norm-breakers," and an Inner Circle as "norm makers" (B. Kachru, 1985a), and her suggestion that the time has come "to have one large circle with everyone inside."

The aim of *Cultures, Contexts, and World Englishes* is to raise awareness of the issues discussed in the volume, and the challenges and possibilities of further investigation and study in world Englishes. We also hope the theoretical, methodological, and applied aspects of the research in world Englishes will stimulate thinking and research in other languages of wider communication in Africa, Asia, Europe, the Middle East, and other regions of the world.

Notes

1. Canagarajah (2005), B. Kachru (1985a, 1988a), Lowenberg (1986b), Pakir (1991), Parakrama (1995); for a conventional Inner Circle view on these topics, see Quirk (1985), 1988, 1989).
2. See the website http://esl.about.com/od/englishlearningresources/f/f_esl market.htm (accessed January 3, 2006).
3. For a discussion of issues related to the teaching and testing of English around the world, see, e.g. Agnihotri and Khanna (1994), Bamgbose *et al.* (1995), Baumgardner (1993), Baxter (1980), Davidson (1993a, 1993b), Gill *et al.* (1995), Gupta and Kapoor (1991), Hinkel (1999), B. Kachru (1976, 1977, 1981b, 1986f, 1988b, 1990a, 1996a), Y. Kachru (1993a, 1994), Lowenberg (1986a, 1988, 1992), Quirk and Widdowson (1985), K. Sridhar (1989), S. Sridhar (1994), K. Sridhar and S. Sridhar (1992), Strevens (1980, 1988), Swales (1985), Tickoo (1991), Tollefson (1995), Widdowson (1979, 1984), Williams (1989), Yap (1978).
4. See, Crawford (2000), Cummins (2001), Glenn (1996), Gomez *et al.* (2005), Nero (2006), Ovando and McLaren (2000), Tosi (1984, 1988), among others.
5. See, e.g. Clyne (1992) for general discussion of norms; see, Agnihotri (2001) for India; Baik (1994) and Baik and Shim (1995) for Korea; Bautista (1997) for the Philippines; Dendrinos (1992) for Greece for varied topics related to language education, including textbooks; and for general issues in education, see, Devaki *et al.* (1990), B. Kachru (1986f, 1988a, 1991, 1992, 1995a, 1996c, 1997b), Nicholls (1995), Pakir (1994, 1997, 1999), Ricento (2000), Smith (1983), Tickoo (1988, 1991, 1995), among others.
6. See, Newbrook (1999) for Thailand; Said and Ng (2000) for Malaysia.
7. e.g. Braine (1999), Honna and Takeshita (1998), Seidlhofer (1999).
8. See, e.g. for code-mixing and switching, Bautista (1990, 1991), T. Bhatia (1992), T. Bhatia and Ritchie (1989), Bhatt (1996), Kamwangamalu (1989), Myers-Scotton (1993a, 1993b), Zhang (2000); and for multilinguals' creativity see, Courtright (2001), Dissanayake (1985), B. Kachru (1986c, 1990b, 1994c, 1995b, 1998b, 2001a, 2002, 2005a), Lim (1993, 1994); Tawake (1990); Thumboo (1985, 1992, 1994, 2001), among others.
9. See, for ownership of language, the discussions in Hayhoe and Parker (1994), Strevens (1982), Widdowson (1994), for literary canon, see, Ashcroft *et al.* (1989), Gates (1992), B. Kachru (1994c, 1995b, 2005a).
10. See, e.g. Hasan and Williams (1996), Hinkel (2002) for issues in literacy; for a discussion of monolingualism vs. bilingualism and monoculturalism vs. multiculturalism, see, e.g. Grosjean (1982), Hakuta (1986), S. Sridhar (1992), S. Sridhar and K. Sridhar (1980); and see, Watson-Gegeo (2004) for a discussion of the interaction between socialization and cognition in second language acquisition.
11. See, Mazaferro (2002), Pennycook (1994), Phillipson (1992), Tsuda (1994, 2002), among others.
12. See, e.g. Phillipson (1998, 2003), Skutnabb-Kangas (2001), Skutnabb-Kangas and Phillipson (1997, 1998). See also the following for a bibliography of writing

on linguistic human rights compiled by Tove Skutnaab-Kangas: http://www.
terralingua.org/Bibliographies/ToveBibA_C.html/.
13. See, Braine (1999), Canagarajah (2000), Seidlhofer (1999), among others.
14. See, e.g. Cummins (2005) for treating heritage languages as learning resource;
    Hornberger (2005) for US and Australian perspectives on heritage language;
    Tavares (2000) for trends in Canada; see Valdés (2005) for research on heritage
    language in SLA contexts.
15. See, Jenkins (2006) and Seidlhofer (2004) for the English as Lingua Franca
    (ELF) approach; see Prodromou (2007) for a critique of this approach.

Further Reading

Ammon, U. (2000) Towards more fairness in international English: linguistic rights
    of non-native speakers? In R. Phillipson (ed.), *Rights to Language: Equity, Power
    and Education. Celebrating the 60th Birthday of Tove Skutnabb-Kangas* (pp. 111–116).
    Mahwah, NJ: Lawrence Erlbaum Associates.
Cummins, J. (2005) A proposal for action: strategies for recognizing heritage language
    competence as a learning resource within the mainstream classroom. *Modern
    Language Journal,* 89(4), 585–592.
Kachru, B. B. (2002) On nativizing *Mantra*: identity construction in Anglophone
    Englishes. In R. Ahrens, D. Parker, K. Stierstorfer, and K.-K. Tam (eds), *Anglophone
    Cultures in Southeast Asia: Appropriations, Continuities, Contexts* (pp. 55–72).
    Heidelberg: Universitätsverlag.
Phillipson, R. (1998) Globalizing English: are linguistic human rights an alternative
    to linguistic imperialism? In P. Benson, P. Grundy, and T. Skutnabb-Kangas (eds),
    Language Rights. Special volume of *Language Sciences,* 20(1), 101–112.
Tsuda, Y. (2002) The hegemony of English: problems, opposing views and
    communication rights. In G. Mazzaferro (ed.), *The English Language and Power*
    (pp. 19–31). Torino: Edizioni dell'Orso.

Suggested Activities

1. Read Tsuda (2002) and B. Kachru (2002) from the list above. Contrast
   the views expressed by these scholars and discuss the relevance of each
   for your own context(s).

2. Read and critically discuss Ammon (2000) from the list above.

References

Abd el-Jawad, H. R. S. (2000) A linguistic and sociopragmatic and cultural study of swearing in Arabic. *Language, Culture, and Curriculum,* 13(2), 217–240.

Abdulaziz, M. M. H. (1991) East Africa (Tanzania and Kenya). In J. Cheshire (ed.), *English around the World: Sociolinguistic Perspectives* (pp. 391–401). Cambridge: Cambridge University Press.

Abercrombie, D. (1951) R. P. and local accent. *The Listener,* 6, 385–386. [Reprinted in D. Abercrombie (ed.) (1965) *Studies in Phonetics and Linguistics* (pp. 10–15). London: Oxford University Press.]

Abercrombie, D. (1967) *Elements of General Phonetics.* Chicago: Aldine Publishing Co.

Achebe, C. (1965) English and the African writer. *Transition,* 18, 27–30.

Adams, T. W. (1987). *Body English: A Study of Gestures.* Glenview, IL: Scott, Foresman.

Agnihotri, R. K. (2001) English in Indian education. In *Language Education in Multilingual India* (pp. 186–209). Edited by C. J. Daswani. New Delhi: UNESCO.

Agnihotri, R. K. and Khanna, A. L. (eds) (1994) *Second Language Acquisition: Sociocultural and Linguistic Aspects of English in India.* New Delhi: Sage.

Albert, E. M. (1972) Culture patterning of speech behavior in Burundi. In J. J. Gumperz and D. Hymes (eds), *Directions in Sociolinguistics: The Ethnography of Communication* (pp. 72–105). New York: Holt, Rinehard and Winston.

Al-Khatib, M. A. (2001) The pragmatics of letter writing. *World Englishes,* 20(2), 179–200.

Allan, K. (1980) Nouns and countability. *Language,* 56(3), 541–567.

Allison, R. (ed.) (1996) *Dictionary of Caribbean English Usage.* Oxford: Oxford University Press.

Allsopp, R. (ed.) (1996) *Dictionary of Caribbean English Usage.* New York: Oxford University Press.

Allsopp, R. and Allsopp, J. (eds) (1996) *Dictionary of Caribbean English Usage, with a French and Spanish Supplement.* Oxford: Oxford University Press.

Ammon, U. (2000) Towards more fairness in international English: Linguistic rights of non-native speakers? In R. Phillipson (ed.), *Rights to Language: Equity, Power and Education. Celebrating the 60th Birthday of Tove Skutnabb-Kangas* (pp. 111–116). Mahwah, NJ: Lawrence Erlbaum Associates.

Anderson, S. and Lightfoot, D. (2002) *The Language Organ: Linguistics as Cognitive Psychology.* Cambridge: Cambridge University Press.

Argyle, M. and Cook, M. (1976) *Gaze and Mutual Gaze.* Cambridge: Cambridge University Press.

Asante, M. K. (1987) *The Afrocentric Idea.* Philadelphia: Temple University Press.

Ashcroft, G. G., Griffith, G., and Helen, T. (1989) *The Empire Writes Back: Theory and Practice in Post-colonial Literatures.* London and New York: Routledge.

Aston, G. (1977) Comprehending value: Aspects of the structure of argumentative discourse. *Studi Italiani di Linguistica Teorica ed Applicata,* 6, 465–509.

Austin, J. L. (1962) *How to Do Things with Words.* Oxford: Clarendon Press.

Baik, M. J. (1994) *Language, Ideology, and Power: English Textbooks of Two Koreas.* Seoul: Thaehaksa.

Baik, M. J. and Shim, R. J. (1995) Language, culture, and ideology in the English textbooks of two Koreas. In M. L. Tickoo (ed.), *Langauge and Culture in Multilingual Societies: Viewpoints and Visions* (pp. 122–138). Singapore: Seameo Regional Language Centre.

Bailey, R. W. (1992) *Images of English.* Cambridge: Cambridge University Press.

Bailey, R. W. and Görlach, M. (eds) (1982) *English as a World Language.* Ann Arbor: University of Michigan Press.

Bamgboṣe, A. (1992) Standard Nigerian English: Issues of identification. In B. B. Kachru (ed.), *The Other Tongue: English across Cultures* (2nd edn) (pp. 148–161). Urbana, IL: University of Illinois Press. [First edn. (1982), pp. 99–111.]

Bamgboṣe, A. (1998) Torn between the norms: Innovations in world Englishes. *World Englishes,* 17(1), 1–14.

Bamgboṣe, A., Banjo, A., and Thomas, A. (eds) (1995) *New Englishes: A West African Perspective.* Ibadan: Mosuro.

Bamiro, E. O. (1991) Nigerian Englishes in Nigerian English literature. *World Englishes,* 10(1), 7–17.

Banjo, A. (1997) Aspects of the syntax of Nigerian English. In E. W. Schneider (ed.), *English around the World 2: Caribbean, Africa, Asia, Australasia: Studies in Honor of Manfred Görlach* (pp. 85–118). Amsterdam and Philadelphia: John Benjamins.

Bao, Z. (2001) Two issues in the study of Singapore English phonology. In V. Ooi (ed.), *Evolving Identities: The English Language in Singapore and Malaysia* (pp. 69–78). Singapore: Times Academic Press.

Bartlett, F. C. (1932) *Remembering.* Cambridge: Cambridge University Press.

Baskaran, L. (1994) The Malaysian English mosaic. *English Today,* 37(10), 27–32.

Basso, K. (1970) "To give up on words": Silence in Western apache culture. *Southwestern Journal of Anthropology,* 26, 213–230.

Bateson, G. (1972) *Steps to an Ecology of Mind: Collected Essays in Anthropology, Psychiatry, Evolution, and Epistemology.* Aylesbury: Intertext.

Baumgardner, R. J. (1987) Using Pakistani newspaper English to teach grammar. *World Englishes,* 6(3), 241–252.

Baumgardner, R. J. (1993) *The English Language in Pakistan.* Karachi: Oxford University Press.

Bautista, Ma. L. S. (1990) Tagalog–English code-switching revisited. *Philippine Journal of Linguistics,* 21(2), 15–29.

Bautista, Ma. L. S. (1991) Code-switching studies in the Philippines. *International Journal of the Sociology of Language,* 88, 19–32.

Bautista, Ma. L. S. (ed.) (1996) *Readings in Philippine Sociolinguistics* (2nd edn). Manila: De La Salle University Press.

Bautista, Ma. L. S. (ed.) (1997) *English is an Asian Language: The Philippine Context.* Sydney: Macquarie Library Pty Ltd.

Bautista, Ma. L. S. and Bolton, K. (eds) (2004) Philippine English: Tensions and transitions. Special issue of *World Englishes*, 23(1), 1–210.

Baxter, J. (1980) How should I speak English? American-ly, Japanese-ly, or internationally? *JALT Journal*, 2, 31–61.

Beaugrande, R. de and Dressler, W. (1981) *Introduction to Text Linguistics*. London: Longman.

Bell, A. and Holmes, J. (1991) New Zealand. In J. Cheshire (ed.), *English around the World: Sociolinguistic Perspectives* (pp. 153–168). Cambridge: Cambridge University Press.

Bell, A. and Kuiper, K. (eds) (1999) *New Zealand English (Varieties of English around the World*, vol. 25). Amsterdam: John Benjamins.

Bhatia, T. K. (1992) Discourse functions and pragmatics of mixing: Advertising across cultures. *World Englishes*, 11(2/3), 195–215.

Bhatia, T. K. and Ritchie, W. (eds) (1989) Code-mixing: English across languages. Special issue of *World Englishes*, 8(3), 261–439.

Bhatia, V. K. (1993) *Analyzing Genre: Language Use in Professional Settings*. London and New York: Longman.

Bhatia, V. K. (1996) Nativization of job applications in South Asia. In R. Baumgardner (ed.), *South Asian English: Structure, Use, and Users* (pp. 158–173). Urbana, IL: University of Illinois Press.

Bhatia, V. K. (ed.) (1997) Genre analysis and world Englishes. Special issue of *World Englishes*, 16(3).

Bhatt, R. (ed.) (1996) Symposium on constraints on code-switching. *World Englishes*, 15(3), 359–404.

Bhatt, S. (1988) Search for my tongue. In *Brunizem*. Manchester: Carcanet.

Biber, D. (1986) Spoken and written textual dimensions in English: Resolving the contradictory findings. *Language*, 62, 384–414.

Black, J. H. (1995) The "think-aloud" procedure as a diagnostic and learning tool for second-language learners. In M. Haggstrom, L. Z. Morgan, and J. A. Wieczorek (eds), *The Foreign Language Classroom: Bridging Theory and Practice* (pp. 21–38). New York: Garland.

Bloch, M. (1991) Language, anthropology and cognitive science. *Man*, 26, 183–197.

Bloom, D. (1986) The English language and Singapore. In B. K. Kapur (ed.), *Singapore Studies: Critical Surveys of the Humanities and Social Sciences* (pp. 337–458). Singapore: Singapore University Press.

Blum-Kulka, S. (1989) Playing it safe: The role of conventionality in indirectness. In S. Blum-Kulka and J. House (eds), *Cross-cultural Pragmatics: Requests and Apologies* (pp. 37–70). Norwood, NJ: Albex.

Bokamba, E. G. (1991) West Africa. In J. Cheshire (ed.), *English around the World: Sociolinguistic Perspectives* (pp. 493–508). Cambridge: Cambridge University Press.

Bokamba, E. G. (1992) The Africanization of English. In B. B. Kachru (ed.), *The Other Tongue: English across Cultures* (2nd edn) (pp. 125–147). Urbana, IL: University of Illinois Press. [1st edn., pp. 77–98.]

Bolton, K. (ed.) (2002) *Hong Kong English: Autonomy and Creativity.* Hong Kong: Hong Kong University Press.

Bolton, K. (2003) *Chinese Englishes: A Sociolinguistic History.* Cambridge: Cambridge University Press.

Bolton, K. (2004) World Englishes. In A. Davies and C. Elder (eds), *The Handbook of Applied Linguistics* (pp. 367–396). Oxford: Blackwell Publishing.

Bolton, K. and Kachru, B. B. (eds) (2006) *World Englishes: Critical Concepts in Linguistics* (Vols 1–6). London: Routledge.

Bolton, K. and Kachru, B. B. (eds) (2007) *Asian Englishes: History and Development of World Englishes* (Vols 1–5). London: Routledge.

Braine, George (ed.) (1999) *Non-native Speaker Educators in English Language Teaching.* Mahwa, NJ: Lawrence Erlbaum.

Branford, J. (1978) *A Dictionary of South African English.* Cape Town: Oxford University Press.

Brown, A. (1986) The pedagogical importance of consonantal features of the English of Malaysia and Singapore. *RELC Journal*, December, 1–25.

Brown, A. (1992) *Making Sense of Singapore English.* Singapore: Federal Publications.

Brown, G. and Yule, G. (1983) *Discourse Analysis.* Cambridge: Cambridge University Press.

Brown, K. (1995) World Englishes: To teach or not to teach? *World Englishes*, 14(2), 233–245.

Brown, K. and Peterson, J. (1997) Exploring conceptual frameworks: Framing a world Englishes paradigm. In L. E. Smith and M. L. Forman (eds), *World Englishes 2000* (pp. 32–47). Honolulu: University of Hawaii Press.

Brown, P. and Levinson, S. C. (1987) *Politeness: Some Universals in Language Usage.* Cambridge: Cambridge University Press.

Brown, R. and Gilman, A. (1960) The pronouns of power and solidarity. In T. A. Sebeok (ed.), *Style in Language* (pp. 253–276). Cambridge, MA: MIT Press.

Burkhardt, A. (ed.) (1990) *Speech Acts, Meaning and Intentions: Critical Approaches to the Philosophy of John R. Searle.* Berlin: W. de Gruyter.

Butler, S. (1996) World English in an Asian context: The Macquarie Dictionary Project. *World Englishes*, 15(3), 347–357.

Butler, S. (1997a) World Englishes in an Asian context: Why a dictionary is important. In L. E. Smith and M. L. Forman (eds), *World Englishes 2000* (pp. 90–125). Honolulu: University of Hawaii Press.

Butler, S. (1997b) Selecting South-East Asian words for an Australian dictionary: How to choose in an English not your own. In E. W. Schneider (ed.), *Englishes around the World 2: Caribbean, Africa, Asia, Australasia: Studies in Honor of Manfred Görlach* (pp. 273–286). Amsterdam and Philadelphia: John Benjamins.

Canagarajah, A. S. (2000) Negotiating ideologies through English: Strategies from the periphery. In T. Ricento (ed.), *Ideologies, Politics and Language Policies: Focus on English* (pp. 121–132). Amsterdam: John Benjamins.

Canagarajah, A. S. (ed.) (2005) *Reclaiming the Local in Language Policy and Practice.* Mahwa, NJ: Lawrence Erlbaum.

Candlin, C., Bruton, C. J., and Leather, J. H. (1976) Doctors in casualty: Applying Components of communicative competence to specialist course design. *International Journal of Applied Linguistics*, 14(2), 245–272.

Candlin, C., Coleman, H., and Burton, J. (1983). Dentist–patient communication: Communicating complaint. In N. Wolfson and E. Judd (eds), *Sociolinguistics and Language Acquisition* (pp. 56–81). Rowley, MA: Newbury House.

Cassidy, F. G. and LePage, R. B. (eds) (2003) *Dictionary of Jamaican English* (2nd edn). Cambridge: Cambridge University Press.

Cenoz, J. and Jessner, U. (2000) *English in Europe: The Acquisition of a Third Language.* Clevedon and Buffalo: Multilingual Matters.

Cervi, D. and Wajnryb, R. (1992) Coping with Aussie English. *English Today*, 8(2), 18–21.

Chafe, W. L. (1972) Discourse structure and human knowledge. In R. O. Freedle and J. B. Carroll (eds), *Language Comprehension and the Acquisition of Knowledge* (pp. 41–69). Washington, DC: V. H. Winston.

Chafe, W. L. (1980) The deployment of consciousness in the production of a narrative. In W. L. Chafe (ed.), *The Pear Stories: Congnitive Cultural, and Linguistic Aspects of Narrative Production* (pp. 41–69). Norwood, NJ: Ablex.

Chafe, W. L. (1982) Integration and involvement in speaking, writing and oral literature. In D. Tannen (ed.), *Spoken and Written Language: Exploring Orality and Literacy* (pp. 35–54). Norwood, NJ: Ablex.

Chambers, J. K. (1991) Canada. In J. Cheshire (ed.), *English around the World: Sociolinguistic Perspectives* (pp. 89–107). Cambridge: Cambridge University Press.

Chan, R. (1991) The Singaporean and Malaysian speech communities. In S. Alladina and V. Edwards (eds), *Multilingualism in the British Isles (Africa, Middle East and Asia)* (pp. 207–220). New York: Longman.

Cheshire, J. (ed.) (1991) *English around the World: Sociolinguistic Perspectives.* Cambridge: Cambridge University Press.

Chisanga, T. (1987) An investigation into the forms and functions of educated English in Zambia. Unpublished doctoral dissertation, York University, UK.

Chishimba, M. M. (1991) Southern Africa. In J. Cheshire (ed.), *English around the World: Sociolinguistic Perspectives* (pp. 435–445). Cambridge: Cambridge University Press.

Cicourel, A. V. (1967) The acquisition of social structure: Towards a developmental sociology of language and meaning. *Rassegna Italiana di Sociologia,* 9. [Reprinted in In A. V. Cicourel (ed.) (1974), *Cognitive Sociology: Language and Meaning in Social Interaction* (pp. 42–73). New York: The Free Press.]

Clyne, M. (1983) *Linguistics and written discourse in particular languages: Contrastive studies: English and German.* Annual Review of Applied Linguistics, 3, 38–49.

Clyne, M. (1992) *Pluricentric Languages: Differing Norms in Different Nations.* Berlin and New York: Mouton de Gruyter.

Coates, J. and Cameron, D. (eds) (1988) *Women in their Speech Communities.* Harlow: Longman.

Collins, P. and Blair, D. (eds) (1989) *Australian English: The Language of a New Society.* St Lucia: University of Queensland Press.

Comrie, B. (1975) Antiergative. In R. E. Grossman, L. J. San, and T. J. Vance (eds), *Papers from the 11th regional meeting of the Chicago Linguistic Society* (pp. 112–121). Chicago: University of Chicago.

Connor, U. and Kaplan, R. (eds) (1987) *Writing across Languages: Analysis of L2 Text.* Reading, MA: Addison-Wesley.

Corbett, G. G. (1976) Address in Russian. *Journal of Russian Studies,* 31, 3–15.

Courtright, M. S. (2001) Intelligibility and context in reader responses to contact literary texts. Unpublished doctoral dissertation, University of Illinois at Urbana-Champaign.

Crawford, J. (2000) *At War with Diversity: US Language Policy in an Age of Anxiety.* Clevedon: Multilingual Matters.

Crewe, W. J. (ed.) (1977) *The English Language in Singapore.* Singapore: Eastern University Press.

Cruz, I. R. and Bautista, Ma. L. S. (eds) (1995) *A Dictionary of Philippine English.* Metro Manila: Anvil Publishing Inc.

Crystal, D. (1998) *Language Play.* Harmondsworth: Penguin.

Cummins, J. (2001) Language, power, and pedagogy: Bilingual children in the crossfire. Clevedon: Mulitlingual Matters.

Cummins, J. (2005) A proposal for action: Strategies for recognizing heritage language competence as a learning resource within the mainstream classroom. *Modern Language Journal,* 89(4), 585–592.

Dautermann, J. (1995) A case for examining professional voices in institutional settings: Nurses in conversation. *Studies in the Linguistic Sciences,* 25(2), 193–213.

Davidson, F. (ed.) (1993a). Symposium on testing across cultures. *World Englishes,* 12(1), 85–125.

Davidson, F. (1993b) Testing English across cultures: Summary and comments. *World Englishes,* 12(1), 113–125.

Davis, J. N. and Bistodeau, L. (1993) How do L1 and L2 reading differ? Evidence from think aloud protocols. *The Modern Language Journal,* 77(4), 459–471.

de Clerk, V. (1996) *Focus on South Africa (Varieties of English around the World,* vol. 15). Amsterdam and Philadelphia: John Benjamins.

De Ersson, E. O. and Shaw, P. (2003) Verb complementation patterns in Indian Standard English. *English World-Wide,* 24(2), 137–161.

de Kadt, E. (1993) Language, power, and emancipation in South Africa. *World Englishes,* 12(2), 157–168.

Dendrinos, B. (1992) The EFL Textbook and Ideology. Athens, NC: Grivas Publications.

Deneire, M. G. and Goethals, M. (eds) (1997) English in Europe. Special issue of *World Englishes,* 16(1), 1–134.

Desai, A. (1978) A Devoted Son. In *Games at Twilight* (pp. 70–81). London: Penguin Books.

Devaki, L., Ramasamy, K., and Srivastava, A. K. (1990) *An Annotated Bibliography on Bilingualism, Bilingual Education and Medium of Instruction.* Mysore: Central Institute of Indian Languages.

Dissanayake, W. (1985) Towards a decolonized English: South Asian creativity in fiction. *World Englishes,* 4(2), 233–242.

Dooling, J. D. and Lachman, R. (1971) Effects of comprehension on retention of prose. *Journal of Experimental Psychology,* 88, 216–222.

D'souza, J. (1988) Interactional strategies in South Asian languages: Their implications for teaching English internationally. *World Englishes,* 7(2), 159–171.

Dubey, V. D. (1991) The lexical style of Indian English newspapers. *World Englishes,* 10(1), 19–32.

Duncan Jr, S. (1980) Some notes on analyzing data on face-to-face interaction. In M. R. Key (ed.), *The Relationship of Verbal and Nonverbal Communication* (pp. 127–138). The Hague: Mouton.

Duncan Jr, S. and Donald W. Fiske (1977) *Face-to-face Interaction: Research, Methods, and Theory.* New York: Lawrence Erlbaum Associates.

Eades, D. (1982) You gotta to know how to talk . . .: Ethnography of information seeking in Southeast Queensland aboriginal society. *Australian Journal of Linguistics,* 2(1), 61–82.

Edelsky, C. (1981) Who's got the floor? *Language in Society,* 10, 383–421.

Eisikovits, E. (1989) Girl-talk/boy-talk: Sex differences in adolescent speech. In P. Collins and D. Blair (eds), *Australian English: The Language of a New Society* (pp. 35–54). Brisbane: University of Queensland Press.

Erickson, F. (1982) Money tree, lasagna bush, salt and pepper: Social construction of topical cohesion in a conversation among Italian-Americans. In D. Tannen (ed.), *Analyzing Discourse: Text and Talk* (pp. 43–70). Washington, DC: Georgetown University Press.

Ericsson, K. A. and Simon, H. A. (1993) *Protocol Analysis: Verbal Reports as Data.* Cambridge, MA: The MIT Press.

Evans-Pritchard, E. E. (1948) *The Divine Kingship of the Shiluk of the Nilotic Sudan.* Cambridge: Cambridge University Press. [Also in E. E. Evans-Pritchard (ed.) (1962) *Essays in Social Anthropology* (pp. 66–86). New York: Free Press of Glencoe.]

Ferdman, B., Weber, R., and Ramirez, A. (eds) (1994) *Literacy across Languages and Cultures.* Albany, NY: State University of New York Press.

Ferguson, C. A. (1976) The structure and use of politeness formulas. *Language in Society,* 5, 137–151.

Ferguson, C. A. (1982) Foreword. In B. B. Kachru (ed.), *The Other Tongue: English across Cultures* (pp. vii–xi). Urbana, IL: University of Illinois Press.

Ferguson, C. A. and Heath, S. B. (1981) *Language in the USA.* Cambridge: Cambridge University Press.

Firth, A. (1991) Discourse at work: Negotiating by telex, fax, and phone. Unpublished doctoral dissertation, University of Aalborg, Denmark.

Firth, J. R. (1957a) *Papers in Linguistics in 1934–1951.* London: Oxford University Press.

Firth, J. R. (1957b) A synopsis of linguistic theory. In F. R. Palmer (ed.) (1968), *Selected Papers of J. R. Firth, 1952–59* (pp. 168–205). London: Longman.

Fishman, P. M. (1983) Interaction: The work women do. In B. Thorne, C. Kramarae, and N. Henley (eds), *Language, Gender and Society* (pp. 89–102). Rowley, MA: Newbury House Publishers.

FitzGerald, H. (2003) *How Different Are We? Spoken Discourse in Intercultural Communication.* Clevedon: Multilingual Matters.

Foley, J. (ed.) (1988) *New Englishes: The Case of Singapore.* Singapore: Singapore University Press.

Foley, J. (1995) English in Mauritius. *World Englishes,* 14(2), 205–222.

Frank, J. (1988) Miscommunication across cultures: The case of marketing in Indian English. *World Englishes,* 7(1), 25–36.

Freebody, P. and Welch, A. R. (1993) *Knowledge, Culture, and Power: International Perspectives on Literacy as Policy and Practice.* Pittsburgh, PA: University of Pittsburgh Press.

Freedle, R. O. (1979) *New Directions in Discourse Processing.* Norwood, NJ: Ablex.

Frenck, S. and Min, S. J. (2001) Culture, reader and textual intelligibility. In E. Thumboo (ed.), *The Three Circles of English* (pp. 19–34). Singapore: University Press.

Gargesh, R. (2004) The phonology of English in India. In R. Mesthrie (ed.), *Varieties of English: Africa/Southeast Asia/India* (pp. 187–197). Berlin: Mouton de Gruyter.

Gates Jr, H. L. (1992) *Loose Canons: Notes on the Culture Wars.* New York: Oxford University Press.

Geertz, C. (1973) *The Interpretation of Cultures: Selected Essays.* New York: Basic Books.

Giles, H. (1973) Accent mobility: A model and some data. *Anthropological Linguistics,* 15, 87–105.

Giles, H. and Coupland, N. (1991) *Language: Contexts and Consequences.* Open University Press.

Giles, H., Mulac, A., Bradack, J. J., and Johnson, P. (1987) Speech accommodation theory: The next decade and beyond. In M. McLaughlin (ed.), *Communication Yearbook 10* (pp. 13–48). Newbury Park: Sage.

Gill, S. K. *et al.* (eds) (1995) *INTELEC '94: International English Language Education Conference, National and International Challenges and Responses.* Bangi, Malaysia: Pusat Bahasa Universiti Kebangsaan Malaysia.

Ginsberg, M. (1932) *Sociology.* London: Oxford University Press.

Givón, T. (1979) *On Understanding Grammar.* New York: Academic Press.

Givón, T. (1989) *Mind, Code and Context: Essays in Pragmatics*. Hillsdale, NJ: Erlbaum.

Glauser, B., Schneider, E. W., and Görlach, M. (1993) *A New Bibliography of Writings on Varieties of English 1984–1992/93*. Amsterdam/Philadelphia: John Benjamins.

Glenn, C. (1996) *Educating Immigrant Children*. New York: Garland Publishers.

Goffman, E. (1955) On face-work: An analysis of ritual elements in social interaction. *Psychiatry: Journal for the Study of International Processes*, 18, 319–346.

Goffman, E. (1967) *Interaction Ritual: Essays in Face-to-face Behavior*. Chicago: Aldine Publishing Company.

Goffman, E. (1974) *Frame Analysis: An Essay on the Organization of Experience*. Cambridge, MA: Harvard University Press.

Gomez, L., Freeman, D., and Freeman, Y. (2005) Dual language education: A promising 50–50 model. *Bilingual Research Journal Online*, 29(1), 145–164.

Goodwin, M. H. (1990) *He-Said-She-Said: Talk as Social Organization among Black Children*. Bloomington: Indiana University Press.

Goody, E. N. (ed.) (1978) *Questions and Politeness*. Cambridge: Cambridge University Press.

Görlach, M. (1991) *Englishes: Studies in Varieties of English 1984–1988*. Amsterdam and Philadelphia: John Benjamin.

Graddol, D. (1997) *The Future of English*. London: The British Council.

Green, G. M. (1989) *Pragmatics and Natural Language understanding*. Hillsdale, NJ: Lawrence Erlbaum.

Greenbaum, S. (1990) Standard English and the international corpus of English. *World Englishes*, 9(1), 79–83.

Greenbaum, S. (1991) ICE: The international corpus of English. *English Today*, 7(4), 3–7.

Greenbaum, S. and Nelson, G. (eds) (1996) Studies on international corpus of English. Special issue of *World Englishes*, 15(1), 1–124.

Grice, H. P. (1975) Logic and conversation. In P. Cole and J. Morgan (eds), *Syntax and Semantics 3: Speech Acts* (pp. 41–54). New York: Academic Press.

Grice, H. P. (1981) Presupposition and conversational implicature. In P. Cole (ed.), *Radical Pragmatics* (pp. 183–198). New York: Academic Press.

Grosjean, F. (1982) *Life with Two Languages*. Cambridge, MA: Harvard University Press.

Gumperz, J. J. (ed.) (1982a) *Discourse Strategies*. Cambridge: Cambridge University Press.

Gumperz, J. J. (ed.) (1982b) *Language and Social Identity*. Cambridge: Cambridge University Press.

Gumperz, J., Jupp, T. C., and Roberts, C. (1979) *Crosstalk: A Study of Cross-cultural Communication*. London: National Centre for Industrial Language Training.

Gupta, A. F. (1993) *The Step-tongue: Children's English in Singapore*. Clevedon: Multilingual Matters.

Gupta, R. S. and Kapoor, K. (eds) (1991) *English in India: Issues and Problems*. Delhi: Academic Foundation.

Guy, G. R. (1991) Australia. In J. Cheshire (ed.), *English around the World: Sociolinguistic Perspectives* (pp. 213–226). Cambridge: Cambridge University Press.

Gyasi, I. K. (1991) Aspects of English in Ghana. *English Today*, 7(2), 26–31.

Hakuta, K. (1986) *Mirror of Language: The Debate on Bilingualism*. New York: Basic Books.

Hall, E. T. (1959) *The Silent Language*. Garden City, NY: Doubleday.

Hall, E. T. (1960) The silent language in overseas business. *Harvard Business Review*, May–June, 87–96.

Hall, E. T. (1966) *The Hidden Dimension*. Garden City, NY: Doubleday.

Hall, E. T. (1984) *The Dance of Life: The Other Dimension of Time.* New York: Doubleday.

Halliday, M. A. K. (1967–1968). Notes on transitivity and theme. *Journal of Linguistics,* 3, 37–81 and 199–244; *Journal of Linguistics,* 4, 179–215.

Halliday, M. A. K. (1973) *Explorations in the Functions of Language.* London: Arnold.

Halliday, M. A. K. (1978) *Language as Social Semiotic.* Baltimore, MD: University Park Press.

Halliday, M. A. K. and Hasan, R. (1976) *Cohesion in English.* London: Longman.

Hansell, M. and Ajirotutu, C. S. (1982) Negotiating interpretations in interethnic settings. In J. J. Gumperz (ed.), *Language and Social Identity* (pp. 85–94). Cambridge University Press.

Hasan, R. and Williams, G. (eds) (1996) *Literacy in Society.* London and New York: Longman.

Hatim, M. (1991) The pragmatics of argumentation in Arabic: The rise and fall of a text type. *Text,* 11, 189–199.

Hayashi, R. (1987) A study of floor management of English and Japanese conversation. Unpublished doctoral dissertation, University of Illinois at Urbana-Champaign.

Hayashi, R. (1988) Simultaneous talk: From the perspective of floor management of English and Japanese speakers. *World Englishes,* 7, 269–288.

Hayashi, R. (1991) Floor structure of English and Japanese conversation. *Journal of Pragmatics,* 16(1), 1–30.

Hayashi, R. (1996) *Cognition, Empathy, and Interaction: Floor Management of Englsih and Japanese Conversation (Advances in Discourse Processes,* vol. LIV). Norwood, NJ: Ablex.

Hayhoe, M. and Parker, S. (1994) *Who Owns English?* Buckingham: Open University Press.

Heath, S. (1983) *Ways with Words: Language, Life, and Work in Communities and Classrooms.* Cambridge: Cambridge University Press.

Hecht, M. L., Larkey, L. K., and Johnson, J. N. (1992) African American and European American perceptions of problematic issues in interethnic communication effectiveness. *Human Communication Research,* 19, 209–236.

Hersey, J. (1989) *A Single Pebble.* New York: Vintage.

Hilgendorf, S. K. (1996) The impact of English in Germany. *English Today,* 47(12), 3–14.

Hill, B., Ide, S., Ikuta, S., Kawasaki, A., and Ogino, T. (1986) Universals in linguistic politeness: Quantitative evidence from Japanese and American English. *Journal of Pragmatics,* 10, 347–371.

Hinds, J. (1980) Japanese expository prose. *Papers in Linguistics,* 13, 117–158.

Hinds, J. (1982) *Ellipsis in Japanese.* Carbondale, IL and Edmonton: Linguistic Research, Inc.

Hinds, J. (1983) Linguistics and written discourse: English and Japanese. *Annual Review of Applied Linguistics,* 4, 75–84.

Hinds, J. (1987) Reader versus writer responsibility: A new typology. In U. Connor and R. B. Kaplan (eds), *Writing across Languages: Analysis of L2 Text* (pp. 141–152). Reading, MA: Addison-Wesley.

Hinkel, E. (ed.). (1999) *Culture in Second Language Teaching and Learning.* Cambridge: Cambridge University Press.

Hinkel, E. (2002) *Second Language Writers' Text: Linguistic and Rhetorical Features.* Mahwa, NJ: Lawrence Erlbaum Associates.

Ho, C. L. (1992) Word in a cultural context: Term selection. In A. Pakir (ed.), *Words in a Cultural Context* (pp. 202–214). Singapore: UniPress.

Holm, J. and Shilling, A. W. (1982) *Dictionary of Bahamian English.* Cold Spring, NY: Lexik House.

Honna, N. and Takeshita, Y. (1998) On Japan's propensity for native speaker English: A change in sight. *Asian Englishes*, 1(1), 117–137.

Hornberger, N. H. (ed.) (2005) Heritage/community language education: US and Australian perspectives. Special issue of *International Journal of Bilingual Education and Bilingualism*, 8 (2&3).

Hosali, P. and Aitchison, J. (1986) Butler English: A minimal pidgin? *Journal of Pidgin and Creole Linguistics*, 1(1), 51–79.

Huddleston, R. (1984) *Introduction to the Grammar of English*. Cambridge: Cambridge University Press.

Hulme, K. (1985) *The Bone People*. New York: Viking Press.

Hundt, M. (1998) *New Zealand English Grammar: Fact or Fiction?* Amsterdam and Philadelphia: John Benajmins Publishing Company.

Hymes, D. (1964) Toward ethnographies of communication: The analysis of communicative events. In P. P. Giglioli (ed.), *Language and Social Context* (pp. 21–44). Harmondsworth: Penguin.

Hymes, D. (1974) *Foundations in Sociolinguistics*. Philadelphia: University of Pennsylvania Press.

Ikoma, T. and Shimura, A. (1994) Pragmatic transfer in the speech act of refusal in Japanese as a second language. *Journal of Asian Pacific Communications*, 5(1, 2), 105–130.

Jääskeläinen, R. (2002) Think aloud protocol studies into translation: An annotated bibliography. *Target*, 14(1), 107–136.

James, A. (2000) English as a European lingua franca: Current realities and existing dichotomies. In J. Cenoz and U. Jessner (eds), *English in Europe: The Acquisition of a Third Language* (pp. 22–38). Clevedon: Multilingual Matters.

Jenkins, J. (2000) *The Phonology of English as an International Language*. Oxford: Oxford University Press.

Jenkins, J. (2006) Current perspectives on teaching World Englishes and English as a lingua franca. *TESOL Quarterly*, 40(11), 157–181.

Jenkins, S. and Hinds, J. (1987) Business letter writing: English, French and Japanese. *TESOL Quarterly*, 21, 327–349.

Jespersen, O. (1933) *Essentials of English Grammar*. London: Allen and Unwin.

Jose, F. S. (1997) Standards in Philippine English: The writers' forum. In Ma. L. S. Bautista (ed.), *English is an Asian Language: The Philippine Context* (pp. 167–169). Sydney: Macquarie Library Pty Ltd.

Jussawalla, F. and Dasenbrock, R. W. (eds) (1992) *Interviews with Writers of the Post-colonial World*. Jackson, MI and London: University Press of Mississippi.

Kachru, B. B. (1965) The Indianness in Indian English. *Word*, 21, 391–410.

Kachru, B. B. (1976) Models of English for the third world: White man's linguistic burden or language pragmatics? *TESOL Quarterly*, 10, 221–239. [Also in A. Brown (ed.), *Teaching English Pronunciation: A Book of Readings* (pp. 31–52). London and New York: Routledge.]

Kachru, B. B. (1977) The new Englishes and old models. *English Language Forum*, 15(3), 29–35.

Kachru, B. B. (1981) The pragmatics of non-native varieties of English. In L. E. Smith (ed.), *English for Cross-cultural Communication* (pp. 15–39). London: Macmillan.

Kachru, B. B. (1983a) *The Indianization of English: The English Language in India*. New Delhi: Oxford University Press.

Kachru, B. B. (1983b) Normes régionales de l'anglais. In É. Bédard and J. Maurais (eds), *La norme linguistique* (pp. 707–730). Quebec: Gourvernement du Quebec, Consel de la Langue Francaise.

Kachru, B. B. (1985a) Standards, codification and sociolinguistic realism: The English language in the Outer Circle. In R. Quirk and H. Widdowson (eds), *English in the World: Teaching and Learning the Language and Literatures* (pp. 11–30). Cambridge: Cambridge University Press.

Kachru, B. B. (1985b) Institutionalized second language varieties. In S. Greenbaum (ed.), *The English Language Today* (pp. 211–226). Oxford: Pergamon Press. [Revised version in B. B. Kachru (1986a), pp. 19–32.]

Kachru, B. B. (1986a) *The Alchemy of English: The Spread, Functions, and Models of Non-native Englishes.* Oxford: Pergamon Press. [Reprinted 1990, Urbana, IL: University of Illinois Press.]

Kachru, B. B. (1986b) Socially-realistic linguistics: The Firthian tradition. *International Journal of the Sociology of Language,* 3, 65–89.

Kachru, B. B. (1986c) The bilingual's creativity and contact literatures. In B. B. Kachru (ed.), *The Alchemy of English: The Spread, Functions, and Models of Non-native Englishes* (pp. 159–173). Oxford: Pergamon Press.

Kachru, B. B. (1986d) The bilinguals' creativity. *Annual Review of Applied Linguistics,* 6, 20–33.

Kachru, B. B. (1986e) Non-native literatures in English as a resource for language teaching. In C. J. Brumfit and R. Carter (eds), *Literature and Language Teaching* (pp. 140–149). London: Oxford University Press.

Kachru, B. B. (1986f) The power and politics of English. *World Englishes,* 5(2/3), 121–140.

Kachru, B. B. (1987) The past and prejudice: Toward de-mythologizing the English canon. In R. Steel and T. Threadgold (eds), *Linguistic Topics: Papers in Honor of M. A. K. Halliday* (pp. 245–256). Philadelphia: J. Benjamin.

Kachru, B. B. (1988a) The spread of English and sacred linguistic cows. In P. Lowenberg (ed.), *Georgetown Round Table on Languages and Linguistics 1987* (pp. 207–228). Washington, DC: Georgetown University Press.

Kachru, B. B. (1988b) ESP and non-native varieties of English: Toward a shift in paradigm. In D. Chamberlain and R. Baumgardner (eds), *ESP in the Classroom: Practice and Evaluation* (pp. 9–28). London: Macmillan.

Kachru, B. B. (1990a) World Englishes and applied linguistics. *World Englishes,* 9(1), 3–20.

Kachru, B. B. (1990b). Cultural contact and literary creativity in a multilingual society. In J. Toyama and N. Ochner (eds), *Literary Relations East and West* (pp. 194–203). Honolulu: University of Hawaii Press.

Kachru, B. B. (1991) Liberation linguistics and the Quirk concern. *English Today,* 7(1), 1–13.

Kachru, B. B. (1992a) The second diaspora of English. In T. W. Machan and C. T. Scott (eds), *English in its Social Contexts: Essays in Historical Sociolinguistics* (pp. 230–252). New York: Oxford University Press.

Kachru, B. B. (ed.) (1992b) *The Other Tongue: English Across Cultures.* Urbana, IL: University of Illinois Press. [2nd Revsd edn.]

Kachru, B. B. (1994a) English in South Asia. In R. Burchfield (ed.), *Cambridge History of the English language* (Vol. V) (pp. 497–553). Cambridge: Cambridge University Press.

Kachru, B. B. (1994b) Englishization and contact linguistics. *World Englishes,* 13(2), 135–154.

Kachru, B. B. (1994c) The speaking tree: A medium of plural canons. In J. E. Alatis (ed.), *Educational Linguistics, Crosscultural Communication, and Global Interdependence. Georgetown Round Table on Languages and Linguistics 1994.* (pp. 6–22). Washington, DC: Georgetown University Press.

Kachru, B. B. (1995a) Teaching world Englishes without myths. In S. K. Gill (ed.), *INTELEC '94: International English Language Education Conference, National and International Challenges and Responses* (pp. 1–19). Bangi, Malaysia: Pusat Bahasa Universiti Kebangsaan Malaysia.

Kachru, B. B. (1995b) Transcultural creativity in world Englishes and literary canon. In G. Cook and B. Seidlhofer (eds) *Principle and Practice in Applied Linguistics: In Honour of Henry Widdowson* (pp. 271–287). Oxford: Oxford University Press.

Kachru, B. B. (1996a) World Englishes: Agony and ecstasy. *Journal of Aesthetic Education*, 30(2), 135–155.

Kachru, B. B. (1996b) English as lingua franca. In H. Goebl, P. H. Nelde, Z. Stáry, and W. Wölck (eds), *Contact Linguistics: An International Handbook of Contemporary Research* (pp. 906–913). Berlin and New York: Walter de Gruyter.

Kachru, B. B. (1996c) The paradigms of marginality. *World Englishes*, 15(3), 241–255.

Kachru, B. B. (1997a) World Englishes and English-using communities. *Annual Review of Applied Linguistics*, 17, 67–87.

Kachru, B. B. (1997b) World Englishes 2000: Resources for research and teaching. In L. E. Smith and M. L. Forman (eds), *World Englishes 2000* (pp. 209–251). Honolulu: University of Hawaii Press.

Kachru, B. B. (1997c) English as an Asian language. In Ma. L. S. Bautista (ed.), *English is an Asian Language: The Philippine Context* (pp. 1–23). Sydney, Australia: Macquarie Publishing House.

Kachru, B. B. (1998a) Language in Indian society. In S. N. Sridhar and N. K. Mattoo (eds), *Ananya: A Portrait of India* (pp. 555–585). New York: The Association of Indians in America.

Kachru, B. B. (1998b) Raja Rao: *Madhyama* and *Mantra*. In R. L. Hardgrave (ed.), *Word as Mantra: The Art of Raja Rao* (pp. 60–87). New Delhi: Katha.

Kachru, B. B. (2001a) World Englishes and culture wars. In C. K. Tong, A. Pakir, K. C. Ban, and R. Goh (eds), *Ariels: Departures and Returns—Essays for Edwin Thumboo* (pp. 391–414). Singapore: Oxford University Press.

Kachru, B. B. (2001b) A medium of Shakti: Metaphorical constructs of world Englishes. *Asian Englishes, An International Journal of the Sociolinguistics of English in Asia/Pacific*, 4(2), 42–53.

Kachru, B. B. (2002) On nativizing *Mantra*: Identity construction in Anglophone Englishes. In R. Ahrens, D. Parker, K. Stierstorfer, and K.-K. Tam (eds), *Anglophone Cultures in Southeast Asia: Appropriations, Continuities, Contexts* (pp. 55–72). Heidelberg, Germany: Universitätsverlag.

Kachru, B. B. (2005a) *Asian Englishes: Beyond the Canon*. Hong Kong: Hong Kong University Press.

Kachru, B. B. (2005b) English in India: A Lexicographical perspective. In A. Cruse, D. Alan, F. Hundsnurscher, and M. Job (eds), *An International Handbook on the Nature and Structure of Words and Vocabulary* (pp. 1274–1279). Berlin and New York: Walter de Gruyter.

Kachru, B. B. and Kahane, H. (1995) *Cultures, Ideologies, and the Dictionary: Studies in Honor of Ladislav Zgusta* (Lexicographica Series Maior 64). Tübingen: Max Niemeyer Verlag.

Kachru, B. B., Kachru, Y. and Nelson, C. L. (eds) (2006) *The Handbook of World Englishes*. Oxford: Blackwell Publishing.

Kachru, B. B., Kachru, Y., and Sridhar, S. N. (eds) (2008) *Language in South Asia*. Cambridge: Cambridge University Press.

Kachru, Y. (1983). Linguistics and written discourse in particular languages: Contrastive studies: English and Hindi. *Annual Review of Applied Linguistics*, 3, 50–77.

Kachru, Y. (1985a) Applied linguistics and foreign language teaching: A non-Western perspective. (ERIC Document Reproduction Service No. ED 256175).

Kachru, Y. (1985b) Discourse analysis, non-native Englishes and second language acquisition research. *World Englishes*, 4(2), 223–232.

Kachru. Y. (1985c) Discourse strategies, pragmatics and ESL: Where are we going? *RELC Journal*, 16(2), 1–30.

Kachru, Y. (1987) Cross-cultural texts, discourse strategies and discourse interpretation. In L. E. Smith (ed.), *Discourse across Cultures: Strategies in World Englishes* (pp. 87–100). London: Prentice Hall.

Kachru, Y. (1988) Writers in Hindi and English. In A. Purves (ed.), *Writing across Languages and Cultures: Issues in Contrastive Rhetoric* (pp. 109–137). Newbury Park, CA: Sage.

Kachru, Y. (ed.) (1991) Symposium on speech acts in world Englishes. *World Englishes*, 10(3), 295–340.

Kachru, Y. (1992) Culture, style and discourse: Expanding noetics of English. In B. B. Kachru (ed.), *The Other Tongue: English across Cultures* (2nd edn) (pp. 340–352). Urbana, IL: University of Illinois Press.

Kachru, Y. (1993a) Review of L. Selinker, *Redicovering interlanguage*. *World Englishes*, 12(2), 265–273.

Kachru, Y. (1993b) Social meaning and creativity in Indian English speech acts. In J. E. Alatis (ed.), *Language, Communication, and Social Meaning. Georgetown Round Table on Languages and Linguistics 1992* (pp. 378–387). Washington, DC: Georgetown University Press.

Kachru, Y. (1994) Monolingual bias in SLA research. *TESOL Quarterly*, 28(4), 795–800.

Kachru, Y. (1995a) Contrastive rhetoric and world Englishes. *English Today*, 11(1), 21–31.

Kachru, Y. (1995b) Cultural meaning and rhetorical styles: Toward a framework for contrastive rhetoric. In G. Cook and B. Seidlhofer (eds), *Principles and Practice in Applied Linguistics: Studies in Honor of H. G. Widdowson* (pp. 171–184). London: Oxford University Press.

Kachru, Y. (1997a) Culture and argumentative writing in world Englishes. In L E. Smith and M. L. Forman (eds), *World Englishes 2000* (pp. 48–67). Honolulu: University of Hawaii Press.

Kachru, Y. (1997b) Cultural meaning and contrastive rhetoric in English education. *World Englishes*, 16(3), 337–350.

Kachru, Y. (1997c) Culture, variation and English language education. In S. Cromwell, P. Rule, and T. Sugino (eds) *On JALT 96: Crossing Borders. The Proceedings of the JALT 1996 Conference on Language Teaching and Learning* (pp. 199–210). Tokyo: n.p.

Kachru, Y. (1997d) Culture and communication in India. In S. N. Sridhar and N. K. Mattoo (eds), *Ananya: A Portrait of India* (pp. 645–663). New York: The Association of Indians in America.

Kachru, Y. (1998a) Culture and speech acts: Evidence from Indian and Singaporean English. *Studies in The Linguistic Sciences*, 28(1), 79–98.

Kachru, Y. (1998b) Context, creativity, style: Strategies in Raja Rao's novels. R. L. Hardgrave (ed.), *Word as Mantra: The Art of Raja Rao* (pp. 88–107). New Delhi: Katha.

Kachru, Y. (1999) Culture, context and writing. In E. Hinkel (ed.), *Culture in Second Language Teaching and Learning* (pp. 75–89). Cambridge: Cambridge University Press.

Kachru, Y. (2001a) Communicative styles in world Englishes. In C. K. Tong, A. Pakir, K. C. Ban, and R. Goh (eds), *Ariels: Departures and Returns—Essays for Edwin Thumboo* (pp. 267–284). Oxford: Oxford University Press.

Kachru, Y. (2001b) Discourse competence in world Englishes. In E. Thumboo (ed.), *The Three Circles of English* (pp. 341–355). Singapore: UniPress, The Centre for the Arts, National University of Singapore.

Kachru, Y. (2001c) World Englishes and rhetoric across cultures. *Asian Englishes: An International Journal of the Sociolinguistics of English in Asia/Pacific*, 3, 54–71.

Kachru, Y. (2003) Conventions of politeness in plural societies. In R. Ahrens, D. Parker, K. Stierstorfer, and K.-K. Tam (eds), *Anglophone Cultures in Southeast Asia* (pp. 39–53). Heidelberg: Univesitatsverlag Winter.

Kachru, Y. (2006) *Hindi*. London Oriental and African Language Library 12. Amsterdam: John Benjamins.

Kachru, Y. and Nelson, C. L. (2006) *World Englishes in Asian Contexts*. Hong Kong: Hong Kong University Press.

Kahane, H. and Kahane, R. (1979) Decline and survival of Western prestige languages. *Language*, 55, 183–198.

Kahane, H. and Kahane, R. (1986) A typology of prestige language. *Language*, 62, 495–508.

Kamwangamalu, N. (1989) A selected bibliography of studies on code-mixing and code-switching (1970–1988). *World Englishes*, 8(3), 433–440.

Kamwangamalu, N. (2001) Linguistic and cultural reincarnations of English: A case from Southern Africa. In E. Thumboo (ed.), *The Three Circles of English: Language Specialists Talk about the English Language* (pp. 45–66). Singapore: UniPress.

Kandiah, T. (1981) Lankan English schizoglossia. *English World-Wide: A Journal of Varieties of English*, 2(1), 63–81.

Kandiah, T. (1991) South Asia. In J. Cheshire (ed.), *English around the World: Sociolinguistic Perspectives* (pp. 271–287). Cambridge: Cambridge University Press.

Kaplan, R. B. (1966) Cultural thought patterns in inter-cultural education. *Language Learning*, 16(1), 1–20.

Karttunen, L. and Peters, S. (1979) Conventional implicature. In C.-K. Oh and D. A. Dinneen (eds), *Syntax and Semantics 11: Presupposition* (pp. 1–56). New York: Academic Press.

Katchen, J. (1982) A structural comparison of American English and Farsi expository writing. *Papers in Linguistics*, 15, 165–180.

Kathpalia, S. S. (1997) Cross-cultural variation in professional genres: A comparative study of book blurbs. *World Englishes*, 16(3), 417–426.

Koreo, K. (1988) Language habits of the Japanese. *English Today*, 15, 19–25.

Krishan, S. (ed.) (1990) *Linguistic Traits across Language Boundaries (A Report of All India Linguistic Traits Survey)*. Calcutta: Anthropological Survey of India.

Kummer, W. (1972) Aspects of a theory of argumentation. In E. Gulich and W. Raible (eds), *Textsorten* (pp. 25–49). Frankfurt: Anthenäum.

Labov, W. (1972a) *Language in the Inner City: Studies in the Black English Vernacular*. Philadelphia: University of Pennsylvania Press.

Labov, W. (1972b) *Sociolinguistic Patterns*. Philadelphia: University of Pennsylvania Press.

Labov, W. (1988) The judicial testing of linguistic theory. In D. Tannen (ed.), *Linguistics in Context: Connecting Observation and Understanding* (pp. 159–182). Norwood, NJ: Albex.

Lakoff, R. T. (1974) What you can do with words: Politeness, pragmatics and performatives. In C. Fillmore, G. Lakoff, and R. Lakoff (eds), *Berkeley Studies in*

Syntax and Semantics, vol. 1 (pp. 1–55). Berkeley: Institute of Human Learning, University of California.

Lakoff, R. T. (1975) *Language and Women's Place.* New York: Harper and Row.

Laver, J. and Hutcheson, S. (eds) (1972) *Communication in Face to Face Interaction.* Harmondsworth: Penguin Books.

Lee, J. S. and Kachru, Y. (eds) (2006) Symposium on world Englishes in popular culture. *World Englishes,* 25(2), 191–308.

Leech, G. (1983) *Principles of Pragmatics.* New York: Longman.

Lee-Wong, S. M. (1994) Imperatives in requests: Direct or impolite—Observations from Chinese. *Pragmatics,* 4(4), 491–515.

Lewis, I. (1991) *Sahibs, Nabobs and Boxwallahs: A Dictionary of the Words of Anglo-India.* Delhi: Oxford University Press.

Li, D. (1995) English in China. *English Today,* 11(1), 53–56.

Liao, C.-C. (1997) *Comparing Directives: American English, Mandarin and Taiwanese English.* Taipei: Crane Publishing Co.

Lim, S. G.-L. (1993) Gods who fail: Ancestral religions in the new literatures in English from Malaysia/Singapore. In C. Y. Loh and I. K. Ong (eds), *S. E. Asia Writes Back!* (pp. 224–237). London: Skoob Books Publishing.

Lim, S. G.-L. (1994) *Writing South East/Asia in English: Against the Grain, Focus on Asian English-language Literature.* London: Skoob Books Publishing.

Lim, S. G.-L. (1998) *What the Fortune Teller Didn't Say.* Albuquerque, NM: West End Press.

Linton, R. (1936) *The Study of Man.* New York: Appleton-Century.

Lisle, B. and Mano, S. (1997) Embracing the multicultural rhetoric. In C. Severino, J. C. Guerra, and J. E. Butler (eds), *Writing in Multicultural Settings* (pp. 12–26). New York: The Modern Language Association of America.

Llamzon, T. A. (1997) The phonology of Philippine English. In Ma. L. S. Bautista (ed.), *English is an Asian Language: The Philippine Context* (pp. 41–48). Manila: De La Salle University Press.

LoCastro, V. (1987) Aizuchi: a Japanese conversational routine. In L. E. Smith (ed.), *Discourse across Cultures: Strategies in World Englishes* (pp. 101–113). New York: Prentice Hall.

Low, E. L. and Brown, A. (2003) *An Introduction to Singapore English.* Singapore: McGraw Hill.

Lowenberg, P. H. (1984) English in the Malay archipelago: Nativization and its functions in a sociolinguistic area. Unpublished doctoral dissertation, University of Illinois at Urbana-Champaign.

Lowenberg, P. H. (1986a) Sociolinguistic context and second language acquisition: Acculturation and creativity in Malaysian English. *World Englishes,* 5(1), 71–83.

Lowenberg, P. H. (1986b) Non-native varieties of English: Nativization, norms, and implications. *Studies in Second Language Acquisition,* 8(1), 1–18.

Lowenberg, P. H. (ed.) (1988) *Language Spread and Language Policy: Issues, Implications and Case Studies. Georgetown University Round Table on Language and Linguistics 1987.* Washington DC: Georgetown University Press.

Lowenberg, P. H. (1991) Variation in Malaysian English: The pragmatics of language in contact. In J. Cheshire (ed.), *English around the World: Sociolinguistic Perspectives* (pp. 364–375). Cambridge: Cambridge University Press.

Lowenberg, P. H. (1992) Testing English as a world language: Issues in assessing non-native proficiency. In B. B. Kachru (ed.), *The Other Tongue: English across Cultures* (2nd edn) (pp. 108–121). Urbana, IL: University of Illinois Press.

Lumbera, B. (1978) Phillipine vernacular literature. In V. Toree (ed.), *A survey of*

Contemporary Philippine Literature in English (pp. 65–71). Philippines: National Book Store, Inc.

McArthur, T. (1986) The power of words: Pressure, prejudice and politics in our vocabularies and dictionaries. *World Englishes*, 5, 209–219.

McArthur, T. (ed.) (1992) *The Oxford Companion to the English Language.* Oxford: Oxford University Press.

McArthur, T. (1993) The English language or the English languages? In W. F. Bolton and D. Crystal (eds), *The English Language* (pp. 323–341). *Penguin History of Literature*, vol. 10. London: Penguin Books.

McArthur, T. (1998) *The English Languages.* Cambridge: Cambridge University Press.

McArthur, T. (2001) World English and world Englishes: Trends, tensions, varieties, and standards. *Language Teaching*, 34, 1–20.

McNeil, D. (ed.) (2000) *Language and Gesture.* Cambridge: Cambridge University Press.

Magura, B. (1985) Southern African Black English. *World Englishes*, 4(2), 251–256.

Makino, S. (1970) *Two Proposals about Japanese Polite Expression—Studies Presented to Robert B. Lees by his Students* (pp. 163–187). Edmonton: Linguistic Research Inc.

Mandelbaum, D. (1970) *Society in India, vol. II: Change and Continuity.* Berkeley: University of California Press.

Martin, S. E. (1964) Speech levels in Japan and Korea. In D. Hymes (ed.), *Language in Culture and Society* (pp. 407–415). New York: Harper & Row.

Matsumoto, Y. (1989) Politeness and conversational universals: Observations from Japanese. *Multilingua*, 8, 207–221.

Mazaferro, G. (ed.) (2002) *The English Language and Power.* Alessandria: Edizioni dell'Orso.

Mencken, H. L. (1936) *The American Language: An Inquiry into the Development of English in the United States* (4th edn). New York: Knopf.

Mesthrie, R. (1992) *English in Language Shift: The History, Structure and Sociolinguistics of South African Indian English.* Cambridge: Cambridge University Press.

Mesthrie, R. (1997) A sociolinguistic study of topicalization phenomena in South African Black English. In E. W. Schneider (ed.), *English around the World 2: Caribbean, Africa, Asia, Australasia: Studies in Honor of Manfred Görlach* (pp. 119–140). Amsterdam: John Benjamins.

MEXT (2003) Regarding the Establishment of an Action Plan to Cultivate "Japanese with English Abilities." Available at: http://www.mext.go.jp/english/topics/03072801.htm.

Meyer, P. G. (1997) *Coming to Know: Studies in the Lexical Semantics and Pragmatics of Academic English.* Tübingen: Gunter Narr Verlag.

Miner, E. (ed.). (1972) *English Criticism in Japan.* Tokyo: University of Tokyo Press.

Minsky, M. (1975) A framework for representing knowledge. In P. H. Winston (ed.), *The Psychology of Computer Vision* (pp. 211–277). New York: McGraw-Hill.

Mishra, A. (1982) Discovering connections. In J. J. Gumperz (ed.), *Language and Social Identity* (pp. 57–71). Cambridge: Cambridge University Press.

Mishra, A. (1992) *English in Cross-cultural Communication.* New Delhi: Creative.

Mitchell-Kernan, C. (1972) Signifying and marking: Two Afro-American speech acts. In J. J. Gumperz and D. Hymes (eds), *Directions in Sociolinguistics* (pp. 325–345). New York: Holt, Rinehart, & Winston.

Mitchell-Kernan, C. (1973) Signifying. In A. Dundes (ed.), *Mother Wit from the Laughing Barrel* (pp. 310–328). New York: Garland.

Modiano, M. (1996) The Americanization of Euro-English. *World Englishes*, 15(2), 207–215.

Molcho, S. (1985) *Body Speech.* New York: St Martin's Press.

Morgan, M. (1996) Conversational signifying: Grammar and indirectness among African American women. In E. Ochs, E. A. Schegloff, and S. A. Thompson (eds), *Interaction and Grammar* (pp. 405–434). Cambridge: Cambridge University Press.

Morris, D. (1977) *Manwatching: A Field Guide to Human Behavior.* New York: Harry N. Abrams.

Morris, D. (1978) *Manwatching.* St Albans: Triad Pnther.

Mufwene, S. S. (ed.) (1997) Symposium on English-to-pidgin continua. *World Englishes,* 16(2), 181–296.

Mukherjee, B. (1972) *The Tiger's Daughter.* Boston: Houghton Mifflin.

Mukherjee, M. (1971) *The Twice Born Fiction: Themes and Techniques of the Indian Novel in English.* Delhi: Arnold-Heinemann.

Myers-Scotton, C. (1993a) *Duelling Languages: Grammatical Structure in Code-switching.* Oxford: Clarendon.

Myers-Scotton, C. (1993b) *Social Motivations for Code-switching: Evidence from Africa.* Oxford: Clarendon.

Narayan, R. K. (1990) *The World of Nagaraj.* London: Heinemann.

NCERT (2000) India: education policies and curriculum at the upper primary and secondary education levels. Available at: http://www.ibe.unesco.org./curriculum/Asia%20Networkpdf/ndrepin.pdf.

Nelson, C. L. (1982) Intelligibility and non-native varieties of English. In B. B. Kachru (ed.), *The Other Tongue: English across Cultures* (pp. 58–73). Urbana, IL: University of Illinois Press.

Nelson, C. L. (1985) My language, your culture: whose communicative competence? *World Englishes,* 4(2), 243–50. [Also in B. B. Kachru (1992b).]

Nelson, C. L. (1995) Intelligibility and world Englishes in the classroom. *World Englishes,* 14(2), 273–279.

Nelson, G. (ed.) (2004) Special issue on the international corpus of English. *World Englishes,* 23(2), 225–316.

Nero, S. (2006) *Dialects, Englishes, Creoles, and Education.* Mahwa, NJ: Lawrence Erlbaum.

Newbrook, M. (ed.) (1999) *English is an Asian Language: The Thai Context.* Sydney: The Macquarie Library Pty Ltd.

Ngũgĩ, wa T. (1981) *Writers in Politics.* London and Exeter, NH: Heinemann.

Ngũgĩ, wa T. (1986) *Decolonizing the Mind: The Politics of Language in African Literature.* London: James Currie.

Ngũgĩ, wa T. (1991) English: A language for the world? *The Yale Journal of Criticism,* 4(2), 283–293.

Nicholls, J. (1995) Cultural pluralism and the multicultural curriculum: Ethical issues and English language textbooks in Canada. In M. L. Tickoo (ed.), *Language and Culture in Multilingual Societies: Viewpoints and Visions* (pp. 112–121). Singapore: SEAMEO Regional Language Centre.

Nihalani, P., Tongue, R. K., and Hosali, P. (1979) *Indian and British English: A Handbook of Usage and Pronunciation.* New Delhi: Oxford University Press.

Nishiyama, K. (1995) *Japan–US Business Communication.* Dubuque, IA: Kendall/Hunt Publishing Company.

Norton, B. and Toohey, K. (2004) *Critical Pedagogies and Language Learning.* Cambridge: Cambridge University.

Nwoye, G. O. (1985) Eloquent silence among the Igbo of Nigeria. In D. Tannen and M. Saville-Troike (eds), *Perspectives on Silence* (pp. 185–191). Norwood, NJ: Ablex Publishing Corporation.

Nwoye, G. O. (1992) Obituary announcements as communicative events in Nigerian English. *World Englishes*, 11(1), 15–27.

Ochs, E. (1979) Planned and unplanned discourse. In T. Givón (ed.), *Discourse and Syntax* (pp. 51–80). New York: Academic Press.

Okara, G. (1964) *The Voice*. London: Heinemann.

Ovando, C. and McLaren, P. (2000) *The Politics of Multiculturalism and Bilingual Education: Students and Teachers Caught in the Cross Fire*. Boston: McGraw-Hill.

Pakir, A. (1991) The status of English and the question of "standard" in Singapore: A sociolinguistic perspective. In M. L. Tickoo (ed.), *Language and Standards: Issues, Attitudes, Case Studies* (pp. 109–130). Singapore: SEAMEO Regional Language Centre.

Pakir, A. (ed.) (1992) *Words in a Cultural Context: Proceedings of the Lexicography Workshop, September, 9–11, 1991*. Singapore: University Press.

Pakir, A. (1994) Education linguistics: Looking to the East. In J. Alatis (ed.), *Educational Linguistics, Cross-cultural Communication, and Global Interdependence* (pp. 370–383). Washington DC: Georgetown University Press.

Pakir, A. (1997) Standards and codification for world Englishes. In L. E. Smith and M. L. Forman (eds), *World Englishes 2000* (pp. 169–181). Honolulu: University of Hawaii Press.

Pakir, A. (1999) Bilingual education with English as an official language: Sociocultural implications. In J. E. Alatis and A.-H. Tan (eds), *Georgetown University Round Table on Languages and Linguistics* (pp. 341–349). Washington DC: Georgetown University Press.

Pandharipande, R. (1983) Linguistics and written discourse in particular languages: Contrastive studies: English and Marathi. *Annual Review of Applied Linguistics*, 3, 118–136.

Pandharipande, R. (1987) On nativization of English. *World Englishes*, 6(2), 149–158.

Parakrama, A. (1995) *De-hegemonizing Language Standards*. London: Macmillan.

Parret, H. (1987) Argumentation and narrativity. In F. van Eemeren, R. Grootendorst, J. Blair, and C. Willard (eds), *Argumentation: Across the Lines of Discipline* (pp. 165–175). Providence, RI: Foris Publications.

Patrick, P. L. (1997) Style and register in Jamaican Patwa. In E. W. Schneider (ed.), *Englishes around the World 2: Caribbean, Africa, Asia, Australasia: Studies in Honor of Manfred Görlach* (pp. 41–55). Amsterdam: John Benjamins.

Patton, M. Q. (2002) *Qualitative Research and Evaluation Methods* (3rd edn). Thousand Oaks, CA: Sage.

Payatos, F. (ed.) (1988) *Cross-cultural Perspectives in Non-verbal Communication*. Toronto: Hogrefe.

Peng, L. and Ann, J. (2001) Stress and duration in three varieties of English. *World Englishes*, 20(1), 1–27.

Pennycook, A. (1994) *The Cultural Politics of English as an International Language*. London: Longman.

Philip, M. N. (1989) Discourse on the logic of language. In *She Tries Her Tongue; Her Silence Softly Breaks*. Charlottetown, Canada: NFS Canada Series.

Philips, S. U. (1983) *The Invisible Culture: Communication in Classroom and Community on the Warm Springs Indian Reservation*. New York: Longman.

Phillipson, R. (1992) *Linguistic Imperialism*. Oxford: Oxford University Press.

Phillipson, R. (1998) Globalizing English: Are linguistic human rights an alternative to linguistic imperialism? In P. Benson, P. Grundy, and T. Skutnabb-Kangas (eds), *Language Rights*. Special volume of *Language Sciences*, 20(1), 101–112.

Phillipson, R. (2003) *English-only Europe? Challenging Language Policy.* London: Routledge.

Phillipson, R. and Skutnabb-Kangas, T. (1997) Lessons for Europe from language policy in Australia. In M. Putz (ed.), *Language Choices: Conditions, Constraints and Consequences* (pp. 115–159). Amsterdam: John Benjamins.

Plank, G. A. (1994) What silence means for education of American Indian children. *Journal of American Indian Education,* 34444(1), 3–19.

Platt, J. (1977) The sub-varieties of Singapore English: Their sociolectal and functional status. In W. Crewe (ed.), *The English Language in Singapore* (pp. 83–95). Singapore: Eastern University Press.

Platt, J. and Ho, M. L. (1989) Discourse particles in Singaporean English: Substratum influences and universals. *World Englishes,* 8(2), 215–221.

Platt, J. and Weber, H. (1980) *English in Singapore and Malaysia: Status, Features, Functions.* Kuala Lumpur: Oxford University Press.

Pope, E. (1976) *Questions and Answers in English.* The Hague: Mouton.

Prodromou, L. (2007) Is ELF a variety of English? *English Today,* 23(2), 47–53.

Proshina, Z. G. (ed.) (2005) Special Issue on Russian Englishes. *World Englishes,* 24(4), 437–532.

Quinn, N. and Holland, D. (1987) *Cultural Models in Thought and Language.* Cambridge: Cambridge University Press.

Quirk, R. (1985) The English language in a global context. In R. Quirk and H. G. Widdowson (eds), *English in the World: Teaching and Learning the Language and Literatures* (pp. 1–6). Cambridge: Cambridge University Press.

Quirk, R. (1988) The question of standards in the international use of English. In P. H. Lowenberg (ed.), *Georgetown Round Table on Languages and Linguistics 1987* (pp. 229–241). Washington, DC: Georgetown University Press.

Quirk, R. (1989) Language varieties and standard language. *JALT Journal,* 11(1), 14–25.

Quirk, R. and Widdowson, H. G. (eds) (1985) *English in the World: Teaching and Learning the Language and Literatures.* Cambridge: Cambridge University Press.

Quirk, R., Greenbaum, S., Leech, G., and Svartvik, J. (1972) *A Grammar of Contemporary English.* London: Longman.

Quirk, R., Greenbaum, S., Leech, G., and Svartvik, J. (1985) *A Comprehensive Grammar of the English Language.* London: Longman.

Rahman, T. (1990) *Pakistani English: The Linguistic Description of a Non-native Variety of English.* Islamabad: National Institute of Pakistan Studies.

Rajadhon, P. A. (1968) *Essays on Thai Folklore.* Bangkok: Editions Duang Kamol.

Rao, G. S. (1954) *Indian Words in English: A Study of Indo-British Cultural and Linguistic Relations.* Oxford: Clarendon Press.

Rao, R. (1963) *Kanthapura.* London: George Allen and Unwin Ltd. [Originally published in 1938.]

Rao, R. (1978a) The caste of English. In C. D. Narasimhaiah (ed.), *Awakened Conscience: Studies in Commonwealth Literature* (pp. 420–422). New Delhi: Sterling.

Rao, R. (1978b) *The Policeman and the Rose.* Delhi: Oxford University Press.

Reyes, S. (1978) The hero in the contemporary Tagalog novel. In V. Toree (ed.), *A Survey of Contemporary Philippine Literature in English* (pp. 72–80). Philippines: National Book Store, Inc.

Reynolds, D. W. (1993) Illocutionary acts across languages: Editorializaing in Egyptian English. *World Englishes,* 12(1), 35–46.

Ricento, T. (ed.) (2000) *Ideologies, Politics and Language Policies: Focus on English.* Amsterdam: John Benjamins.

Riesbeck, C. K. and Schank, R. C. (1978) Comprehension by computer: Expectation-

based analysis of sentences in context. In W. Levelt and G. Flores d'Arcais (eds),
Studies in the Perception of Language (pp. 247–294). New York: Wiley.

Romaine, S. (1991) The Pacific. In J. Cheshire (ed.), *English around the World:
Sociolinguistic Perspectives* (pp. 619–636). Cambridge: Cambridge University Press.

Romaine, S. (1997 [2006]) British heresy in ESL revisited. In S. Elinsson and
R. H. Jahr (eds) *Language and its Ecology: Essays in Memory of Einar Haugen*
(pp. 419–432). The Hague: Mouton. [Reproduced in K. Bolton and B. Kachru
(eds) (2006) *World Englishes: Critical Concepts in Linguistics.* (pp. 140–153). London:
Routledge.]

Rubin, J. and Jernudd, B. (eds) (1971) *Can Language be Planned? Sociolinguistic Theory
and Practice for Developing Nations.* Honolulu: The University Press of Hawaii.

Rushdie, S. (1991) "Commonwealth Literature" does not exist. In *Imaginary
Homelands: Essays and Criticism* (pp. 61–70). New York: Viking.

Russell, R. (1999) *How Not to Write the History of Urdu Literature and Other Essays on Urdu
and Islam.* New Delhi: Oxford University Press.

Sa'adeddin, M. A. (1989) Text development and Arabic–English negative
interference. *Applied Linguistics,* 10, 36–51.

Sacks, H. (1972) On the analyzability of stories by children. In J. J. Gumperz and
D. Hymes (1986) (eds), *Directions in Sociolinguistics* (pp. 325–345). New York: Holt,
Rinehart, & Winston.

Sacks, H., Schegloff, E. A., and Jefferson, G. (1974) A simplest systematics for the
organization of turn-taking for conversation. *Language,* 50, 696–735.

Sadock, J. M. (1974) *Toward a Linguistic Theory of Speech Acts.* New York: Academic
Press.

Said, H. M. and Ng, K. S. (eds) (2000) *English is an Asian Language: The Malaysian
Context.* Persatuan Bahasa Moden Malaysia and The Macquarie Library Pty Ltd.

Sanford, A. J. and Garrod, S. C. (1981) *Understanding Written Language.* Chichester:
Wiley & Sons.

Saro-Wiwa, K. (1989) *Four Farcical Plays.* London: Saros Int. Pub.

Savignon, S. and Berns, M. (1984) *Initiatives in Communicative Language Teaching.*
Reading, MA: Addison-Wesley.

Saville-Troike, M. (1982) *The Ethnography of Communication: An Introduction.* London:
Basil Blackwell. [Third edn (2003) Oxford: Blackwell.]

Schachter, J. and Celce-Murcia, M. (1983) Some reservations concerning error
analysis. In B. W. Robinett and J. Schachter (eds), *Second Language Learning:
Contrastive Analysis, Error Analysis, and Related Aspects* (pp. 272–284). Ann Arbor:
University of Michigan Press.

Schachter, J. and Rutherford, W. (1983) Discourse function and language transfer.
In B. W. Robinett and& J. Schachter (eds), *Second Language Learning: Contrastive
Analysis, Error Analysis, and Related Aspects* (pp. 303–315). Ann Arbor: University
of Michigan Press.

Schank, R. C. and Abelson, R. (1977) *Scripts, Plans, Goals and Understanding.* Hillsdale,
NJ: Lawrence Erlbaum.

Schegloff, E. A. (1968) Sequencing in conversational openings. *American Anthropologist,*
70, 1075–1095.

Schegloff, E. A. (1979) The relevance of repair to syntax-for-conversation. In T. Givón
(ed.), *Discourse and Syntax* (pp. 261–285). New York: Academic Press.

Schegloff, E. A. and Sacks, H. (1973) Opening up closings. *Semiotica,* 8, 289–327.

Schilling-Estes, N. (2000) Redrawing ethnic dividing lines through linguistic creativity.
American Speech, 75(4), 357–359.

Schneider, E. W. (ed.) (1997) *English around the World: Studies in Honor of Manfred
Görlach.* Vol. 1, *General Studies: British Isles, North America: Görlach;* Vol. 2, *Caribbean,*

Africa, Asia, Australasia. In the series *Varieties of English around the world.* Amsterdam: John Benjamins.

Schneider, E. W. (2003) Evolutionary patterns of New Englishes and the special case of Malaysian English. *Asian Englishes,* 6(2), 44–63.

Scollon, R. and Scollon, S. (1981) *Narative, Literacy, and Face in Interethnic Communication.* Norwood, NJ: Ablex.

Scollon, R. and Scollon, S. W. (1994) Face parameters in East–West discourse. In S. Ting-Toomey (ed.), *The Challenge of Facework* (pp. 133–157). Albany, NY: State University of New York Press.

Scribner, S. and Cole, M. (1981) *The Psychology of Literacy.* Cambridge, MA: Harvard University Press.

Searle, J. (1969) *Speech Acts: An Essay in the Philosophy of Language.* Cambridge: Cambridge University Press.

Searle, J. (1975) Indirect speech acts. In P. Cole and J. L. Morgan (eds), *Speech Acts. Syntax and Semantics* (Vol. 3) (pp. 59–82). New York: Academic Press.

Searle, J. R. (1979) *Expression and Meaning.* Cambridge: Cambridge University Press.

Seidlhofer, B. (1999) Double standards: teacher education in the Expanding Circle. *World Englishes,* 18(2), 233–245.

Seidlhofer, B. (2001) Closing a conceptual gap: the case for a description of English as a lingua franca. *International Journal of Applied Linguistics,* 11, 133–158.

Seidlhofer, B. (2004) Research perspectives on teaching English as a lingua franca. *Annual Review of Applied Linguistics,* 24, 200–239.

Selinker, L. (1972) Interlanguages. In B. W. Robinett and J. Schachter (eds), *Second Language Learning, Error Analysis, and Related Aspects* (pp. 173–196). Ann Arbor: University of Michigan Press.

Sey, K. A. (1973) *Ghanaian English: An Exploratory Survey.* London: Macmillan.

Shah, A. B. (1968) *The Great Debate: Language Controversy and University Education.* Bombay: Lalvani Publishing House.

Shi, D. (2000) Topic and topic-comment constructions in Mandarin Chinese. *Language,* 76(2), 383–408.

Shields, K. (1989) Standard English in Jamaica: A case of competing models. *English World-Wide,* 10, 41–53.

Shim, R. J. (1999) Codified Korean English: Process, characteristics, and consequences. *World Englishes,* 18(2), 247–258.

Singh, A. and Altbach, P. G. (eds) (1974) *The Higher Learning In India. Bombay:* Vikas Publishing House Pvt. Ltd.

Silva, P. (1997) The lexis of South African English: Reflections of a multilingual society. In E. W. Schneider (ed.), *Englishes around the World 2: Caribbean, Africa, Asia, Aystrakasua: Studies in Honor of Manfred Görlach* (pp. 159–176). Amsterdam: John Benjamins.

Silva, P., Dore, W., Mantzel, D., Muller, C., and Wright, M. (eds) (1996) *A Dictionary of South African English on Historical Principles.* Oxford: Oxford University Press.

Silva, T. and Brice, C. (2004) Research in teaching writing. *Annual Review of Applied Linguistics,* 24(1), 70–106.

Simo-Bobda, A. (1994a) *Aspects of Cameroon English Phonology.* Berne: Peter Lang.

Simo-Bobda, A. (1994b) Lexical innovation in Cameroon English. *World Englishes,* 13(2), 245–260.

Sinclair, J., Forsyth, I. H., Coulthard, M., and Ashby, M. C. (1972) *The English Used by Teachers and Pupils.* Mimeo. Birmingham: University of Birmingham.

Singh, K. (1959) *I Shall Not Hear the Nightingale.* London: John Calder.

Skutnabb-Kangas, T. (2000) *Linguistic Genocide in Education or Worldwide Diversity and Human Rights?* Mahwah, NJ and London: Lawrence Erlbaum Associates.

Skutnabb-Kangas, T. (2001) Linguistic human rights in education for language maintenance. In L. Maffi (ed.), *Language, Knowledge and the Environment: The Interdependence of Cultural and Biological Diversity* (pp. 397–411). Washington, DC: The Smithsonian Institute.

Skutnabb-Kangas, T. and Phillipson, R. (1997) Linguistic human rights and development. In C. Hamelink (ed.), *Ethics and Development: On Making Moral Choices in Development Co-operation* (pp. 56–69). Kampen: Kok.

Skutnabb-Kangas, T. and Phillipson, R. (1998) Linguistic human rights. In C. Hamelink (ed.), *Gazette. The International Journal for Communication Studies.* Special volume on human rights, 60(1), 27–46.

Sledd, J. H. (1993) Standard English and the study of variation: "It all be done for a purpose." In A. W. Glowka and D. M. Lance (eds), *Language Variation in North American English: Research and Teaching* (pp. 275–281). New York: The Modern Language Association of America.

Slobin, D. I. (1963) Some aspects of the use of pronouns of address in Yiddish. *Word,* 19, 193–202.

Smith, L. E. (ed.) (1981) *English for Cross-cultural Communication.* London: Macmillan.

Smith, L. E. (ed.) (1983) *Readings in English as an International Language.* Oxford: Pergamon.

Smith, L. E. (ed.) (1987) *Discourse across Cultures: Strategies in World Englishes.* London: Prentice Hall.

Smith, L. E. (1992) Spread of English and issues of intelligibility. In B. B. Kachru (ed.), *The Other Tongue: English across Cultures* (pp. 75–90). Urbana, IL: University of Illinois Press.

Smith, L. E. and Bisazza, J. A. (1982) The comprehensibility of three varieties of English for college students in seven countries. *Language Learning,* 32, 259–269. [Reprinted in L. Smith (ed.) (1983) *Readings in English as an International Language* (pp. 59–67). Oxford: Pergamon Press.]

Smith, L. E. and Forman, M. L. (eds) (1997) *World Englishes 2000.* Honolulu: University of Hawaii Press.

Smith, L. E. and Nelson, C. L. (1985) International intelligibility of English: Directions and resources. *World Englishes,* 4(3), 333–342.

Smith, L. E. and Rafiqzad, F. N. (1979) English for cross-cultural communication: the question of intelligibility. In L. Smith (ed.) (1983), *Readings in English as an International Language.* Oxford: Pergamon Press.

Smitherman, G. (1995) If I'm lyin', I'm flyin': An introduction to the art of the snap. In J. L. Percelay, S. Dweck, and M. Ivey (eds), *Double Snaps* (pp. 14–33). New York: Quill/William Morrow.

Sridhar, K. K. (1989) *English in Indian Bilingualism.* New Delhi: Manohar Publications.

Sridhar, K. K. (1991) Speech acts in an indigenized variety: Sociocultural values and language variation. In J. Cheshire (ed.), *English around the World: Sociolinguistic Perspectives* (pp. 308–318). Cambridge: Cambridge University Press.

Sridhar, K. K. and Sridhar, S. N. (1992) Bridging the paradigm gap: Second language acquisition theory and indigenized varieties of English. In B. B. Kachru (ed.), *The Other Tongue: English across Cultures* (pp. 91–107). Urbana, IL: University of Illinois Press. [Earlier version in *World Englishes,* 5(1), 1986, 3–14.]

Sridhar, S. N. (1992) The ecology of bilingual competence: language interaction in indigenized varieties of English. *World Englishes,* 11(2/3), 141–150.

Sridhar, S. N. (1994) A reality check for SLA theories. *TESOL Quarterly,* 28(4), 800–805.

Sridhar, S. N. (1996) Toward a syntax of South Asian English: Defining the lectal range. In R. Baumgardner (ed.), *South Asian English: Structure, Use, and Users* (pp. 55–69). Urbana, IL: University of Illinois Press.

Sridhar, S. N. and Sridhar, K. K. (1980) The syntax and psycholinguistics of bilingual code-mixing. *Canadian Journal of Psychology*, 34(4), 407–416.

Stalnaker, R. C. (1978) Assertion. In P. Cole (ed.), *Syntax and Semantics 9: Pragmatics* (pp. 315–332). New York: Academic Press.

Stanlaw, J. (2003) *Japanese English: Language and Culture Contact.* Hong Kong: Hong Kong University Press.

Strevens, P. (1980) *Teaching English as an International Language.* Oxford: Pergamon.

Strevens, P. (1982) World English and the world's Englishes: Or, whose language is it, anyway? *Journal of the Royal Society of Arts*, CXX, 418–431.

Strevens, P. (1988) Language learning and language teaching: Toward an integrated model. In D. Tannen (ed.), *Linguistics in Context: Connecting Observation and Understanding* (pp. 299–312). Norwood, NJ: Ablex Publishing Corporation.

Stubbe, M. and Holmes, J. (1999) Talking Maori or Pakeha in English: Signaling identity in discourse. In A. Bell and K. Kuiper (eds) *New Zealand English* (pp. 249–278). Amsterdam: John Benjamins.

Swales, J. (1985) ESP—The heart of the matter or the end of the affair. In R. Quirk and H. G. Widdowson (eds), *English in the World: Teaching and Learning the Language and Literatures* (pp. 212–223). Cambridge: Cambridge University Press.

Swales, J. (1990) Genre analysis—English in Academic and Research Settings. Cambridge: Cambridge University Press.

Taiwo, O. (1976) *Culture and the Nigerian Novel.* New York: St Martin's Press.

Takahashi, T. and Beebe, L. (1993) Cross-linguistic influence in the speech act of correction. In G. Kasper and S. Blum-Kulka (eds), *Interlanguage Pragmatics* (pp. 138–157). New York: Oxford University Press.

Take Two: Teaching English for Intercultural Communication (1983) James Baxter (project Director), Cliff Clarke, Deena Levine, Shelia Ramsey, and K. M. Young. Videotape and training manual. Palo Alto, CA: CATESOL and Intercultural Relations Institute.

Tannen, D. (1981) New York Jewish conversational style. *International Journal of the Sociology of Language*, 30, 133–149.

Tannen, D. (1982a) *Analyzing Discourse: Text and Talk.* Washington, DC: Georgetown University Press.

Tannen, D. (ed.) (1982b) *Spoken and Written Language: Exploring Orality and Literacy.* Norwood, NJ: Ablex.

Tannen, D. (1984) *Conversational Style: Analyzing Talk among Friends.* Norwood, NJ: Ablex.

Tannen, D. (1989) *Talking Voices: Repetition, Dialogue, and Imagery in Conversational Discourse.* Cambridge: Cambridge University Press.

Tannen, D. and Saville-Troike, M. (eds) (1985) *Perspectives on Silence.* Norwood, NJ: Ablex.

Tavares, A. J. (2000) From heritage to international languages: Globalism and Western Canadian trends in heritage language education. *Canadian Ethnic Studies*, XXXII(1), 156–167.

Tawake, S. K. (1990) Culture and identity in literature of the South Pacific. *World Englishes*, 9, 205–213.

Tawake, S. K. (1993) *Reading The Bone People* cross-culturally. *World Englishes*, 12(3), 325–333.

Tawake, S. K. (ed.) (1995) Symposium on world Englishes in the classroom. *World Englishes*, 14(2), 231–300.

Tay, M. W. J. (1986) Lects and institutionalized varieties of English: The case of Singapore. *Issues and Developments in English and Applied Linguistics*, 1, 93–107.

Tay, M. W. J. (1991) Southeast Asia and Hong Kong. In J. Cheshire (ed.), *English around the World: Sociolinguistic Perspectives* (pp. 319–332). Cambridge: Cambridge University Press.

Tay, M. W. J. (1993) *The English Language in Singapore: Issues and Developments*. Singapore: UniPress, The Centre for Arts, National University of Singapore.

Teo, A. (1995) Analysis of newspaper editorials: A study of argumentative text structure. Unpublished doctoral dissertation, University of Illinois at Urbana-Champaign.

Thirabutana, P. (1973) *Little Things*. London: Fontana. [First published 1971.]

Thornton, R. (1988) Culture: A contemporary definition. In E. Boonzaier and J. Sharp (eds), *South African Keywords: Uses and Abuses of Political Concepts* (pp. 17–28). Cape Town: David Phillip.

Thumboo, E. (1985) Twin perspectives and multi-ecosystems: Tradition for a commonwealth writer. *World Englishes*, 4(2), 213–222.

Thumboo, E. (1992) The literary dimensions of the spread of English. In B. B. Kachru (ed.), *The Other Tongue: English across Cultures* (pp. 255–282). Urbana, IL: University of Illinois Press.

Thumboo, E. (1994) Language into languages: Some conjugations of choice in Singapore. In T. Kandiah and J. Kwan-Terry (eds), *English and Language Planning: A Southeast Asian Contribution* (pp. 106–123). Singapore: Times Academic Press.

Thumboo, E. (ed.) (2001) *The Three Circles of English: Language Specialists Talk about the English Language*. Singapore: UniPress, The Centre for the Arts, National University of Singapore.

Tickoo, M. L. (1988) In search of appropriateness in EF(S)L teaching materials. *RELC Journal*, 19(2), 39–50.

Tickoo, M. L. (ed.) (1991) *Language and Standards: Issues, Attitudes, Case Studies*. Singapore: SEAMEO Regional Language Centre.

Tickoo, M. L. (ed.) (1995) *Language and Culture in Multilingual Societies: Viewpoints and Visions*. Singapore: SEAMEO Regional Language Centre.

Ting-Toomey, S. (ed.) (1994) *The Challenge of Facework: Cross-cultural and Interpersonal Issues*. Albany, NY: State University of New York Press.

Ting-Toomey, S. and Cocroft, B. K. (1994). Facework in Japan and the United States. *International Journal of Intercultural Relations*, 18, 469–506.

Tirkkonen-Condit, S. (1985) *Argumentative Text Structure and Translation*. Jyväskylä, Finland: University of Jyväskylä.

Todd, L. and Hancock, I. (1986) *International English Usage*. London: Croom-Helm.

Tollefson, J. W. (ed.) (1995) *Power and Inequality in Language Education*. Cambridge: Cambridge University Press.

Tongue, R. (1974) *The English of Singapore and Malaysia*. Singapore: Eastern Universities Press. [Reprinted 1976; 2nd edn. 1979.]

Tosi, A. (1984) *Immigration and Bilingual Education: A Case Study of Movement of Population, Language Change and Education within the EEC*. New York: Pergamon Press.

Tosi, A. (1988) The jewel in the crown of the modern prince. The new approach to bilingualism in multicultural education in England. In T. Skutnabb-Kangas and J. Cummins (eds), *Minority Education: From Shame to Struggle* (pp. 79–103). Clevedon: Multilingual Matters.

Tripathi, P. D. (1990) English in Zambia. *English Today*, 6(3), 34–38.

Tsuda, Y. (1994) The diffusion of English: Its impact on culture and communication. *Keio Communication Review*, 16, 49–61.

Tsuda, Y. (2002) The hegemony of English: Problems, opposing views and communication rights. In G. Mazzaferro (ed.), *The English Language and Power* (pp. 19–31). Torino: Edizioni dell'Orso.

Valdés, G. (2005) Bilingualism, heritage language learners, and SLA research: Opportunities lost or seized? *Modern Language Journal,* 89(3), 410–426.

Valentine, T. (1988) Developing discourse types in non-native English: Strategies of gender in Hindi and Indian English. *World Englishes,* 7(2), 143–158.

Valentine, T. (1991) Getting the message across: Discourse markers in Indian English. *World Englishes,* 10(3), 325–334.

Valentine, T. (1995) Agreeing and disagreeing in Indian English discourse: Implications for language teaching. In M. L. Tickoo (ed.), *Language and Culture in Multilingual Societies: Viewpoints and Visions* (pp. 227–250). Singapore: SEAMEO Regional Language Centre.

Valentine, T. (2001) Reconstructing identities and gender in discourse: English transplanted. In B. B. Kachru and C. L. Nelson (eds), *Diaspora, Identity, and Language Community.* Special issue of *Studies in the Linguistic Sciences,* 31(1), 193–212. Urbana, IL: University of Illinois.

van Dijk, T. (1980) *Macrostructure: An Interdisciplinary Study of Global Structures in Discourse, Interaction and Cognition.* Hillsdale, NJ: Lawrence-Erlbaum Associates.

Vavrus, F. K. (1991) When paradigms clash: The role of institutionalized varieties in language teacher education. *World Englishes,* 10(2), 181–195.

Vyas, B. S., Tiwari, B. N., and Srivastava, R. N. (1972) *Hindii VyaakaraN aur Racnaa* (Hindi Grammar and Composition). Delhi: National Council of Educational Research and Training.

Watson-Gegeo, K. A. (2004) Mind, language, and epistemology: Toward a language socialization paradigm for SLA. *The Modern Language Journal,* 88(3), 331–350.

Watson, O. M. (1970) *Proxemic Behaviro: A Cross-cultural Study.* The Hague: Mouton.

Werlich, E. (1976) *A Text Grammar of English.* Heidelberg: Quelle and Meyer.

White, S. (1989) Backchannels across cultures: A study of Americans and Japanese. *Language in Society,* 18, 59–76.

Whitworth, G. C. (1982) *Indian English.* New Delhi: Bahri Publications. [First published 1907.]

Widdowson, H. (1979) *Explorations in Applied Linguistics.* London: Oxford University Press.

Widdowson, H. (1984) ESP and the curse of Caliban. In H. Widdowson (ed.), *Explorations in Applied Linguistics 2* (pp. 189–200). Oxford: Oxford University Press.

Widdowson, H. (1994) The ownership of English. *TESOL Quarterly,* 26(2), 337–389.

Wierzbicka, A. (1985) *Lexicography and Conceptual Analysis.* Ann Arbor: Karoma.

Williams, J. (1989) Language acquisition, language contact and nativized varieties of English. *RELC Journal,* 20(1), 39–67.

Wilma, V. M. (1987) *A Study of Sentence-final Particles in Singapore English. Academic Exercise.* Singapore: Department of English Language and Literature, National University of Singapore.

Wiltshire, C. and Moon, R. (2003) Phonetic stress in Indian English vs. American English. *World Englishes,* 22(3), 281–303.

Winford, D. (1991). The Caribbean. In J. Cheshire (ed.), *English around the World: Sociolinguistic Perspectives* (pp. 565–584). Cambridge: Cambridge University Press.

Wolff, K.H. (1964) Intelligibility and inter-ethnic attitudes. In D. Hymes (ed.) *Language in Culture and Society* (pp. 310–328). New York: Harper & R. W.

Wolfgang, A. (ed.) (1984) *Nonverbal Behavior: Perspectives, Application, Intercultural Insights.* New York: C. J. Hofrege, Inc. Lewinston.

Wong, J. (2004) The particles of Singapore English: A semantic and cultural interpretation. *Journal of Pragmatics,* 36(4), 739–793.

Yamada, H. (1992) *American and Japanese Business Discourse: A Comparison of Interactional Styles.* Norwood, NJ: Ablex.

Yamanashi, M. (1974) In On minding your p's and q's in Japanese: A case study from honorifics. In M. W. Lagaly, R. A. Fox, and A. Bruck (eds) *CLS 10. Papers from the Tenth Regional Meeting of the Chicago Linguistic Society* (pp. 760–771). Chicago: Chicago University Press.

Yap, A. (1978) *Language Education in Multilingual Societies.* Singapore: Singapore University Press.

Yngve, V. H. (1970) On getting a word in edgewise. In *Papers from the Sixth Regional Meeting of the Chicago Linguistic Society,* April 16–18, 567–578. Chicago: University of Chicago, Department of Linguistics.

Young, L. W. L. (1982) Inscrutability revisited. In J. J. Gumperz (ed.) (1984), *Language and Social Identity* (pp. 72–84). Cambridge: Cambridge University Press.

Yule, H. and Burnell, A. C. (1886) *Hobson-Johnson: A Glossary of Colloquial Anglo-Indian Words and Phrases and of Kindred Terms, Etymological, Historical, Geographical, and Discursive.* [New edition W. Crooke (1903) London: J. Murray.]

Zgusta, L. (ed.) (1980) *Theory and Method in Lexicography: Western and Non-western Perspectives.* Columbia, SC: Hornbeam Press.

Zhang, A. (2000) Language switches among Chinese/English bilinguals. *English Today,* 16, 53–56.

Zhao, Y. and Campbell, K. P. (1995) English in China. *World Englishes,* 14(3), 377–390.

Index